PAGAN

PAGAN IRELAND
Ritual and belief in another world

John Waddell

Word_well_

First published in 2023
Wordwell Ltd
Unit 9, 78 Furze Road,
Sandyford Industrial Estate,
Dublin 18
www.wordwellbooks.com

Cover image: 'The winter solstice sun in Newgrange' by Ken Williams (www. shadowsandstone.com).

ISBN: 978-1-913934-92-7 (trade paperback)

British Library Cataloguing-in-Publication Data.
A catalogue record for this book is available from the British Library.

Typeset in Ireland by Wordwell Ltd
Copy-editor: Emer Condit
Cover design and artwork: Wordwell Ltd
Printed by: SprintPrint, Dublin

Contents

Illustrations

Acknowledgements and sources of illustrations

I am very grateful to Ken Williams, who generously provided me with a number of his superb photographs. Sincere thanks are due to Jane Conroy, Carleton Jones, Sam Moore and Regine Maraszek for their help with some illustrations. Máirín Ní Dhonnchadha kindly drew my attention to several publications. I am also grateful to all those archaeologists who made their illustrations and other material readily available online or in published form.

Sources of illustrations are as follows: Lissivigeen, Co. Kerry: Ken Williams. 1.1: Paul Naessens. 1.2: R.A.S. Macalister. 1.3: J. Geber *et al.* 1.4: Carleton Jones. 2.1: Ken Williams. 2.2: Ulrich Boser and John Waddell. 2.3: Wikimedia Commons. 2.4: Geraldine Stout. 2.5: William O'Brien. 2.6: Kristian Kristiansen. 2.7–2.8: National Museum of Ireland. 2.9–2.10: John Waddell, from *Archaeology and Celtic myth*. 2.11: Barry Raftery. 3.1: Archaeological Survey of County Sligo. 3.2: William O'Brien. 3.3: Rory Sherlock. 3.4: George Willmot. 3.5: Charles Thomas. 4.1–4.3: William O'Brien. 5.1: L. Hackett and J. Twomey. 5.2: National Museum of Ireland. 5.3: From Mary Cahill and Maeve Sikora. 5.4: Andrew Fitzpatrick. 6.1: Ken Williams. 6.2: National Gallery of Ireland. 6.3: Martin Doody. 6.4: Brendon Wilkins, Rubicon Heritage Services Ltd. 7.1–7.2: John Lehane and Debbie Leigh. 7.3: Laurent Olivier. 7.4: Ian Stead. 7.5: National Historical Museum Stockholm: Creative Commons. 7.6: Wellcome Collection. 8.1: Carleton Jones. 8.2: Anna Brindley and Jan Lanting. 9.1: National Museum of Ireland. 9.2: George Eogan. 9.3: Richard Warner. 10.1: Eamonn Cotter. 10.2: G. Eogan. 10.3: B. Ó Ríordáin. 10.4: Mary Cahill. 11.1: Archaeological Survey of County Galway. 11.2: Conor Newman. 11.3: From E. FitzPatrick, E. Murphy, R. McHugh, C. Donnelly and C. Foley. 12.1–12.2: Sam Moore. 12.3: Frank Coyne. 12.4: Stefan Bergh. 12.5: Cambridge University Collection of Aerial Photography. 13.1–13.2: Claire Cotter and the Discovery Programme. 13.3 (1): E. Aner and K. Kersten. 13.3 (2): R.A. Smith. 13.4: J. de Courcy Ireland. 14.1: National Museum of Ireland. 14.2: Ros Ó Maoldúin. 14.3: R.A. Smith. 14.5: Sabine Gerloff. 15.1: Chris Lynn. 15.2: Rose M. Cleary. 15.3: Conor Newman. 15.4: H.O'N. Hencken. 16.1–16.2: Ken Williams. 16.3: M.J. O'Kelly. 16.4: G. Eogan and K. Cleary, and digital image courtesy of the Discovery Programme. 16.5: M.J. O'Kelly. 16.6: Ken Williams. 16.7: Ken Williams and Christiaan Corlett. 16.8: R.A.S. Macalister. 16.9: Howard Morphy. 17.1: Chris Lynn. 17.2: © Crown DfC Historic Environment Division. 17.3: From John Waddell, *Archaeology and Celtic myth* (A: © Crown DfC Historic Environment Division; B: J.P. Mallory and T.P. McNeill; C: J. Auboyer). 17.4: R.J. Williams *et al.* 17.5: R. Poulton. 17.6: John Irwin. 17.7: Barry Raftery. 18.1: Image reproduced courtesy of the National Library of Ireland MS

700. 18.2: Wellcome Collection. 18.3: Eamonn O'Donoghue. 18.4: Conor Newman. 19.1: Landesamt für Denkmalpflege und Archäologie Sachsen-Anhalt and Karol Schauer. 19.2: Uno Holmberg. 19.3: George Eogan. 19.4: From Joseph Cooper Walker's *Historical essay on the dress of the ancient and modern Irish* (1818). 19.5: Barry Raftery. 19.6: Elizabeth O'Brien. 19.7: George Coffey. 19.8: Raghnall Ó Floinn. 20.1: Bryony Coles. 20.2: Barry Raftery. 20.3–20.4: Michael Stanley. 20.5: Eve Campbell and Ros Ó Maoldúin; replica created by Archaeological Management Solutions, the Pallasboy Project, Digital Heritage Age and CEAMC. 20.6: Hajo Hayen. 21.1: From the *Dublin Penny Journal*. 21.2: Mark Brennand and Maisie Taylor. 21.3: Con Manning. 21.4: René Wyss. 22.1: Paul Naessens. 22.2: Göran Burenhult. 22.3: Christy Cunniffe. 22.4: Barry Raftery. 23.1: Martin Byrne. 23.2: Finbar McCormick *et al.* 23.3: Göran Burenhult. 24.1: Musée national du Moyen Âge, Paris. 24.2: Neil Carlin. 24.3: Shadreck Chirikure. 24.4: R. Poulton. 25.1: E.P. Kelly. 25.2: Raghnall Ó Floinn. 26.1: William O'Brien. 26.2: M.J. O'Kelly. 26.3: Miranda Green and S. Read, M. Henig and L. Cram. 26.4–26.5: P.-M. Duval. 26.6: Barry Raftery. 26.7–26.8: V. Kruta. 27.1: National Museum of Ireland. 27.2: Thomas Barron. 27.3: Barry Raftery. 27.4: M.V. Duignan and the Discovery Programme. 27.5–27.6: Barry Raftery. 28.1: J. Rodríguez-Corral. 28.2: National Museum of Denmark. 28.3: Aubrey Beardsley. 28.4: Barry Raftery; R. and V. Megaw. 28.5: Conor Newman. 29.1–29.2: Helen Lanigan Wood, Anne Cassidy and R.B. Warner. 29.3: A.J. Daubney; R.E.M. and T.V. Wheeler; Fraser Hunter *et al.* 29.4: William O'Brien. 29.5: Image reproduced courtesy of the National Library of Ireland MS 700. 29.6: J.C. Leyendecker. 30.1: Paul Stevens. 30.2: Ken Williams. 30.3: Ordnance Survey Memoirs. 30.4: John Waddell. 30.5: Finbar McCormick. 30.6: Angélique Day and Royal Irish Academy.

Introduction:
a pagan tapestry

'The past is never dead. It's not even past'
—William Faulkner

A ritual stone circle at Lissivigeen, near Killarney, Co. Kerry.

In the nineteenth century various writers described a small stone circle at Lissivigeen, Co. Kerry, as a druidical monument, noting that it was known locally as the 'Seven Sisters'. Celtic druids were popular at the time as an explanatory label for many prehistoric monuments, but this circle is a much older ritual site. In fact, it was probably in use in the Bronze Age before 1000 BC. We do not know what pagan rites were performed here but it was probably frequented by priests or ritualists of some description. It was certainly a place with sacred connotations, as its circular plan implies. As we shall see, such ceremonial circles defined sacred space and their architecture was an expression of a belief in a circular, cyclical cosmos, as witnessed in the path of the sun and the fixed stars and in the rhythm of the year.

1

'Behind all Irish history hangs a great tapestry, even Christianity had to accept it and be itself pictured there. Nobody looking at its dim folds can say where Christianity begins and Druidism ends ...'. So wrote W.B. Yeats in 1937, when he praised the work of scholars like John O'Donovan who, a century before, had recorded so many of the names and legends of the country in their labours for the Ordnance Survey.

This tapestry contains images that are much older than Yeats imagined, for archaeological traces of pagan themes and activities, as at Lissivigeen, can be traced back in time for thousands of years and continued long after the introduction of the new religion. Indeed, the earlier centuries of Christianity's existence in Ireland were more complex and contradictory than commonly believed.

Archaeology, history, folklore and mythology all have something to tell us about past religious traditions. These reflect a belief in the supernatural in a world that was very different from the present. Archaeology in particular has the capacity to reveal something about beliefs and rituals in Irish prehistory over many thousands of years.

As is well known, the name 'pagan' and the concept of paganism were created by early Christians to describe the idol-worshippers and heathens of other religions. It became a derogatory and problematic expression and today some writers would prefer to use terms such as primal, traditional or indigenous religion to designate pre- or non-Christian belief systems. In an Irish context, however, pagan (or paganism) is as good a term as any to describe a remarkably diverse range of ancient indigenous beliefs and practices that, in some instances, helped to shape or even co-existed with more recent Christian phenomena. The concepts of a dying god and a virgin birth were just two pagan themes adopted by early Christianity. As the theologian James P. Mackey once wrote of paganism: 'properly appreciated ... primal religions provide the basic structures that receive the shape and sustain the existence of all those so-called world religions that strut the stage of human history for as long as each may last'. These great religions, of which Christianity is but one, all started as obscure cultural experiments.

In the past, myths and symbols were keepers of memory, and sacred spaces and monuments were created to facilitate communication with the supernatural and with ancestral figures. The concept of religion as a discrete area of human activity is a relatively modern one. In ancient societies there was no difference between the religious and secular worlds because the sacred or supernatural penetrated all areas of activity. It was embedded in the political, social and economic life of the community and in commonplace, everyday experience. In contrast, today religion, in the sense of a system of institutionalised beliefs, practices and texts, is very much separated from daily life.

A belief in the supernatural is as old as humanity and probably had its origins in a predisposition to detect agency in nature. Religious beliefs are an intrinsic part of human life and may be defined as attempts to give meaning to the world, employing a range of supernatural concepts. This otherworldly realm may include divine figures and spirits in great variety, and myths and ceremonial activities often reflect an engagement with this domain. The objective may be personal or communal benefit, but an important aspect may be the fact that the participants believe that they acquire a measure of meaningful control of the world in which they live.

The religious practices of pagan Ireland embodied a myriad of variable forms spanning many thousands of years. There is an impressively rich body of archaeological evidence to show how they mutated and changed over time. We can confidently see their early traces in the megalithic monuments of the Neolithic era from around 4000 BC. We now know that these stone structures were more than just resting-places for the remains of the dead. Monumentality had deeper meanings. The complex architecture of court tombs, for instance, with their multiple cells and elaborate forecourts, those 'gaunt grey ghostly gossips' as James Joyce called them, speak to us about more than just building skills and social complexity.

Functional interpretations embracing factors like communal expertise and organisation may well be true, but these were also religious monuments. They were the focus of complex rituals: they embodied ancestral memories and myths and were places for communion with the gods. The orientation of some monuments—and Newgrange is only the best known—tells us that solar phenomena were an important part of the religious cosmology of their builders. While great stone tombs of this sort are very visible expressions of ancient beliefs, many rituals have left little or no trace.

Some years ago the archaeologist Timothy Insoll recorded a ritual sacrifice that he observed in 2002 at a place called Dafra in Burkina Faso, west Africa. Led by a man whom he describes as a priest, the participants entered a forested gorge in which stood a large natural boulder. The stone was smeared with blood and butter extracted from nuts of a local tree. Chickens were sacrificed here and those present were asked to name the animals that they themselves would sacrifice to the gods if their wishes were granted. The celebrant then fed some of the chicken entrails to sacred catfish in an adjacent pool. He rubbed some of the butter from the stone on the hands of each participant, reminding them not to wash them with hot water for the next 24 hours. This concluded the ceremonies. Insoll pointed out that these complicated rites at a sacred place were undertaken by people who firmly believed that they would produce results. Important though these activities at Dafra may have been, an archaeologist would be all too aware that these sorts of rituals would also leave no enduring archaeological expression.

The study of the customs and beliefs of culturally distinct indigenous peoples elsewhere in the world, as at Dafra, is a useful tool, but only in so far as it may broaden our imagination and help to test our modern western ways of thinking. Some prehistoric standing stones or natural boulders decorated with rock art in Ireland may well have been a focus for ceremonial visits and treated like the Dafra boulder. The use of ethnographic analogy can remind us of overlooked aspects of human behaviour but, of course, a custom in a far-off community, no matter how intriguing, is no proof that a similar practice occurred in an Irish context.

Though there has been much debate on what constitutes the evidence for ritual action in archaeology, there is general agreement that the discipline does have the capability to identify ritual customs that tell us something of the ideologies and practices of times gone by. In short, there is merit in the widespread recognition that ritual action is representational, that it is mainly an expression of human attitudes and beliefs.

For some writers performance is a key feature of ritual, be it religious or secular. This might consist of formal acts that reflect social attitudes and beliefs and symbolically communicate a message. Performance, particularly the successful execution of certain actions, and the careful adherence to certain conventions have both been considered important characteristics. Of course, rituals and belief systems change over time and—to complicate matters—in preliterate societies variation may stem from the fact that rituals are imperfectly remembered from generation to generation.

In an archaeological context, repetitive action is one important component but not all repetitive acts are necessarily ritual in nature. Repetitive technological activity is one example but, once again, some repetitive tasks of a transformative kind (like metalworking) did have this kind of ritual dimension. In short, the recognition of patterns in the archaeological record may sometimes be correlated with actions with a religious significance.

Some decades ago there was a tendency in archaeological studies to apply the term 'ritual' to any action that could not be easily explained or to an object whose function was not understood. For this reason its use often invited much scepticism. Today there is a very large body of literature on the study of ritual practice and many valuable insights have been provided by social anthropology and religious studies. Of course, not all rituals have a religious meaning—the ceremonies attached to wedding or birthday cakes today are sometimes cited as good examples of this. In an archaeological context it is a challenge to identify those that have a sacral character rather than a secular dimension.

Varied practices such as sacrifices, offerings in special places, foundation deposits and burial rites may all be assumed to address a supernatural world peopled by spirits, ancestors or gods. The same may be true of some rituals associated with gift-giving, feasting, agriculture, the deliberate fragmentation of objects, the building of monuments and houses, and a host of other activities. Identifying the religious concepts behind these rituals is especially challenging and we must always be cautious when making claims about the beliefs of peoples distant in time. Nonetheless, it is sometimes possible to make plausible inferences. Some rites undoubtedly had cosmological significance and were concerned with bringing meaning and order to the world. We can be sure that fertility and solar mythology were of enduring importance. When St Patrick, in his *Confessio*, declared that 'the splendour of the material sun, which rises every day at the bidding of God, will pass away, and those who worship it will go into dire punishment', he was offering historical proof that the sun was indeed worshipped in Ireland in pagan times. And there is archaeological evidence as well, as we shall see.

The earliest inhabitants of this island have left little trace of their rituals and beliefs, but ethnographic evidence suggests that simple and relatively egalitarian hunter-gatherer groups generally hold fewer religious opinions and participate in less ritual than more complex societies. Their religious activities may include sacred rites such as hunting rituals, healing dances and ceremonies marking life events like birth, puberty and death. They believe in gods and spirits with limited powers who are typically not omniscient. Their gods usually lack any concern for morality and any interest in human affairs. For the most part, they are indifferent to the trivial actions of humans.

Of course, there is considerable variation among such people around the world but to a varying degree their belief systems may include animism, namely the acceptance that all natural things, such as plants, animals and even such phenomena as thunder, have intentionality or a vital force and can have an influence on human lives. A belief in an afterlife is also common. Shamanism—the presence of male or female ritualists who act as intermediaries with a spirit world or as healers and problem-solvers—is also widespread. So, too, is ancestor worship, in which the dead remain active in another realm where they may affect this world and can be influenced by the living.

These traits may also be found in the belief systems of more complex societies but here more powerful interventionist deities seem to proliferate. These were gods—sometimes benevolent, sometimes vengeful—who intervened in human affairs with punishments and rewards, and who demanded loyalty. The major factor in the emergence of a belief in vigilant deities concerned with the actions of mere mortals was probably the need for greater social cooperation and control in early agricultural communities where lives were governed by the seasons. In turn, these new gods induced greater cooperation and trust among their adherents. Those communities with religious beliefs and behaviours that promoted social cohesion may have had a competitive advantage over other groups.

The new gods were a significant element in the ideology of the early farming communities who, with their great ceremonial enclosures and megalithic tombs, left an indelible imprint on the European landscape. Rituals to engage with these 'high gods' to ensure their approval became, in time, more formal, elaborate and costly. In Ireland, the extravagant monuments of the Neolithic, like Newgrange, are visible testimony to the influence of such powerful supernatural figures. That perception of the gods should change is unsurprising. Today Christianity promotes the notion of a loving and caring deity, a striking contrast to the vindictive figure of some centuries ago.

1

Manipulating bones and bodies

1.1—Cairn K, Carrowkeel, Co. Sligo.

In 1911 R.A.S. Macalister, the newly appointed professor of Celtic archaeology in University College Dublin, the naturalist Robert Lloyd Praeger and E.C.R. Armstrong of the National Museum investigated a number of hilltop cairns on Carrowkeel, Co. Sligo. Praeger discovered these monuments when engaged in fieldwork for his pioneering *Irish topographical botany* in 1896. Fourteen cairns were partly investigated in just three visits in April, June and October over a total period of twelve days. Several were found to contain burial chambers and these were examined in a straightforward fashion: cairn material was removed until an entrance was located, the tomb contents were then extracted and the monument was planned and photographed. This was not scientific excavation in the modern sense—the position of every bone deposit and every artefact was not meticulously recorded. Tomb-raiding is probably an accurate term to use.

Their description of one tomb is characteristically brief. The entrance to the tomb in Cairn K, as it was labelled, was identified late on 14 April and its contents removed the following morning:

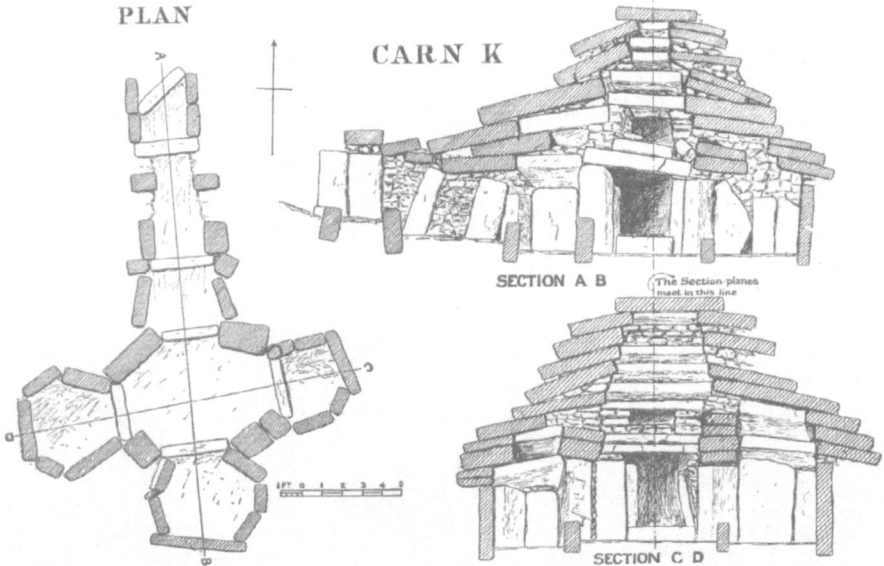

1.2—Macalister's plan and section of Cairn K, Carrowkeel.

'In design this fine carn resembles G, but, though rather larger, is, from the point of view both of construction and artistic finish, vastly its inferior. A poor, rotten stone has been used, and all the lintels are in consequence cracked: some of the side-stones have also settled. It is, indeed, rather surprising that the whole chamber has not collapsed. The chamber is much higher in K than in G, though it is in this respect less than the great ruined chamber in F: the maximum height is 12 feet 2 inches. The mound itself is about 20 feet in height and 71 feet in diameter ...'

The contents were described with equal brevity and included burnt and unburnt human bones, fragments of pottery, bone pins, stone beads and pendants. Macalister's father, Alexander Macalister, a professor of anatomy at Cambridge University who participated in some of the work, provided a summary account of the bones for the excavation report.

Today we know that such finds are typical in tombs of the passage tomb class, and Carrowkeel is famous as one of the two great cemeteries in County Sligo. Over a century ago, Newgrange in the Boyne Valley, with its cruciform plan of side cells and end cell, offered an obvious parallel for Carrowkeel tombs like Cairn K. Since Newgrange was then dated to the Bronze Age (mainly on the basis of its famous spiral ornament, believed to have been inspired by similar designs in far-off Mycenae), Macalister claimed a similar date for Carrowkeel. We know now that the construction and primary use of these monuments date from a time some centuries after the beginning of the Neolithic period, c. 3600–c. 2900 BC.

Thanks to further study of the finds from Carrowkeel we also know a lot more about the burial rites of the people who built them. Using techniques undreamt-of by Macalister, the ever-growing field of archaeological science includes sophisticated bone analysis, isotope and trace-element analysis to identify geographical origins and nutritional variations, high-resolution accelerator mass spectrometry radiocarbon dating and the study of ancient DNA.

The artefacts from the early investigations in 1911 were deposited in the National Museum and most of the human remains were preserved in Cambridge. Recent multidisciplinary studies have provided new and exciting information. The bone assemblage consists of a mix of cremated (5.7kg) and unburnt (9.7kg) human bone but the precise context was not always recorded. It seems that at least 22 individuals are present in the burnt material and eighteen in the unburnt; adult males and females and children are all represented. The nature of the heat-cracking on the burnt bone suggests that corpses were cremated in a fleshed condition. The bone fragments are relatively clean and may have been sorted and perhaps washed before deposition.

The largest sample of unburnt bone comes from Cairn K. The bones from this tomb and from others show no signs of weathering or bleaching. This is an important detail because the presence of disarticulated human bones in megalithic tombs is often assumed, and with good reason, to denote the practice of natural excarnation, in which the corpse is allowed to decay and deflesh when exposed to the elements and to the attention of scavenging animals or birds of prey. In one Bronze Age burial in England the regurgitated food pellet of such a bird was actually found within the skull. Ridding the body of flesh may have been seen as a way of freeing the spirit. Once defleshed, selected bones, such as skulls and long bones, might then be placed in the tomb. No evidence of carnivore gnawing was found on the Carrowkeel examples, however, so exposure seems unlikely.

The identification of cut-marks on a number of bones was a very significant discovery. A minimum of 91 such marks occurred on about a dozen bones of an adult individual from two separate monuments, Cairns H and K. Executed with a sharp stone blade of flint, chert or quartz, they were shallow grooves near the attachment places for tendons or ligaments, and represented the careful dismemberment of shoulder, elbow, hip, knee and foot joints at or near the time of death. They indicate detailed anatomical knowledge of certain tendons that connect muscle to bone and

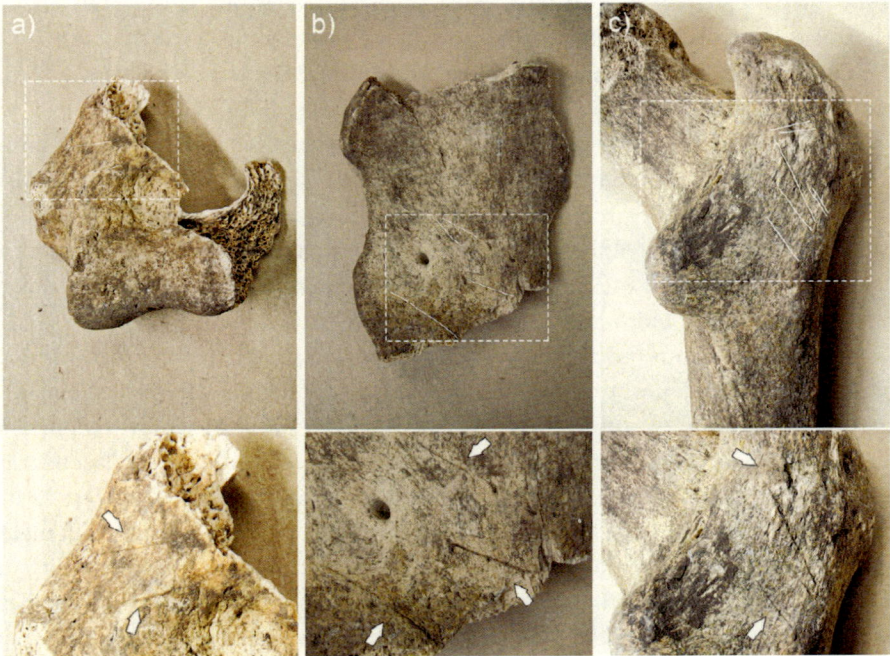

1.3—Cut-marks on human bones from Cairn K, marked in white (above) and magnified (below): on a left arm bone (a), a hip bone (b) and a thigh bone (c).

ligaments that connect one bone to another. Clearly the treatment of human remains, both unburnt and burnt, was a very complicated process. In some cases at least it involved the careful dismemberment of the body.

Judging from the dates obtained, the varied range of burial practices in Carrowkeel at first focused on the deposition of disjointed unburnt human body parts along with cremation, and then simply on cremated burial until around 2880 BC. Some burnt antler and skull bones of deer from Cairns E and K were dated to the period from 3641–3382 to 3366–3165 BC (presumably placed therein with human remains) and represent the earliest dated activity here. These animal parts may have been deliberately placed on a funeral pyre.

It was interesting that aDNA analysis at Carrowkeel found no evidence for direct kinship among the individuals whose bones were deposited in the tombs, even though five of the six samples came from the one monument (Cairn K). This suggests that in this case close family groupings may not have been the basis for deposition. There are, however, kinship links with an individual buried in Listoghil in Carrowmore, with those in a monument with passage tomb affinities at Millin

Bay, Co. Down, and with an unusual male burial in Newgrange. That such relationships extended across the island suggests that these passage tomb individuals had networks with a high degree of social interaction. Since stable isotope analysis also hints at a rich diet of meat and animal products among passage tomb users, these people may have been a privileged and élite segment of the population.

Their burial rites may have been impressive occasions, perhaps involving animal sacrifice. Cremation of human bodies and animal remains was possibly a dramatic and public phenomenon. Post-mortem processing of the bodies may have been the main focus of the funerary rites and it too may have been a spectacular event. Presumably defleshing also involved washing and cleaning the bones. It must have included evisceration, but what happened to the entrails, organs and skin is not known. Their disposal would have been some of the many mortuary practices invisible in the archaeological record. It is not impossible that some body parts were eaten, and the heart, skull and brain may have been a focus of particular attention. Parts of the body may have been distributed as mementoes or relics. Blood may have been drunk as part of these rites. Indeed, there are some disconcerting references to the practice of drinking the blood of the deceased as a mourning ritual in early Irish tradition, and even in a number of literary and historical sources of more recent date. Why treat the human body in so many different ways?

The manipulation of human corpses was a frequent and widespread practice from Palaeolithic times onwards not only in Europe but also in Africa and Asia. Extensive ethnographic evidence serves as a reminder of how varied and intricate mortuary rites once were. For instance, even though mainly a Muslim people, the Dii of Cameroon in central Africa remained preoccupied with the question of natural or unnatural death as recently as the early twentieth century. The latter was attributed to witchcraft or sorcery of one sort or another. Accidental death was often suspect. Only children and those who died in combat were above suspicion.

To determine whether the death was natural, the body of the deceased was laid on its side in his or her house and carefully examined. This involved opening the body to reveal the entrails, liver, lungs and heart. It was then the task of the elders and the blacksmiths to determine what sort of sorcery was involved. If examination revealed a pale heart (empty of blood), it was concluded that death was due to the action of a sorcerer who had stolen the heart of the deceased and brought it home. If the stomach contained blood or the intestines were rotten or displayed black marks, other forms of sorcery were involved. If all seemed normal, nothing else had to be done and the extracted body parts were buried behind the house. The corpse was filled with leaves of a particular tree, stitched up with fibres of a kind of hemp and then interred. If witchcraft was diagnosed, there might be a trial to determine who was responsible or the family might seek revenge on the presumed sorcerer by magical means.

In contrast, among the Asabano of central New Guinea we find a very different ritual response to death in the same period. They believed that the world had always existed but that ancestral heroes had changed the landscape and established people there. When a man or woman of good standing died, his or her body was placed on a platform built some distance from the settlement. The body was protected, covered by bark and branches, and allowed to decay naturally.

After decomposition, men either collected or abandoned the bones. Individuals thought to possess special or greater abilities than others were more likely to have their bones preserved because all such abilities derived from that person's spiritual power. Bones of those considered unskilled and thus without powerful connections to the supernatural were just left at the exposure site. Men carried individual bones for success in hunting, painted skulls to give them power in battle, and buried bones in gardens beneath sacred Cordyline plants to ensure a good harvest. The skulls of important women were preserved in net bags in communal houses where families slept. The Asabano also curated certain bones as memory aids to preserve accounts of ancestral activities. During initiations, bones of named relatives and ancestors were displayed, and stories and songs of their accomplishments were shared. Evidently the dead continued as a significant spiritual presence among the living.

We naturally look at the remote past through modern eyes and tend to impose modern concepts on the materials and peoples that we investigate. An examination of the beliefs and practices of non-Western societies like the Dii and the Asabano does not tell us what our past was like, but the use of ethnographic analogy does alert us to different ways of doing things.

Numerous animal bones were found in the early Carrowkeel excavations but little attention was paid to them. The animal skeletal remains included cattle, sheep or goat, dog or wolf, pig, red deer and hare. Cairn K produced some red deer bones, including cremated antler and skull fragments. Interestingly, this suggests that a deer skull with antlers still attached could have been placed on a cremation pyre. It is often assumed that animal bones from burial contexts are the remains of ceremonial funeral feasts, and this may be the case in many instances. It is also possible, however, that animal sacrifice may have been a dramatic part of the rituals at Cairn K and elsewhere.

At Ashleypark, near Nenagh, Co. Tipperary, a cairn covered a rectangular Neolithic tomb that contained the disarticulated bones of an elderly adult male and a child, and some bones of cattle, sheep and pig. More animal bones were found in the cairn and represented cattle and pig. In many cases the cattle bones were split

1.4—Parknabinnia, Co. Clare, before excavation.

or broken for marrow extraction and sometimes displayed butchering marks, indicating that they were discarded food remains. Thus the consumption of food does seem to have been part of the rituals enacted here, but some of these animals may have been ceremonially slaughtered as part of the feasting process. It is worth remembering that the sacrificial killing of large and valuable cattle may have been an especially important act.

Interesting evidence comes from a small court tomb at Parknabinnia, in the Burren, Co. Clare, that contained the disarticulated remains of some twenty individuals, including males, females and children. It seems that people moved bones around in episodes of tomb-cleaning and further deposition: larger bones were moved more, while smaller bones tended to stay closer to where they were first placed. The main period of use extended over quite a number of centuries from 3700 BC to about 2800 BC, and during this long timespan there may have been a number of episodes of deposition, clearance and cleaning, and sealing, before the next event. The very small amount of cremated bone found represents later insertions in the latter part of the third millennium.

The contemporary animal bone assemblage was dominated by hare bones, and it seems that whole and partly dismembered hares were deposited in the tomb along with the human remains. Young dog and young cattle and pig were also represented, so the deposition of juveniles in spring is a possibility and perhaps associated with fertility rites. The prominence of hares, some with their forelimbs deliberately removed, indicates formal killing. It is a very intriguing depositional pattern that probably associated hares in particular with regeneration. Their forelimbs may have been taken as amulets or charms. They may have been used to cure bodily ailments: as late as the seventeenth century, according to his diaries, Samuel Pepys cured himself of a bout of colic with his hare's foot.

The hare figures in the popular beliefs of many peoples around the world and some considered it a sacred animal. Certain Classical writers thought that it was a hermaphrodite or that it breathed through its ears. A pope in the eighth century reminded Christians that the eating of jackdaws, crows and storks along with beavers, hares and wild horses was strictly forbidden. Hares also have a somewhat negative reputation in Irish folklore, being mainly associated with old women who had the ability to transform themselves into hares to steal butter or milk. This 'witch as hare' motif was widespread in medieval Europe, too. On a more positive note, it is good to know that the Easter Bunny was originally a hare and a symbol of rebirth at the time of the full moon that follows the spring equinox.

These rituals of death that entailed the religious manipulation of human and animal remains were imbued with complex meanings. It seems that death, the ultimate rite of passage, was linked with regeneration. Particular parts of human and animal bodies evidently had special significance. Defleshing and disarticulating the human corpse may have been seen as a means of purifying it and speeding its transition to a world of ancestors. The stone tomb itself may have been a monumental indication that the dead were never far away.

Looking at the evidence from sites such as Carrowkeel and Parknabinnia, a modern reader might well ask why dismember a human body? Why deliberately destroy it on a funeral pyre?

It is possible that such destructive acts can tell us something about the deeper religious beliefs of these ancient peoples. We cannot be certain, of course, but some clues may lie in sophisticated Indo-European concepts of life and death. There was a belief that the world (and thus all of humanity) was created from the dismembered body of the first man and, while there are a number of variations on a very complicated scenario, essentially the earth was made of his flesh, mountains of his bones and plants of his hair. Variations on this theme of dismemberment are to be found in diverse mythologies around the world, from the Rig Veda in India to Scandinavian mythology. Man is transformed into distinct elements of the cosmos and death itself becomes a creative act. This was just as coherent a philosophy as any belief in a single omnipotent Creator. That ritual performance involving the dismemberment of the body should replicate primordial events is unsurprising. We see this sort of action in a Christian context, where the Eucharist is a re-enactment of the Last Supper and baptism has its origin in older rites of purification.

The Indo-European evidence should at least remind us that at Carrowkeel and Parknabinnia, and at other places, the sacrificial dismemberment of humans and animals was a deeply religious act. While it may have been a repetition of an original creative event in which the body of a primordial being served as the raw material from which the physical universe was made, the fundamentally important aim of these varied rituals was to sustain creation. These repetitive sacrifices had a cosmological significance, for they represented a concept of how the world worked and a consciousness of cyclical time that was reflected in the changing seasons, in the heavens and in the rhythms of nature.

2

Veneration of the sun

2.1—The winter solstice sun in Newgrange passage tomb.

In Peter Shaffer's epic drama *The Royal Hunt of the Sun*, the Inca Atahuallpa, son of the sun god Inti, declares: 'If you kill me tonight, I will rise at dawn, when my Father first touch my body with light … I will swallow death and spit it out of me'. Atahuallpa is killed one night in 1593 at the behest of the *conquistador* Francisco Pizarro. He actually believed in this solar myth and fully expected the Inca to rise again. Atahuallpa's people also believed—just as the Inca did—that his resurrection would coincide with the rising sun. In a faith-shattering scene of extraordinary power, the sun rises but the murdered Inca does not—failing to respond to the rays of the sun as they touch his body.

Veneration of the sun is probably as old as humanity and has taken many forms around the world, from the Inca of ancient Peru to the Greek Helios and Persian

Mithra. It is easy to forget how human activity was dictated by sunrise and sunset and how the power of the sun influenced the seasons. Since solar observation was one of the major factors in structuring the agricultural calendar, it is not surprising that it also had a significant impact on the monumentalisation of the European landscape in early prehistory.

Several hundred Neolithic circular enclosures or rondels have been found in recent decades, mainly in central Europe. Many have significant solar orientations marked by entrances on the south-east or south-west towards sunrise or sunset; some have been called 'solar temples'.

2.2—Above: the reconstructed Goseck circle. Below: the double palisades at Goseck as reconstructed.

One of the earliest, dating from about 4900 BC, is at Goseck, south-west of Leipzig in Germany. The Goseck rondel consists of a circular ditch about 71m in diameter with two concentric timber palisade circles inside it, 56m and 49m across respectively. There are several entrances to the interior but the principal pair on the south-east and south-west are orientated towards the midwinter sunrise and sunset respectively. One other entrance is orientated to the north but with an error of a few degrees.

This was a place where significant celestial observations formed part of seasonal rituals. The enclosing elements might imply that access was restricted to certain special members of the community but in fact it may have been a place of pilgrimage for a wider audience. The two enclosing palisades with several metres between them and the various astronomical alignments do imply some internal order and orientation. The circle was a sacred space with cosmic significance, for in much of the ancient world the cosmos was perceived as circular. The earth was flat, and the star-studded sky above was bowl-shaped. The periodical movements of the sun, moon and stars helped to structure time and to determine critical dates for certain human events. The sun, itself a disc, journeyed in a great circle across the heavens and then beneath the earth to rise again. Large ritual enclosures, like Goseck, were conceived as miniature representations of the cosmos, and the various components, such as entrances and boundary palisades, were rich in symbolic meaning.

Archaeologists often see large monuments as expressions of social competition or of a desire for ostentatious display. They note the probability that their construction may often have included performance and spectacle, and that they may have had a role in creating a sense of community and in promoting social cohesion. All of this may be true, but sites like Newgrange and Goseck remind us of the importance of intense religious experience—with a solar focus—that was a feature of the lives of many traditional societies.

The winter solstice, the shortest day of the year in the northern hemisphere, was a moment in time that marked the rejuvenation of the sun. In many farming communities it was probably a time of celebration, and it has been claimed that various winter festivals may originally have been linked to this event. The Welsh 'Mari Lwyd' folk custom, in which a horse's skull is paraded through the streets by a man covered in cloth and ribbons to ensure good fortune in the year to come, is just one example, but establishing a clear link between midwinter festivities and the solstice is difficult.

Many European megalithic tombs have a general eastern or western orientation and are believed to be aligned on the rising or setting sun. Some are also meant to face noteworthy features in the landscape, such as significant hilltops or other

2.3—Bryn Celli Ddu passage tomb.

important monuments. Some are aligned on the winter solstice, that profoundly important astronomical juncture that marks the regeneration of the sun. A small number are focused on the summer solstice.

The great passage tomb at Bryn Celli Ddu on Anglesey in Wales is one that is orientated on the midsummer solstice. Its round mound covers a polygonal chamber containing a tall pillar stone on one side and approached by a long passage. A beam of light from the rising sun penetrates the passage and illuminates the end wall of the chamber. This passage was extended and blocked with stones shortly after the monument was constructed, sealing the burnt and unburnt bones of the dead. When the tomb was closed, the sun's rays could only penetrate the chamber through a narrow slot above the blocking. It has been suggested that this was a solstice alignment created to nourish the dead rather than the living. Those who understood the symbolic meanings of the different elements of the monument, including its pillar stone and its solar magic, were the possessors of powerful secret knowledge.

Winter or summer solstice alignments appear to occur at about a dozen Irish passage tombs, including Townley Hall, Co. Louth (summer sunrise), and Knockroe, Co. Kilkenny (winter sunrise eastern tomb, winter sunset western tomb). The winter phenomenon at Newgrange is undoubtedly the best known. This famous tomb was constructed around 3200 BC and its long passage leads to an impressive cruciform chamber. Its stones were laboriously transported from different locations and may have been imbued with special significance.

The discovery of what has been called the 'roof-box' above the entrance to the passage on the south-east indicates that the face of the great mound probably

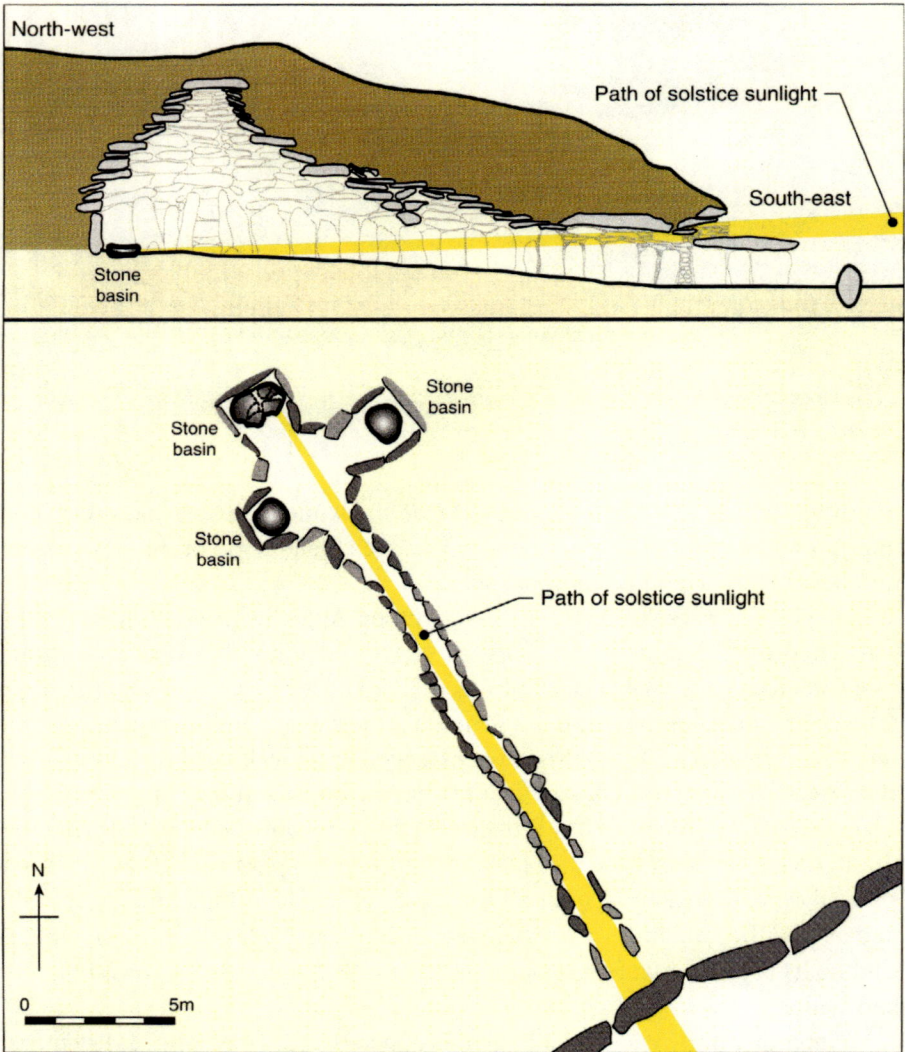

North-west

Path of solstice sunlight

South-east

Stone
basin

Stone
basin

Stone
basin

Stone
basin

Path of solstice sunlight

N

0   5m

2.4—The path of the sun in Newgrange.

turned inwards at this point. This stone-built slot was constructed beneath a decorated lintel and over a gap between the first two roof-slabs in an extension to the
passage. At dawn on the midwinter solstice the rays of the rising sun shine through
the roof-box and briefly illuminate the chamber. In the past the spectacle would
have lasted for several days and irradiated the interior more than it does today.

Clearly, solar phenomena had a central place in the magico-religious beliefs and practices of those who built this monument, but reconstructing the rituals that may have surrounded this event is difficult, to say the least. We can be sure that it was a profoundly important time of midwinter renewal. Participants may have been a privileged few. A fragment of the skull of an adult male from the 1960s excavations has been subjected to DNA analysis with exceptional results. This individual has proved to be the child of a first-degree incestuous union. In other words, he was the product of a union between a brother and sister or between a parent and off-spring. A radiocarbon date of 3338–3028 BC places this deposition at the time of the tomb's primary usage.

Incest is and has been taboo in most societies, but in those where it has been socially sanctioned, as in ancient Egypt, it has been an élite practice to maintain a dynastic bloodline. Usually it has taken the form of mating between siblings of ruling families whose perceived divinity exempted them from social convention. It was the custom among Inca rulers, too. The Inca peoples did not have a written language and much of what we know comes from sixteenth- and early seventeenth-century accounts written in Spanish. The ruling Inca was expected to marry his full sister. In doing so he emulated his mythical ancestor, the first Inca, Manco Capac, whose father was the sun, and who in one version of the story married his sister. In Inca mythology, the sun, who married his sister the moon, preserved the purity of the divine royal line and gave legitimacy to his heirs' right to the throne in both the male and female lines.

Presumably the practice of sibling incest reflects the emergence of a dynastic system with a strong sense of descent from a common ancestor, a process that ultimately culminated in the emergence of a superior caste. It raises the possibility that the rulers of the great passage tombs in the Boyne Valley were members of royal lineages headed by quasi-divine kings.

It was also established that this Newgrange individual had kin in Sligo at Carrowkeel and at Carrowmore, and in County Down. Such significant relationships extending across the island might suggest that pilgrimages between these special places were a part of rites directed to varied ends throughout the ritual year.

While the solstice ceremonies in Newgrange may have been the preserve of a privileged minority, there may have been nocturnal events and cult feasts for a larger number in the vicinity at this special time. There were probably festivals at other times of the year as well. The Boyne was a sacred river and provided the stones used in the great cairn. It and its waters may have had a role in prolonged and complex ceremonies. The periodic salmon runs may have been important seasonal happenings.

Atahuallpa, whom Shaffer depicts as having a sceptical view of Christian beliefs and practices, would have appreciated such ritual diversity. The Inca year was highly ritualised. In January sacrifices were made with fasts and penance, and people covered themselves in ashes and put ash on their doorways. They held processions to various temples of the sun and of the moon, and went, led by priests, from hilltop to hilltop. In February the Inca king sacrificed great quantities of gold, silver and animals at monuments or natural places for the sun, the moon and the stars, and at the highest mountain peaks during a season of scarcity and hunger. March was considered a time of plenty, but more animals were sacrificed in ceremonies led by priests. Various fiestas took place in April and May, which was the time of harvest.

June was the winter solstice (in the southern hemisphere) and the festival of Inti, when the sun received offerings of gold, silver and shells and children were sacrificed at shrines throughout the land. Different ritual sacrifices took place in July and the following months. September was devoted to the festival of the moon, the wife of the sun, and the Inca king deployed his armies to drive out pestilence from the land. They did this by shouting for the disease to leave and hurling burning embers from their slings. In October rites focused on rainfall, and feasts for dead ancestors were held in November. In December there was another festival of the sun, accompanied by sacrifices.

At Newgrange the combination of mystery, secret knowledge and the orchestration of ritual performance may have been a pursuit of divine legitimacy—to gain the approval of the gods. Ceremonies at the tomb and in the surrounding countryside probably played an important role in both the legitimisation of authority and the maintenance of social order. The veneration of the sun was only one element in a much wider spectrum of recurrent ceremonial activity that may have varied over time and from community to community.

While the custom of building passage tombs, large and small, lasted for almost 1,000 years, the evidence for a preoccupation with solar matters would persist and manifest itself in different ways in the following millennia. This is evident at a number of Bronze Age stone circles, such as Drombeg, near Glandore, Co. Cork, that are aligned on the rising or setting sun.

At Drombeg the solar alignment runs midway between two tall entrance stones on the north-east, and across a flat-topped recumbent stone on the opposite side, in the direction of an indentation in the hills beyond. The sun sets in this notch on the horizon on the winter solstice. Just as at Newgrange, the days and nights on and around 21 December must have been especially important for the people of Drombeg. The interior of the circle was a sacred space and excavation revealed that it had been covered with compacted gravel. Beneath this gravel five small pits were found, three containing shattered stones that must have come from the shaping of the stones in the circle and were then used to sanctify the enclosed area. This may

2.5—Drombeg stone circle, Co. Cork.

also have been the purpose of two pits that held a little cremated bone. One of these token burials, that of an adult male, was accompanied by fragments of a plain pottery vessel. Some charcoal adhering to the pot provided a radiocarbon date of around 1000 BC, presumably indicating construction of the circle in the later Bronze Age.

It is very possible that Drombeg folk had, among their solar myths, the belief that the sun travelled in a boat or a horse-drawn vehicle in its journey across the heavens. The latter is attested by the famous 'chariot of the sun' from Trundholm, Denmark, as we shall see. Other visual imagery of the Bronze Age clearly indicates a belief that the sun might also traverse the heavens in a mythical boat. This was probably a widespread European concept but in the Bronze Age it only finds pictorial expression in rock art and metalwork in Scandinavia, where boat imagery is particularly common (some boats having a horse's head on prow or stern), and on some metalwork in central and northern Europe. Some of these images refer to a mythological narrative of the daytime and night-time journeys of the sun.

This is the accepted interpretation of the Trundholm sun chariot—to be considered later. This is undoubtedly the best-known Bronze Age solar symbol. A gold-plated bronze disc, mounted on a two-wheeled vehicle, is drawn by a horse (mounted on four wheels) from left to right and depicts the sun's westward route across the heavens. When reversed, the back of the disc, which was apparently never

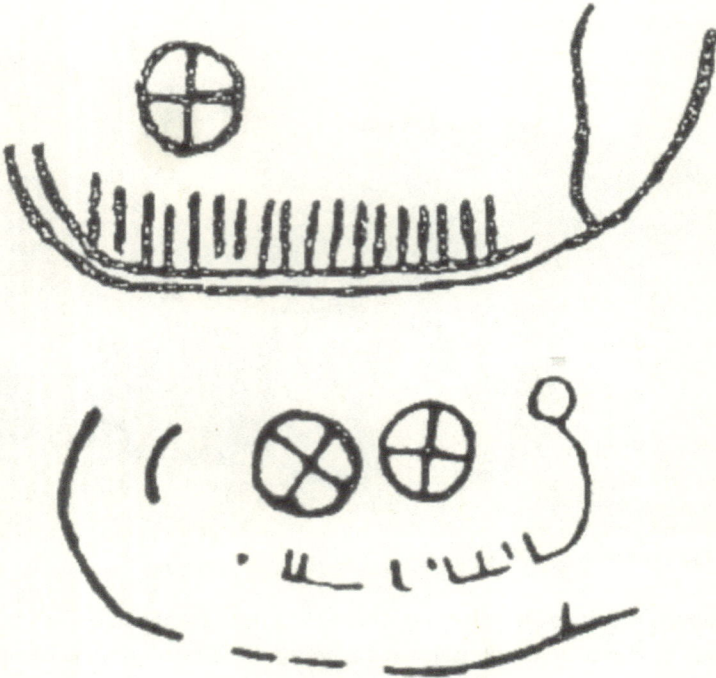

2.6—Two rock art images from Scandinavia depicting (above) a solar symbol in a boat and (below) a pair of suns in a boat.

gold-covered, is pulled by the horse from right to left, and this is taken to represent the sun's nocturnal journey under the land or under the sea towards the dawn in the east. An image of twin suns may carry the same message. These, too, are found in Scandinavian rock art.

The presence of a pair of solar symbols in the one boat is exceptionally interesting; one may be a daytime sun, the other a night-time sun in its underworld journey. A clue to the meaning of some of the earliest Irish goldwork may lie in this particular rock art symbol.

Over twenty decorated discs of sheet gold are known, and they are invariably poorly documented finds. In about half a dozen cases they form matching pairs, and they vary in diameter from about 4cm to about 11cm. A majority also bear a cruciform design, usually a simple double cross with a ladder pattern set within a circle. Centrally placed pairs of perforations were presumably for attaching these discs to something such as cloth or leather. They have been called 'sun discs' for many years.

2.7—The Coggalbeg find.

Gold lunulae are the commonest objects made of this precious metal in the Irish early Bronze Age around 2000 BC. The name, a diminutive of the Latin *luna*, 'moon', was first given to these crescent-shaped objects in the middle of the eighteenth century, and their shape and size have long convinced many writers that they must have been decorative collars. Just over 90 examples have been found in Ireland and many of these have no information recorded about find-spot or context.

A typical lunula is a decorated crescent of burnished, thin, sheet gold with impressed or incised geometric ornament on one face only, where it is invariably confined to the horns of the crescent and the edges of the widest part. Obvious signs of prehistoric use have been detected on very few and they may not have been used as personal ornaments very often, if at all. They may even have decorated inanimate objects like wooden idols. None have come from certain burials—a context that might offer a clue as to their ornamental purpose if, indeed, they were ever worn.

A discovery at Coggalbeg, south-west of Strokestown, Co. Roscommon, raises some intriguing questions about their symbolic significance. Here a lunula and two discs were found at a depth of some 2m in a bog in the course of turf-cutting. This unique Irish association of a curving lunula with a pair of discs with characteristic cross-shaped motifs has prompted Mary Cahill to consider how the two forms may have functioned in combination. She agrees that the different motifs on the gold discs are probably solar symbols and suggests that an arrangement of a pair of discs and a lunula, as at Coggalbeg, might represent twin suns in a solar boat. Other pairs

2.8—The Petrie Crown.

of Irish sun discs may well have carried this meaning, too, when ceremonially displayed with a gold lunula. Perhaps they never were personal ornaments but were objects for display in a place where ceremonies had the sun as the focus of attention.

It is an interesting illustration of the partial and fragmentary nature of the archaeological record that almost 2,000 years must pass before the enduring belief in the voyage of the solar ship is clearly depicted once again in an Irish context.

The Petrie Crown is a tiny but finely decorated object. It is a very small fragmentary piece, only 15cm in maximum height. It now consists of a band of openwork sheet bronze with a pair of slightly dished discs attached to the front. Each disc apparently supported a bronze horn, one of which survives. This horn is made of a sheet of hammered bronze folded to a conical shape. Each element—the band, the discs and the horn—is very skilfully ornamented with an elegant symmetrical

26

2.9—The sun ship is clearly represented on the right-hand disc of the Petrie Crown.

design of thin and elongated trumpet curves, some terminating in different sorts of birds' heads. It is named after the nineteenth-century antiquary George Petrie because it was once in his collection of antiquities. He did not record—or never knew—its provenance, so we know nothing about its find circumstances. If ever used as a crown, given its size it can only have decorated the head of a doll-sized wooden idol.

Various writers have described the decoration on the circular discs in divergent ways. One has described it as having 'an elusive zoomorphic aspect, suggesting creatures with rounded muzzle and large button nose beneath spiral eyes'. Another thought that it looked like a face with an upturned curling moustache. The belief that this sort of La Tène or Celtic art had a sort of playful element in it has a long history. Often abstract or ambiguous or both, this is sometimes an understandable interpretation of some stylised elements in this art style.

2.10—Solar symbolism: (1) On a late Bronze Age bucket from Nyírlugos, eastern Hungary. (2) Two rows of solar boats one above the other on another bucket known as the Vienna situla. (3) An Iron Age bronze torc from Attancourt, Haute-Marne. (4) Iron Age bronze torc from the Marne region.

The design on the disc below the surviving horn is particularly interesting because the bird's-head terminals flank a circle set in a crescent form. In fact, this is a representation of the solar boat with bird's-head prow and stern. In Bronze Age central European solar symbolism birds' heads replace horse heads as the dominant creature on sun ships.

These images are found on fine metalwork in the thirteenth–twelfth centuries BC. On a Hungarian bronze bucket the image consists of a large roundel flanked by birds' heads with two interesting reversed images on either side (with the birds' heads facing inwards). This reversal is significant and possibly reflects the sun's nocturnal journey through the underworld. The representation of two horizontal zones of solar boats, one above the other, on a bucket known as the Vienna situla may have a similar meaning. A series of Iron Age torcs from the Marne region display variations on the theme: a pair of sun ships on one flank a cluster of three roundels,

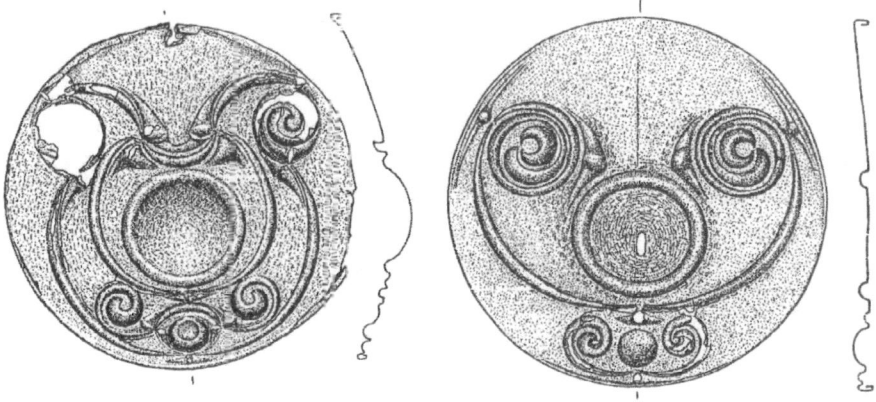

2.11—The Monasterevin discs.

possibly a triple sun, and a wheel-shaped device flanked by birds occurs on another.

It is significant that the left-hand disc on the Petrie Crown displays a reversed motif. In this case the birds enclose a solar roundel in an inverted design that presumably represents an upside-down boat. This juxtapositioning of such contrasting designs presents the viewer with images of a sophisticated cosmological narrative of the daytime and night-time voyages of the sun. When the sun sank in the west, it was believed that it journeyed beneath the earth, through an inverted otherworld, to rise again in the east. As we will see, in one ninth-century text the many marvels and fearful spectacles of this underworld are described. These include a lofty sea of fire, black valleys, the enclosure of the beast, the dark tearful plain with dragons who have been placed under the mist, and flocks of birds who sing many songs.

Such a night-time journey of the sun through a very different underworld is an imaginative concept and, since this nether world was conceived as a reversed or inverted version of this one, its representation in reversed solar imagery in this fashion is unsurprising. It is found on other bronze metalwork as well. One example is a pair of bronze discs from Monasterevin, Co. Kildare. Nothing is known about their discovery and their purpose is unknown. Made of sheet bronze, they are about 30cm in diameter. The solar roundel is clearly set in a broad boat-shaped device but the flanking birds' heads on both are so highly stylised as to be barely recognisable. They are reduced to swirling curves, spiralling inwards on one disc and outwards on the other Once again this reversal is a reference to the sun's nocturnal crossing. It may have held other meanings too, perhaps replicating the division of the year into winter and summer halves.

On these discs the artist seems to be seeking to hide the solar symbol or, more likely, trying to reduce it to its essential elements and, in so doing, to give greater emphasis to its inherent strength. In a very deliberate act, a traditional symbol is altered to give it a new or different or more powerful meaning. Just as repetition, such as triplism, may accentuate the power of an image, so dissection may expose its inner qualities.

Like some gold discs and lunulae, and the Petrie Crown, these discs may once have been attached to wooden or leather supports. They may have been displayed on ceremonial occasions when the story of the journeys of the sun was recounted. It is tempting to think that this may have been a form of sacred theatre accompanied by singing and chanting of mythical tales. Solar mythology and the veneration of the sun were still a fact of life 3,000 years after its worship at Newgrange.

3

The cosmic circle

3.1—Circular passage tomb cairns on Carrowkeel, Co. Sligo.

The large ceremonial circle at Goseck in Germany, dated to around 4900 BC, is an early example of the replication of the cosmic circle in monumental form. The round cairns of passage tombs, as at Carrowkeel, are further expressions of this concept. Stone circles in Ireland, like those at Lissivigeen and Drombeg, are later and smaller examples of the same phenomenon, many with a solar focus.

The circle, a universal symbol, actually takes many forms in early Ireland. From the great circular mound at Newgrange to early medieval enclosures, it is not only found in a ritual context but also was an integral part of secular social practice. The image is so familiar that we no longer pay much attention to what was implicit in it, yet over thousands of years it had a socially accepted cosmological significance. In this long timespan it was a symbol intrinsically bound up with the changes in burial and settlement forms that took place and it evidently represented shifting ideologies.

The sun provided a double image of the circle, both in its form and in its movement in the sky. It helped to shape people's concepts of the world and offered a blueprint for many social actions, from planning a house to enclosing a settlement or building a burial mound. In many countries, archaeological and ethnological evidence shows time and again how people replicated their circular and cyclical concept of the nature of the world in aspects of their daily lives. Elements of temples, tombs, tents, houses, settlements and the landscape itself often reflected this understanding of the cosmos.

That the shape of a circular monument might have had various symbolic meanings would not surprise a Christian worshipper in early medieval Ireland. The quadrangular form of their churches had sacred connotations, too: they echoed the shape of Solomon's Temple and a harmonious quadripartite world created by God with its four seasons, four elements, four humours and so forth. Even the antae which monumentally emphasise the four corners of some early churches gave added expression to the symbolic significance of the quadrilateral form. Facing eastwards to pray, towards the rising sun and the location of the Garden of Eden, was also a deeply symbolic act since the earliest days of Christianity when Christ was declared 'the Sun of Righteousness' (Malachi 4:2).

As already mentioned, the round cairn of a passage tomb, like those at Carrowkeel, set within a retaining circle of stones is one illustration of the embodiment of cosmological principles in funerary architecture. The circle becomes a sacred delimitation between a timeless world, that of the ancestors, and a temporal world, that of the living. The centrally placed burial chamber is the focal point and a metaphor for the *axis mundi*, the centre of the world. Prominent mounds and their frequent location in high places had similar connotations. These monuments were meant to be eternal, in contrast to contemporary domestic dwellings. Each time a passage tomb was built at Carrowkeel, for instance, the creation of the world was re-enacted. Since this was a mystical concept, there could be any number of such central places without any logical inconsistency. The orientation of the entrance of a tomb too, whether facing the rising sun, another monument or a landscape feature, had a story to tell.

As Mircea Eliade has written, a new era begins with every new construction: 'what is important is that man has felt the need to reproduce the cosmogony in his constructions, whatever be their nature; that this reproduction made him contemporary with the mythical moment of the beginning of the world, and that he felt the need of returning to that moment, as often as possible, in order to regenerate himself'. Of course, the metaphysical concept of cyclical time, geared to the changing seasons, the heavens and all the rhythms of nature, does not logically exclude a notion of linear time—an appreciation of sequential events and the memory of ancestors demonstrate this.

The circle finds another monumental expression in the great timber and pit circles and earthen enclosures of the later Neolithic, and in those smaller stone circles as well. The impressive embanked enclosure at Dowth in the Boyne Valley has an internal diameter of some 170m and is enclosed by a huge earthen bank. There is a definite entrance on the south-west and a second, less certain one opposite it on the north-east. A tremendous amount of labour went into its construction, and it was a project of religious significance. This enclosure, and others like it, were great ceremonial sites, and it is highly likely that celestial observations were a part of these activities—as in the more modest stone circles.

Small or large, all these circular monuments had a cosmic charge. A diminutive circle of five stones at Knocknaneirk, near the village of Crookstown, Co. Cork, is only about 4m across. The main axis of these Cork–Kerry circles is usually aligned

3.2—Stone circle at Knocknaneirk, Co. Cork; the axial stone is in the foreground.

3.3—Reconstruction of a Bronze Age round house at Killydonoghoe, Co. Cork.

on the rising and setting sun, but Knocknaneirk is one that does not conform to this pattern. Its recumbent or axial stone, opposite a pair of portal or entrance stones, is on the north. Nonetheless, its diminutive enclosure encapsulated the same essential meaning as the great earthen ring at Dowth.

The sixteenth century BC witnesses the emergence of a formal round house architecture in Bronze Age Ireland. Many hundreds of examples are now known. One, revealed by excavation at Killydonoghoe, between Watergrasshill and Cork city, was a fairly typical single house, simply formed by one circle of timber posts some 6.4m in diameter with an entrance on the south-east. A central hearth was set in a deep, roughly circular pit, and some stake-holes may have marked internal partitions. Quantities of oak and hazel charcoal suggested that the posts may have been oak and supported wall panels of woven hazel. This house was dated to around the twelfth century BC.

The circular house in Britain has been a fruitful area of study for those who believe that life in such places was ritually structured. In many cases these houses display a consistent orientation towards the east and towards a rising sun that nourished both house and inhabitants. Internal organisation was based around the central hearth, with periphery and entrance also important—as the occasional votive offering suggests. This is broadly the case in Ireland too. To what extent there were strict rules is uncertain, however, though the persistent use of a circular plan does suggest a shared cosmology. Not every central hearth may have been perceived as an *axis mundi*, for there are good practical reasons for placing a fireplace in the centre of a timber house, but it is possible that the mystical and the functional were combined in this configuration.

There is abundant ethnographic evidence to demonstrate how the domestic dwelling might be redolent with symbolic meaning, the house being a microcosm in which controlled ritual space may have embodied a number of social and religious meanings. The Kaguru are a Bantu people who live in what is today east-central Tanzania in east Africa. Their round houses have male and female symbolic connotations. The hearth, with its associations of warmth, sustenance and comfort, is a woman's domain, and terms for fire, hearthstones and cooking pots sometimes represent women and their qualities. A tall central post near the hearth, sometimes hung with male symbols such as weapons, is said to represent men. The main timber posts in a rectangular structure might have a similar meaning. The house as a whole, then, conjoins male and female principles and represents social order and security.

In the cosmology of the Inuit people of the Canadian Arctic, it was believed that each dwelling had a particular soul, its *inua* (soul or living spirit), which created a spiritual bond between the inhabitant and the house. In addition to this soul, the house was thought of as a protective female body, reflected in some of the descriptive vocabulary of the house. For example, the word *paa* (entrance) was also a vulva, a *quingaq* (ventilation hole) a nose, and a *quilak* (arch of the door) a roof of the mouth. This body was then considered a person that encompassed, nourished and protected its inhabitants. Surprisingly, the hearth seemed to have no bodily designation.

The circular theme is also dominant in the funerary sphere throughout much of prehistory. Round mound, ring-ditch, embanked ring-ditch and ring-barrow are widespread monument types. The principal distinguishing feature of both ring-barrow and embanked ring-ditch is a bank and inner ditch, and in many cases these are annular. Some have an entrance through the bank and a corresponding causeway across the ditch, often on the eastern side; examples with two opposed entrances are also known. A number occur in groups or cemeteries, often along with other monuments—as on the Hill of Tara, Co. Meath.

Two embanked ring-ditches were excavated on Carbury Hill, Co. Kildare, in 1936. One was exceptionally large, with an overall diameter of over 51m. Its ditch,

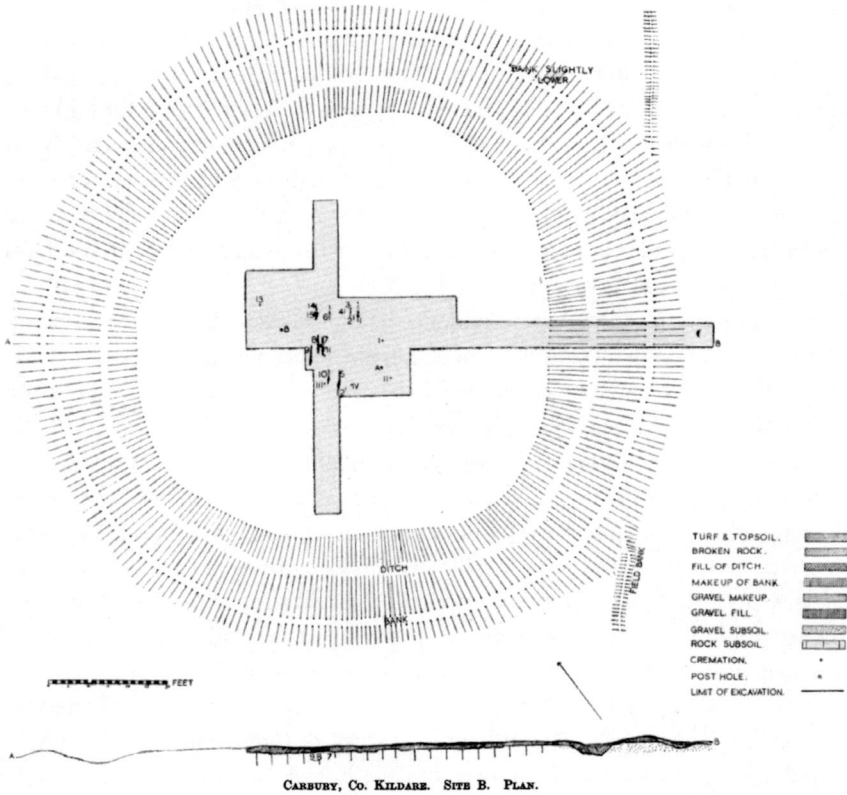

TURF & TOPSOIL.
BROKEN ROCK.
FILL OF DITCH.
MAKEUP OF BANK.
GRAVEL MAKEUP.
GRAVEL FILL.
GRAVEL SUBSOIL.
ROCK SUBSOIL.
CREMATION.
POST HOLE.
LIMIT OF EXCAVATION.

CARBURY, Co. KILDARE. SITE B. PLAN.

3.4—Plan of an embanked ring-ditch on Carbury Hill, Co. Kildare.

inside the bank, was substantial and rock-cut, being over 4m wide and 1m deep. This arrangement of internal ditch and external bank is quite common. We see it at great ceremonial enclosures like Navan Fort, where it is clearly the reversal of the normal defensive order—with ditch outside a rampart—to repel any external assault. It was configured to symbolically contain the forces of the Otherworld within the sacred precincts of the monument.

The Carbury Hill ring-ditch was only partially excavated, and a mix of burials was revealed in the central area. Four cremations were found, two of them apparently disturbed by later unburnt burials. One of the cremated deposits was accompanied by two small iron rings and a pin-shaped fragment. There were also fifteen unburnt burials, three disturbed by other later interments. All the undisturbed burials were extended with heads to the south-west. The excavator, George Willmot, a young English archaeologist particularly interested in Beaker pottery, must have

36

been disappointed at the lack of finds and of dating evidence. The human bones were preserved, however, and several decades later would tell an interesting story.

Four have now been radiocarbon-dated and six subjected to strontium and oxygen isotope analysis in which tooth enamel can indicate a person's place of origin or where they spent their childhood. One male skeleton is dated to the third or fourth century AD and represents one of the earliest cases of the new burial rite of extended inhumation. He originated in the west of Ireland. One female of fourth- or fifth-century date also came from the west. Another female, slightly later in date, came from somewhere on the Kerry coast in the far south-west. Both were adults, 45–60 years old, when they died and were buried on this hill. Three other burials, all male, were of local origin. Carbury Hill was certainly a special place and it was a privilege to be buried there.

The hill figures in early Irish mythology as Síd Nechtain, the otherworldly home of Nechtan, the husband of Boand, goddess of the River Boyne. There is a rich mythology attached to the well of Segais at the foot of the hill, the source of the sacred river. It is possible that the two women, interred in what was an ancestral burial place, represent important marriage alliances between a Kildare dynasty and distant communities.

The following year, in 1937, Willmot excavated two Bronze Age round mounds at Carrowbeg North, Co. Galway, with limited results. In the 1940s he served as one of the 'Monuments Men' in Germany, engaged in the task of recovering and protecting cultural and artistic treasures looted during the war. He then became keeper of the Yorkshire Museum in York.

Circular architecture is a noteworthy aspect of great Iron Age ceremonial centres like Tara, Navan Fort, Rathcroghan and Dún Ailinne. Excavation at Navan Fort has revealed an extraordinary sequence of circular structures over a long time-span of nearly 1,000 years. A great enclosure with rampart and internal ditch, multiple circular features, a huge timber shrine and a great mound raised in the first century BC are an exceptional illustration of a repetitive circular architecture that time and again reflected the creation of the world and was a physical expression of a complex reflection on the cosmos.

This powerful ideology did not die with the advent of Christianity. It evolved into something new and equally powerful symbolically. The circular enclosure of many an early ecclesiastical site is an expression of a sacred place invested with a new spiritual force and divine protection. It was, moreover, a place where the sun-wise or *deiseal* movement was an integral part of the ritual circuit.

A striking illustration of this sacred circle is the plan of Tech Moling, the monastery of the seventh-century St Moling in County Carlow, as depicted in a sketch

+ ST. MARK
+ JEREMIAH
+
HOLY SPIRIT
+
+
ST. LUKE
+   +
ISAIAH
+ CHRIST WITH HIS
APOSTLES
ST. MATTHEW
+   +
DANIEL
+ EZEKIEL
+ ST. JOHN

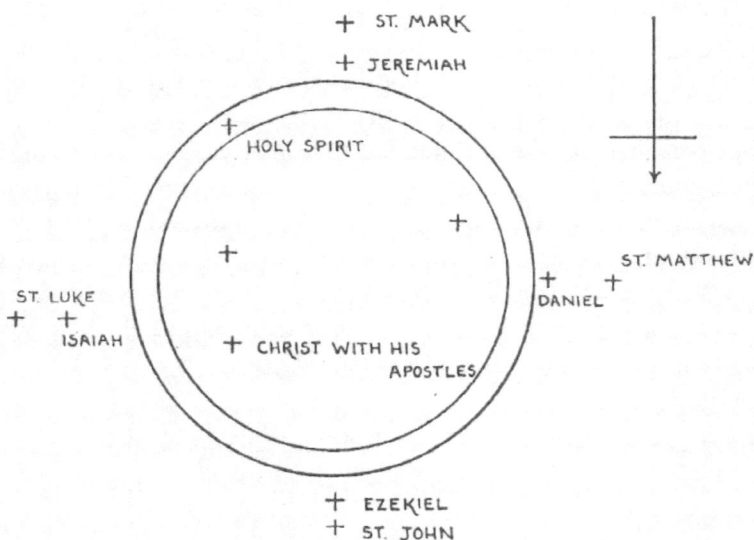

3.5—Charles Thomas's rendering of the schematic plan of the ideal circular monastic enclosure as depicted in the Book of Mulling.

in the eighth-century Book of Mulling. Though damaged and difficult to interpret in places, this drawing shows eight crosses outside the enclosure at the cardinal points of the compass. Each of these pairs combines the names of an Evangelist and a prophet. The inscriptions attached to the crosses within the enclosure are partly illegible. Charles Thomas saw this drawing as a representation of the model enclosure plan. Although often distorted by the facts of local topography, the ideal was undoubtedly a circular one.

Other elements of early insular Christianity may also have some pagan roots. It is possible that this is true of the cult of relics, long believed to be an essentially Christian invention. It is widely assumed to be an integral part of the Christian package and of Mediterranean origin, inspired by the enshrinement of the remains of early martyrs. Martin Carver, however, has rightly noted that the curation of body parts, keeping them as mementoes or souvenirs, has a long prehistory in these islands, from Neolithic to Iron Age times. We will see many examples, and the local adaptation of a pre-existing practice may well have been a major part in the development of this aspect of the new Christian cult.

Like so many other elements of older belief systems, such as a slain god, a virgin birth and a divine child, the cosmic circle was just one very visible symbol appropriated and transmuted by the new religion.

4

Small offerings in hallowed places

4.1—Megalithic tomb at Altar, Co. Cork.

The active reuse of monuments long after they were constructed is a well-documented occurrence in prehistoric archaeology. Secondary burials in megalithic
tombs are well known. Human bones, animal remains, pottery sherds and other
artefacts testify to this. Small offerings of a less tangible sort were probably very
common too but are less easy to identify; indeed, many would not survive in the
archaeological record. Just this sort of thing was described by William Wilde in the
nineteenth century. Writing in his *Irish popular superstitions* in 1852, he recounted
some of the folk customs that followed sudden and unexplained deaths that were
often attributed to fairy folk or 'good people' who had spirited the deceased away:

'Decomposition may indeed afford the physiologist proof positive that the
vital spark has fled, but that avails little with a people who firmly believe

he is "with the fairies on the hill of Rawcroghan (Rath Croghan), or the Fort of Mullaghadooey, where there is plenty of neighbours gone before him". So rooted is this belief, that we have known food of different kinds, bread, meat, and whiskey to be brought by the relatives of deceased persons, and laid for weeks after in these places for their comforts. Fairy-women are often employed to "set a charm" and bargain for their release with the king and queen of the *gentry*.'

The hill at Rathcroghan is a great prehistoric mound, and Mullaghadooey a prominent burial mound near Castlerea, Co. Roscommon, where Wilde was born. Local cult practices like these illustrate the former importance of folk religion and the role that many archaeological monuments continued to play in this sphere well into the nineteenth century.

One megalithic tomb has certainly displayed a long and remarkable pattern of what would seem to be unremarkable small offerings. This simple monument in the townland of Altar, near Schull in west Cork, overlooks Toormore Bay and stands on level grassy ground above a rocky shoreline. It seems to have been deliberately aligned on the pointed summit of Mizen Peak, 13km to the west-south-west, near the end of the peninsula.

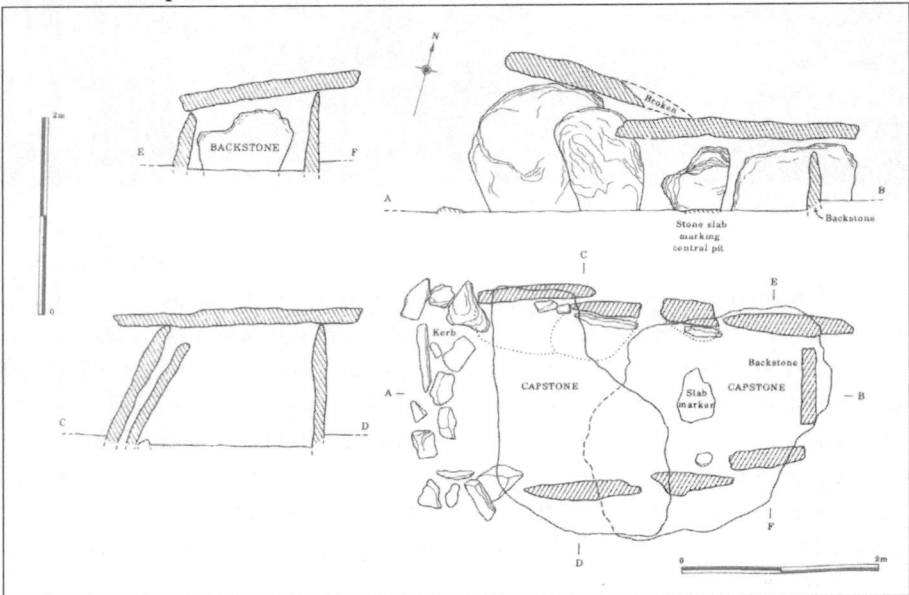

4.2—Simplified plan and cross-section of the Altar wedge tomb after reconstruction, with side slab on north-east and end stone replaced.

Altar is a slab-built structure with two capstones. Only 3.42m in length, each side was formed of three stones and its entrance faced west-south-west. The tomb slopes downwards from front to back, and it also narrows towards the rear, giving it a characteristic wedge-shaped ground-plan. Excavation by William O'Brien revealed that the entrance to the chamber had been marked by a low kerb of a single course of medium to large boulders. It was not clear how the tomb entrance had been sealed. Two large pieces of white quartz had been deliberately placed in the kerb at either end. Two pits containing some stone flakes were found beneath this kerb. These fragments were the product of extracting and shaping the stones of the tomb, which had been sourced nearby, an act that was obviously thought worthy of commemoration. This recalls the three pits in the stone circle at Drombeg, Co. Cork, which contained some shattered stone that came from the shaping of the surrounding stones and were perhaps used to consecrate the enclosed area. Some bones of a whale or dolphin had also been placed below the kerb at Altar, and a fair amount of quartz was found scattered around the tomb.

Apart from two flint flakes, no artefacts were found in the chamber, which produced a little cremated bone—just 15g. These were of a human adult and were found near the entrance. A single unburnt tooth, some charcoal from two pits near the rear of the chamber and some deposits of shellfish such as periwinkles and limpets were also discovered. At first glance these results might be considered unpromising, but a programme of radiocarbon dating of a number of samples from a variety of carefully selected contexts revealed an astonishing pattern of prehistoric depositional events and a sequence of ritual activity that sheds considerable light on the later use of the monument.

The unburnt tooth associated with some cremated bone found inside the tomb entrance dated initial activity to 2316–1784 BC; this deposit is probably broadly contemporary with the construction of the monument. Thus, like other tombs of this wedge-shaped category, it dates from the Chalcolithic or Copper Age. These wedge tombs were the last type of megalithic tomb to be built, but Altar would be remembered for many generations to come.

Some charcoal from a small pit near the centre of the chamber was dated to 1250–832 BC and indicates some sort of depositional activity later in the Bronze Age which could have included small offerings of food or some other perishables. Some more charcoal found near the rear of the chamber provided slightly later dates of 998–560 BC and 766–404 BC.

Charcoal from a small pit on the south side of the chamber dates from the Iron Age period, 356 BC–AD 68. A deposit of periwinkle and limpet shells inside the entrance is of later date: 2 BC–AD 230. A pit in the centre of the chamber had a complicated history. It contained various deposits of shells (periwinkle and limpet) and fish bones (wrasse and eel); three dates for the upper fill place some of this activity in the second century AD. Some charcoal and shell from a very small deposit near the entrance are not precisely dated but indicated some medieval activity.

The ritual sequence at Altar initially seems to have involved just the deposition of token deposits of human remains, but the placing of food offerings, including fish and shellfish, may have figured prominently particularly in later prehistoric times. In fact, the placing of perishable offerings of food in burial contexts may have been common: burnt sea shells, including unopened mussels and oysters, were found along with some cremated bone in one of the small passage tombs at Carrowmore, Co. Sligo. They were very probably contributions for the dead and in some cases may have been placed on the funeral pyre. Food offerings of one sort or another may have been quite widespread in a variety of contexts.

There was some unusual ritual activity before the building of a passage tomb on the summit of Baltinglass Hill, just north-east of the village of Baltinglass, Co. Wicklow. A layer of burnt material contained two concentrations of charred hazelnut shells, and a polished stone axehead was found near one of these deposits. A quantity of charred wheat grains was also discovered in a separate concentration of burnt material. Evidently fires were lit here, and offerings of foodstuff were made as part of some preparatory rites on the hilltop.

It would appear that the depositional emphasis at Altar may have shifted from human remains to votive offerings of other materials in the course of the second millennium BC. Late prehistoric people obviously also regarded the monument as a special place. This seems to have been a location that retained a sacred character for over 2,000 years, when it may variously have been remembered as an ancestral burial place and a gateway to an Otherworld occupied by potent forces for good or evil. It is a good illustration of the fact that monuments are about memory and may govern the lives of later generations.

The fact that the tomb is aligned on the pointed summit of Mizen Peak to the south-west, the Carn Uí Neid of early Irish legend, may be noteworthy too, for it was associated with the mythical Tuatha Dé Danann, the immortal people of the goddess Danu. This may also have been an orientation towards the setting sun at Samhain in early November, the point on the horizon beyond the ocean where the sun began its nocturnal journey through the underworld. This reminds us that the surrounding landscapes and seascapes of such monuments were also imbued with mythological significance in prehistory.

Another tomb in Toormore townland, 750m to the north-west, was excavated too. Radiocarbon dating suggested that it was built around 1900 BC, so it may have been broadly contemporary with Altar. It had a very different story to tell, however—there was no evidence of prolonged later reuse. No human bones or artefacts were found but it was revered in another way. There was a deliberate setting of white quartz pebbles in the entrance area, and four pits contained stone flakes that came from working the stones of the tomb—as at Altar. The offering of 58 quartz pebbles placed on the floor of the tomb was an early deliberate deposit.

It is not certain that the scatter of quartz fragments and pebbles around the Altar monument was deliberate, but it probably was, and their presence may have magically charged the area. When they are water-rolled, quartz stones appear as white pebbles. Such 'shining stones' had a symbolic significance and have been found in a number of other megalithic tombs, and on some later prehistoric sites and burials as well. For example, a standing stone, one of a pair on the upper slopes of the Barrees Valley near Eyeries, Co. Cork, had an offering of small boulders of white quartz placed next to it. Two deposits of cremated bone were found nearby, one in a pit also containing some white quartz. This burial was dated to 1260–980 BC.

Quartz stones are well documented on a small number of early medieval church sites and cemeteries too. Throughout the ages they may have been a symbol of rebirth. In folklore they sometimes have curative powers or otherworldly associations. Quartz is also luminescent, reflecting both moonlight and firelight, and when struck or rubbed together it appears to glow. It has been linked to both solar and lunar symbolism—in recumbent stone circles and passage graves, for instance—and consequently may also have associations with death. Indeed, it has been suggested that ancient peoples may have seen fragments of the moon itself in scatters of quartz that glittered brilliantly in the moonlight.

Over two millennia after the two quartz stones were placed at Altar, the protective power of such white stones is graphically depicted in Adomnán's Life of St Columba, who is said to have blessed a white pebble and used it to cure an ailing Pictish king. The stone was dipped in water and floated on the surface instead of sinking; the king then drank this water and recovered. He kept the magical stone thereafter in the royal treasury, where it healed many others.

Columba's stone may have had curative powers but in other Christian contexts quartz pebbles may have had a different meaning. Thousands have been found in an early monastic settlement on Inishark, off the Connemara coast, where they were associated with a number of stone-built altar stations (*leachta*). These ritual monuments were part of a *turas* or pilgrimage path on the island in medieval times. All of the quartz stones were water-worn, rounded and polished by the sea, and collected on the nearby shore. The smoothness and colour of the pebbles must have

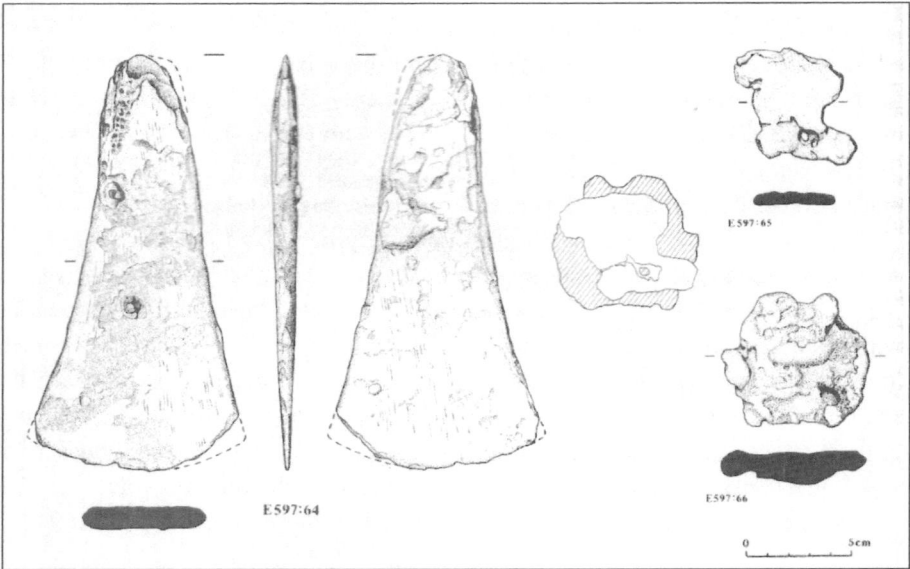

4.3—Bronze axehead and two pieces of copper from Toormore.

had some special meaning for the monks and pilgrims who gathered and handled them, and then left them as individual offerings. Unusual stones, like other unprecedented phenomena, possibly revealed the majesty of God's power over creation, and their white colour may have had some association with spiritual purity.

Apart from the quartz pebbles, there were no offerings in the Toormore tomb, but a notable deposit had been placed at the tomb entrance. Though modest in size, it was presumably much more important than a gift of shellfish. It comprised a small bronze axehead and two pieces of raw copper. Though corroded, it is evident that the axehead is decorated with multiple longitudinal strokes on its flat faces (a so-called rain pattern) and possible lozenge-shaped marks on its narrow sides. It was a prestigious object, possibly an emblem of authority, and along with the copper pieces this was a valuable votive deposit. Indeed, we may underestimate its significance. If the axehead was as valuable as an ox or a horse, we should possibly consider this a bloodless propitiatory sacrifice and very different from a small offering.

5

Crouched burial

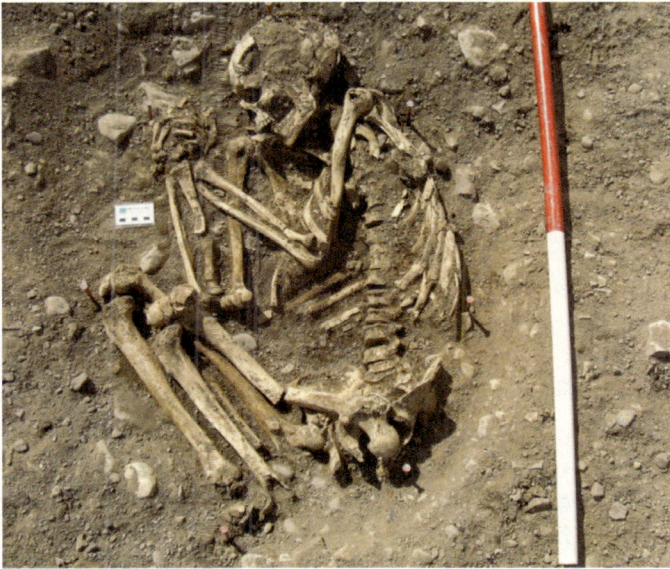

5.1—Excavation of a burial at Mullamast, Co. Kildare.

Excavations in 2007 in the townland of Mullamast, near Ballitore, Co. Kildare, revealed a solitary burial in a shallow pit grave. The skeleton, that of an adult male
about 40 years old, had been placed in a crouched position, face to the west, with
hands apparently clasped together. There were no grave-goods but presumably the
body had been wrapped in a shroud that bound the corpse with legs drawn up in
this fashion. The only find in the grave was a gallstone, suggesting that he had a
fat-rich high-cholesterol diet. Radiocarbon dating indicated that he died in the Iron
Age, around 500 BC. This was a time when cremation was the norm, so he was accorded this unusual rite of crouched unburnt burial. This might be seen as just an
eccentric deviation but there are probably deeper meanings here.

Today the dead are discreetly cremated, or the extended and coffined corpse is ceremonially buried in consecrated ground. A few eccentric souls with a contrary inclination and the financial means have done it differently, of course. Samuel Grubb of Castlegrace, Co. Tipperary, who died in 1921, was famously buried upright in a tall conical cairn that stands today on a hillside near Clogheen with panoramic views of the surrounding countryside. Adolphus Cooke of Cookesborough, Co. Longford, who believed that his father would be reincarnated as a bee and who allegedly thought that he himself would be reincarnated as a fox, had himself interred in a beehive-shaped mausoleum in the mid-nineteenth century. This structure is still to be seen in the grounds of the Church of Ireland church at Reynella, Co. Westmeath.

The fashion of burying an individual in a crouched or foetal position in a grave was popular in Ireland in two distinct periods: in the Chalcolithic and early Bronze Age, between about 2200 BC and 1600 BC, and again, briefly, in the Iron Age, especially in later times, from the second century BC to the first century AD. The term 'crouched burial' includes those bodies buried in a flexed position with the bent knees drawn up towards the abdomen and those whose limbs and torso were evidently tightly bound together, with knees touching the chest.

In studying these people archaeologists are well aware that they have a duty of respect and care. In these close encounters with the past they are equally conscious that in trying to interpret these remains they are investigating a world in which people probably thought very differently about life and death. In some cases burials are a window on social organisation, offering insights into rank and status. The presence of valuable objects may denote a prestige burial but our notion of what is valuable may be misplaced. Their absence, as at Mullamast, may tell nothing about the status of the deceased. Graves containing daggers may not be those of warriors, for not all burials are expressions of status or identity. Grave-goods, whether fine pottery vessels or flint knives, may have a symbolic value for the living rather than the dead. Artefacts may have been selected for many different reasons and placing them in a grave may have been part of a public mortuary ritual for the benefit of the living.

The deposition of human bodies, in part or in whole, may have served other purposes. The occasional secondary burial in an older monument, for example, may have been an offering to the past by a community, perhaps an expression of an ancestor cult.

As already mentioned, while cremation was the dominant burial rite in the Iron Age, crouched unburnt burials of this period are known in some numbers, mainly in the eastern half of the country. Fourteen such burials have been found in the vicinity of the great mound at Knowth, Co. Meath, and a number of them were

5.2—Crouched burial in a reconstructed cist from Keenoge, Co. Meath.

accompanied by necklaces or armlets of glass beads. Strontium and isotope analysis that may trace geographical origins suggests that several of these individuals came from northern England. Some other crouched burials from County Meath have produced similar results, so it seems reasonable to conclude that this rite was introduced by incomers. Indeed, one man buried on the edge of a cemetery at Betaghstown, Co. Meath, may have originated in North Africa. His remains were dated to AD 381–621 and a small number of others are dated more firmly to early medieval Christian times. Whether the late retention of this burial posture was a deliberate mark of paganism is uncertain.

At a time when cremation was the principal rite, the centuries before and after 2000 BC also witness the appearance of crouched burials in significant numbers. A grave at Keenoge, near Duleek, Co. Meath, was a cist built of large stones and was one of fourteen graves in a flat cemetery in which the majority of graves were simple pits. It contained the unburnt crouched skeleton of an adult woman lying on her left side, head to north-east and facing south-east. A pottery bowl had been

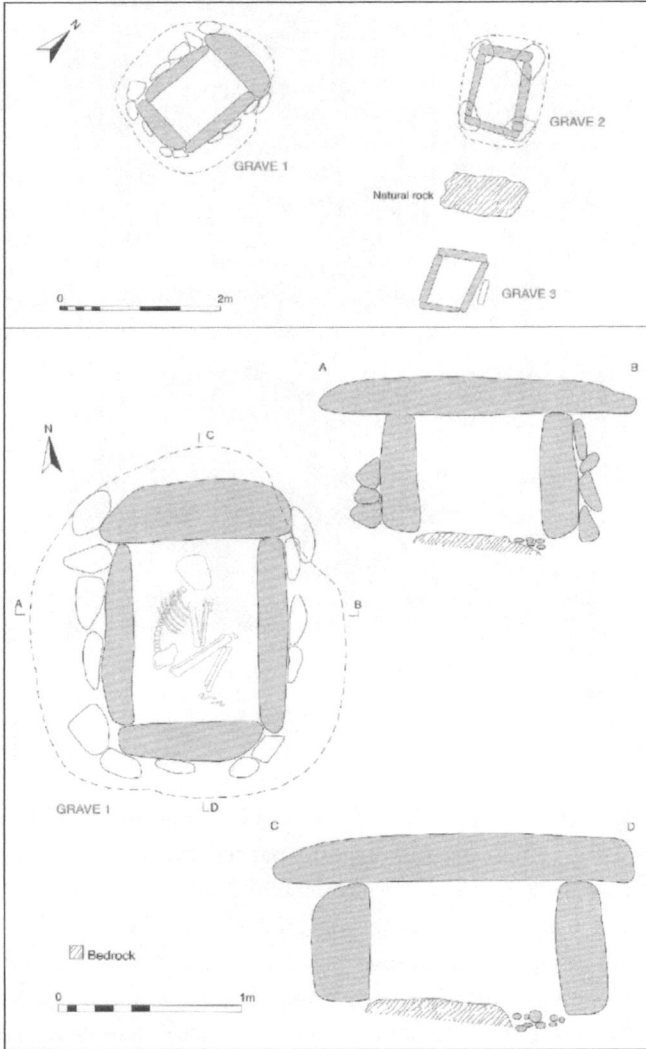

5.3—Cist and crouched burial at Redmondstown, Co. Westmeath.

placed in front of her head. One of the pit graves in the cemetery had a paved floor and contained the crouched skeleton of another adult female, two bowls, a small bronze knife and several flints; a small deposit of cremated bone was found beneath and behind the head of her skeleton. She too was laid on her left side, but with her head to the south and facing west. The tight contraction of the leg bones suggested that her corpse had been tightly bound.

In contrast, an adult male in the largest of three cists found at Redmondstown, near Castletown Geoghegan, Co. Westmeath, lay on his left side but with his head to north and facing east. Even though this positioning of the corpse in a crouched posture was a widespread and socially prescribed ritual practice, and there is a tendency to place pottery bowls near the skull, there is a bewildering variety in associated mortuary rites. Body posture cannot be clearly correlated with sex, for instance, but men do tend to have their heads to the north, as at Redmondstown, while women's heads tend to lie in a southerly direction.

There may be many reasons for the numerous variations in burial practice. Amongst the Nuer, in what is today South Sudan, the anthropologist E.E. Evans-Pritchard recorded:

'The grave is dug to the depth of a man's chest as he stands in it. Nuer say that were a man to be buried in a shallow grave and his corpse to be scratched up by hyenas he would haunt those responsible. The corpse is shaved and all ornaments removed from it before burial. A man goes to the grave as naked as he was born. A woman is buried in her loin skin, closely drawn between the legs. The legs of both sexes are flexed and one arm is placed under the head and the other over it as the corpse lies on its right side on a strip of ox-hide. Another strip of ox-hide is placed over it and pieces are also placed over the ears to prevent earth entering them. I believe that in western Nuerland a man is buried facing east and a woman facing west, but in eastern Nuerland both sexes are buried facing west. Nuer have told me that this is because the eastern Nuer came originally from the west and that it is in western Nuerland that their ancestors were created ...'

A stone-built cist may conceivably have had the same purpose as a very deep grave among the Nuer—simply to protect the body and perhaps to prevent any possibility of a return to the land of the living. It is possible, too, that some crouched bodies were buried facing the land of their ancestors—or even their nearby settlement—but even here caution is necessary. Peter Ucko once alerted archaeologists to the perils of ethnographic analogy and the limitations of inferences drawn from funerary data. When the Ashanti of west Africa went to bury their dead, the general rule was that the corpse should *not* face the village. However, there were those who believed that the dead in the grave turned to face the village immediately after burial, so some buried the dead facing the village in the certain knowledge that they would reverse themselves and conform to the rule to face the forest.

There are close similarities between the Irish tradition of single burial in a crouched position and contemporary mortuary practices among Beaker-using peoples in Britain. Both reflect an evident emphasis on individual status and rank. There are some important differences, however, notably in the types of accompanying pottery vessels. Furthermore, in Scotland and parts of England a sex-based pattern in body posture has been recognised for many years: males tend to be laid on the left, females on the right.

Strontium and oxygen isotope analyses and the study of ancient DNA offer the prospect of new insights into likely contact patterns. The genomic signature of three men from two graves at Glebe on Rathlin Island is an important indication of migratory disruption. One of these was an adult found in a crouched position in a cist and accompanied by a bowl bearing Beaker-inspired ornament. His DNA and

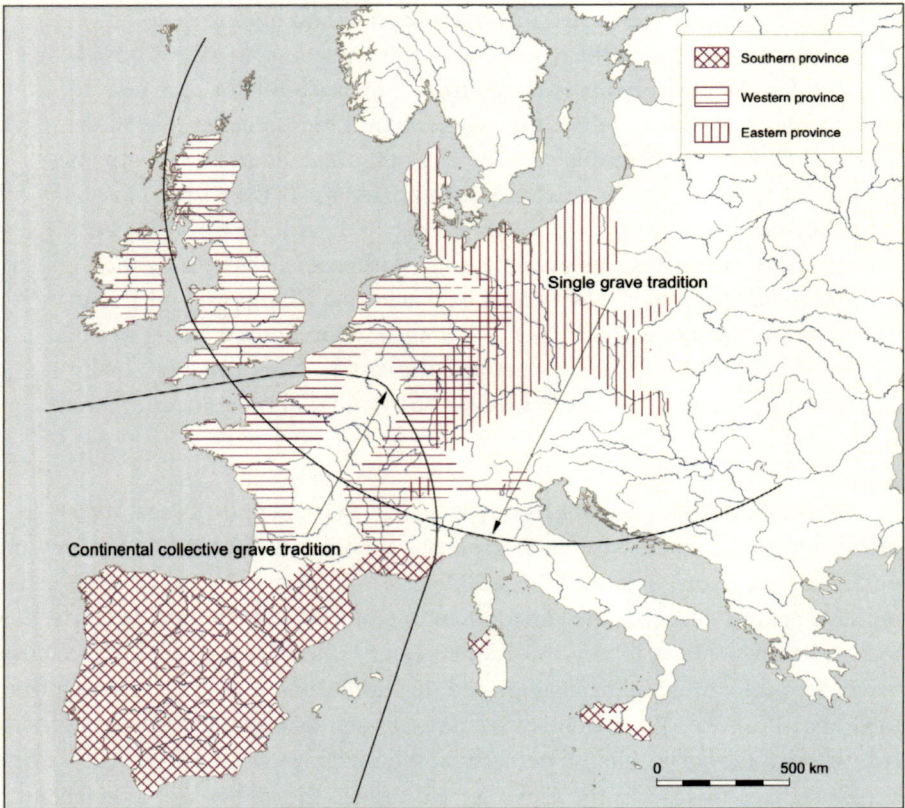

5.4—General distribution of the European single burial tradition.

that of the others indicate a measure of genetic discontinuity compared with the Neolithic. Though the Irish evidence is still limited, it seems likely that the migration of Beaker-using people was indeed a part of the story and that the appearance of crouched burial in Ireland and in Britain was due to both cultural transmission and human migration. Trade in copper between Ireland and Scotland may have been one significant factor in the emergence of this tradition in a modified form on this island.

This rite of single burial has a remarkable Continental distribution. It is found in western, central and parts of northern Europe, from the Vistula to the Rhine. Consistent features include crouched single burial, weapons in male graves and pottery vessels in both male and female burials. The study of ancient DNA now suggests a significant influx of people into central Europe from the east, from the southern Russian steppes north of the Caspian Sea or beyond. Not surprisingly, some have proposed that this might be the archaeological reflection of the expansion of Indo-European-speakers, the ancestors of many European languages.

It is a long way from Keenoge to Kiev, and over this wide geographical area pottery styles and other grave-goods did vary. Nevertheless, crouched single burial is the one constant feature and it is here, surely, in the study of these long-dead individuals, that an explanation will eventually be found for such an extensive mortuary phenomenon. Archaeology may never fully explain this particular rite but it probably had cosmological significance. It does denote a persistent belief system that at times reinforced identities and emphasised sex. Perhaps it was meant to mimic a sleeping posture at a moment of transition between one world and another, to ease the passage from a community of the living to a community of the dead and thus ensure that the departed pose no threat to those they leave behind. Death, like sleep, may have been considered as a normal and transient condition. It is also possible that the grave itself was a conceptual womb and that the dead individual, in this embryonic state, was in the process of becoming an ancestor. While prehistoric concepts of the self may have been very different from our own, there is certainly a new emphasis on the individual. Maybe some of these beliefs were part of a new and widespread pan-European religion.

6

The funeral pyre

6.1—Recreation of a funeral pyre in the shadow of Knowth.

Cremation of the dead was the dominant burial rite for most of Irish prehistory, but until relatively recently the rites of cremation have not received the archaeological attention they deserve. Skulls, bones and bog bodies may be displayed in museums from time to time, but tiny fragments of burnt bone, just the meagre end result of a long process, obviously do not have the same compelling attraction. Cremation is another way of fragmenting the body and the use of fire is a new medium that, with its transformative qualities, gave deeper symbolic meaning to the destructive act. In fact, it added a new dimension to the proceedings, for the destruction by fire of a human body on an open pyre was a slow, intense, dramatic and multisensory event.

Howard Williams has shown that cremation on an open pyre was far from being a quick, clean and clinical method of disposing of a body. He has offered a reconstruction of an Anglo-Saxon cremation:

'Once the pyre had been lit, the fire rapidly broke down the composed image of the deceased. The cremation would have lasted around ten hours … this was a visual spectacle of transformation that would be remembered by the mourners. The forensic and ethnographic literature provides us with an expectation of what might have occurred as the body was transformed during cremation into a series of physical and sensory components including heat, smoke, steam, bone and charred flesh.

The inside of the body became visible as its many layers and surfaces were breached and fragmented. Firstly, the coverings of wood, bark, hides, leather or textile … were burnt off to reveal the body. Next, the clothing, hair, skin and fat were sequentially destroyed revealing the muscles, organs and bone. As the body was heated, the evaporation of the bodily liquids may have occurred so speedily that jets of steam sprayed from the body.

Once heated, the body fat upon the clothed cadaver would perpetuate the cremation process, the corpse itself seemingly accentuating the transformation initiated by the fire. The muscles can tighten under the effects of heat followed by the charring of the muscles and organs before they were consumed by the flames. As the cremation continued, the bony frame of the body including the rib-cage and the skull was revealed, penetrated and fragmented by the fire. For hours until the pyre had cooled, the fragmented bones might have remained visible as indications of the continued presence of the body that had earlier been "composed" on the pyre.'

Sounds and smells would add to the drama of the spectacle. The contraction of muscles and sinews during rapid heating might make the limbs appear to twitch and the corpse appear to writhe as if alive. The expansion of internal liquids and gases would have made the body change colour, and bodily fluids would descend through the pyre, reacting with the heat and flames. The corpse might also emit a range of sounds because of gases expanding in the chest, and all this in addition to the noise of the snapping and cracking of wood. Mourners, perhaps participating in various ceremonies around the pyre and in impassioned lamentation, would also smell the distinctive and memorable acrid odour of burnt flesh.

The centrepiece in a splendid painting by Jacques-Louis David in the National Gallery of Ireland is a gigantic funeral pyre some 5m high. Entitled *The Funeral of*

6.2—J.-L. David, *The Funeral of Patroclus* (1778), in the National Gallery of Ireland. Before a huge funeral pyre, Achilles (in a red cloak) embraces the body of his friend Patroclus. The naked body of Hector, tied to a chariot, is on the ground below.

Patroclus, it depicts a famous episode in the Trojan War. As described in Homer's *Iliad*, Patroclus is killed by Hector, the greatest of warriors and son of Priam, king of Troy. Hector in turn is slain by Achilles and his body dragged behind a chariot before the walls of Troy. At the funeral of Patroclus, Achilles celebrates his own victory and the death of his friend.

David's panoramic work conflates a number of different episodes in the conflict. These include a huge pyre of logs being constructed on the orders of Agamemnon, king of Mycenae; in front of it lies the body of Patroclus, embraced by Achilles in a red cloak. The body of Hector, tied to a chariot, is on the ground below. On the left, twelve Trojan captives are being killed to be sacrificed in the flames. Animals for sacrifice are depicted on the right.

All great Homeric heroes, including Hector and Achilles, were honoured with a funeral pyre and complex mortuary rites. The prominent presence of the naked body of Hector may well remind a modern visitor to the National Gallery how Priam, seeking a decent burial for his son, had to beg Achilles for his body. In Michael

Longley's memorable and poignant lines that resonate with the need for compromise and reconciliation in today's world, he is said to exclaim, 'I get down on my knees and do what must be done—And kiss Achilles' hand, the killer of my son'.

Homer's description of the exceptional rites for Patroclus are rendered in Samuel Butler's nineteenth-century translation of the *Iliad* as follows:

'... Those who were about the dead heaped up wood and built a pyre a hundred feet this way and that; then they laid the dead all sorrowfully upon the top of it. They flayed and dressed many fat sheep and oxen before the pyre, and Achilles took fat from all of them and wrapped the body therein from head to foot, heaping the flayed carcasses all round it. Against the bier he leaned two-handled jars of honey and unguents; four proud horses did he then cast upon the pyre, groaning the while he did so. The dead hero had had house-dogs; two of them did Achilles slay and threw upon the pyre; he also put twelve brave sons of noble Trojans to the sword and laid them with the rest, for he was full of bitterness and fury.'

In theory at least, the cremation of great heroes may have demanded dramatic animal and human sacrifice. As Jim Mallory has shown, however, we have no record of any of Ireland's ancient heroes being cremated, and it is surprising that not one warrior was indulged in this fashion in all of the great corpus of epic literature. Even though cremation was the dominant Iron Age burial rite and was still occasionally practised in early medieval times, almost all mention of this pagan custom seems to have been expunged from the written record. There are a few brief allusions in medieval Irish literature to the scattering of the ashes of an individual in water where it seems to be a mark of disfavour. The ashes of the heart of Mechi, son of the mythical Morrígan, were cast into the River Barrow, and in one text, the *Agallamh Bheag*, Oisín threatens to burn the followers of St Patrick and cast their ashes into a stream.

It is also the case that the archaeological evidence for funeral pyres is surprisingly scarce in any period. A few Bronze Age claimants are rather doubtful: a low mound surrounded by a ditch at Dalystown, north of Tyrrellspath, Co. Westmeath, was dated to the late Bronze Age. It covered a number of pits, at least one of which contained a minute quantity of cremated bone. Some other pits to the east also contained burnt remains. The bone deposits in fifteen pits represented just 1,369g in total and, since an entire adult body might produce 1,600–3,500g, these were obviously token burials. In two instances the bones lacked the fissuring characteristic of burnt fleshed bone and defleshed corpses may have been cremated there. The

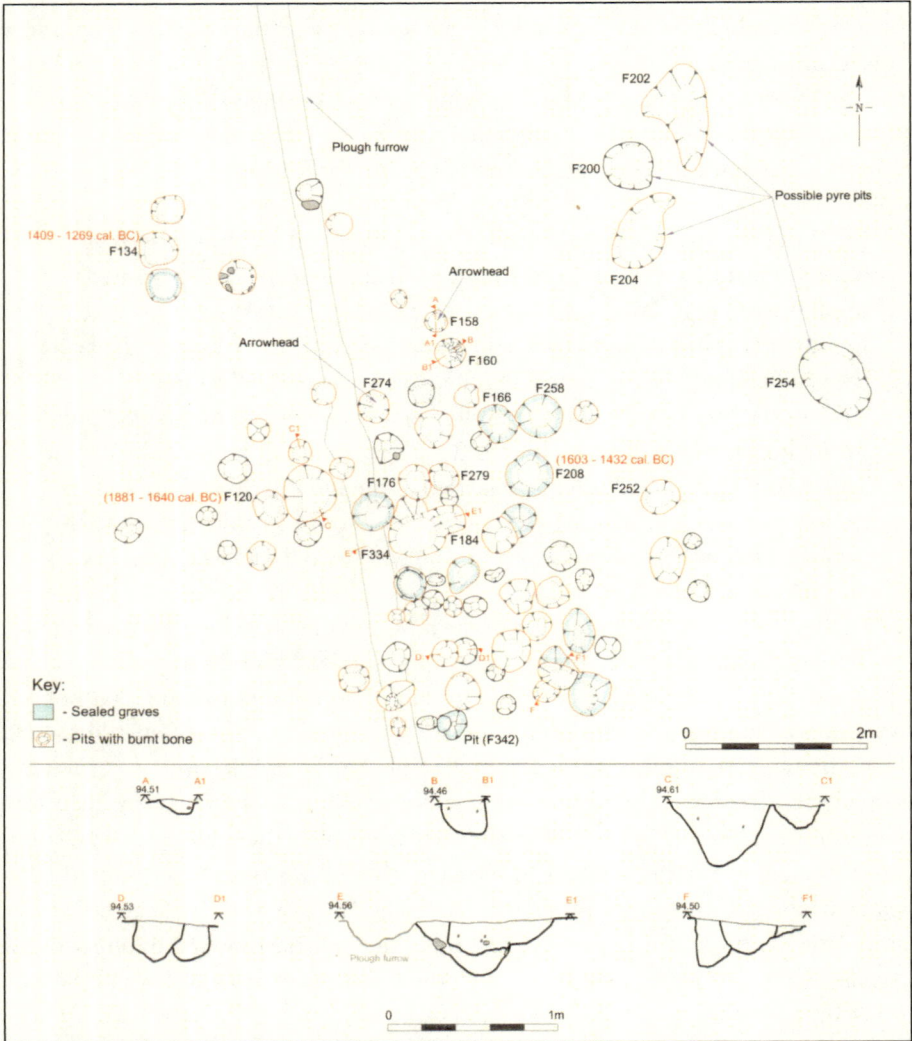

6.3—Burials at Templenoe, Co. Tipperary.

brief excavation report is confusing, but it was claimed that the site of a possible pyre was discovered beneath the mound. This was a natural depression measuring about 1.5m in length and 0.95m in width with an unspecified number of stakeholes in its base. The hollow contained 'evidence for *in situ* burning as well as charcoal-rich fills'. A long, shallow pit beneath a pyre would improve the flow of air to aid combustion, but there is no mention of the bone fragments which might be expected.

A flat cemetery at Templenoe, south of Cashel, Co. Tipperary, comprised 74 pits, of which 57 contained cremated bone. Human remains were identified with certainty in 31 of these and were token deposits, mostly less than 10g of bone. Two also contained the burnt remains of animals (dog and sheep or goat). The cemetery seems to have been in use for several centuries.

Several features all to the north-east of the pits were claimed as possible pyre sites. They were of irregularly oval or triangular shape, with maximum lengths of just over 1m and depths of up to 44cm—very different in size and shape from the other pits. There was no evidence of burning in them or on the surrounding ground surface. They did contain a little charcoal, though much less than from some of the cemetery pits. Again the absence of bone fragments, even minute pieces, is puzzling, but it has been suggested that they had been cleaned out after use. It seems much more likely that they and the feature at Dalystown had some other role in the ritual process and that the pyre itself was some distance away.

The burning of a defleshed corpse begs the question of what was done to skin, organs and entrails. Exposure is a possibility and the relatively frequent presence of disarticulated bones in early Bronze Age graves has often been assumed to reflect this. Almost 20% of the unburnt burials studied by Charles Mount in the south-east were disarticulated and had been exposed or stored elsewhere before final burial. If they were not exposed to decompose naturally, there may have been other means of disposing of the soft tissue and body parts. The puzzling features at Dalystown and Templenoe, and an equally perplexing small circle of burnt timber posts at Caherdrinny, south of Mitchelstown, may have had some role in these particular rites.

A plausible pyre site was found near an early Bronze Age cemetery of over twenty graves at Cloughskelt, near Banbridge, Co. Down, but remains unpublished. It consisted of a thick black deposit containing minute fragments of cremated bone and a single sherd of coarse pottery. It covered a large area measuring some 9m by 6m and may have been used more than once.

Another likely pyre site was excavated in the townland of Newford, just south-west of Athenry, Co Galway. Among a scatter of various cremation pits, post-holes and other features there was one large pit, 2.6m long, 2m wide and 75cm deep. It was thought that this pit was indeed dug to improve the air draught beneath a pyre. It was rich in charcoal and contained some stones and some burnt human and animal bone (amounting to 685g, of which only 72g could be certainly identified as human). There was a distinct lens of cremated bone in its upper fill and, as far as could be ascertained, these bones represented just one adult individual. The animal remains were mostly unidentifiable but pig, red deer antler and sheep or goat were

6.4—Section of a pyre pit at Newford, Co. Galway.

recognised. Animals or animal parts were evidently cremated too. Timbers used included oak, hazel, ash and willow. Three quartz pebbles were also found and may have been ritual offerings. Two radiocarbon samples from bone suggest a date around 700 BC.

Up to about half a ton of dry timber is normally required for the full cremation of a human corpse, and oak was the commonest wood used. It was widespread in prehistoric times and is an excellent fuel, capable of reaching the minimal 500°C necessary to get body fats burning well. Animal fats would also accelerate combustion. Presumably dry wood that had been stored for some time was used.

At Templenoe it appears that the same sorts of wood were consistently used over the lifetime of the cemetery for the cremation of all members of the community, regardless of age or sex. These included oak, ash and pomaceous fruitwood such as crab-apple and hawthorn. Wood remains possibly from the pyres were buried both with the human remains and in the empty pits, implying that the pyre itself was ritually important. Pomaceous fruitwoods have excellent combustion properties but may have been used because they also emitted a pleasant smell. Some cremation deposits produced charred cereal grains, so plants may also have been added to the pyre.

Whether bones are clean or sooty may tell us something about the process. Sooty bones possibly come from pyres that died out slowly, whereas clean bones may come from a pyre put out quickly. At Templenoe most cremations were recovered with clean bone, and this may indicate that a token amount of bone was collected from the top layers in the collapsed pyres. In other words, just some bone was specifically selected from the pyre material for burial at a particular time. As with token deposits generally, the rest was disposed of in some other way. These minimal burials are typical of the later Bronze Age. Larger cremations occur at an earlier date and often imply the careful collection of much of the burnt remains. One of the largest comes from a cist at Straid, near Claudy, Co. Derry, where an adult male was represented by over 2,700g of bone.

Animals were sometimes added to the funeral pyre. Bones of a dog came from one Templenoe deposit and the remains of another mammal (dog or sheep or goat) came from another. The remains of animals have rarely been reported in Bronze Age burials, but unidentified examples have been found from time to time. Burnt bones of unidentified animals were found with several human cremations at Carmanhall, Co. Dublin (where the corpses were cremated when still fresh or flesh-covered), but whether they represent joints of meat or sacrificed animals is not known.

Cremated bone from one of the Templenoe pits was crushed or pounded—a ritual occasionally noted elsewhere. At Raheennamadra, south of Knocklong, Co. Limerick, for instance, two isolated pits each contained small amounts of cremated bone of an adult. The bones had been deliberately pulverised before burial. If this was a public ceremony devoted to a sample of bone from each cremation, again it serves as a reminder of just how complicated mortuary ritual may be.

Even without the cries of animals to be sacrificed, the cremation itself must have been an extraordinary performance. We do not know whether the corpse on the pyre was normally wrapped in skins or textiles, or whether it was laid in a crouched position copying the common unburnt rite in earlier times. Like that Anglo-Saxon cremation described by Williams, the fire and smoke, the noisy disintegration of the wood and the corpse, the smell of burning flesh and the blazing light of the fire would all combine to create a scene of high drama.

Those present would have been well aware that they were witnessing the transformation of a body and its transition to another state of being. It was not a mere process of destruction; the deliberate handling and selection of the burnt bones taken from the pyre prove that they were still full of meaning. All of this preceded the complicated rituals associated with their burial. There may have been a hierarchy of practice around the funeral flames. People of higher status quite probably had more extravagant events—but so far, at least, the archaeological evidence has not been found.

7

Inversion and reversal

7.1—Excavation of an inverted urn at Ballynacarriga, Co. Cork.

A small ring-ditch in Ballynacarriga, just north of Fermoy, Co. Cork, was excavated in advance of the construction of a section of the M8. The ditch had an entrance on the south-east and was 6m in internal diameter. It enclosed two burials: one was a cremation of a juvenile and an infant placed in a small pit, and the other was in a larger pit in the centre of the enclosure. A large urn containing a substantial quantity of burnt bone had been placed mouth downwards in this grave and fragments of a small vase were found beside it. The bones in the urn were those of a woman 20–25 years of age, along with the remains of a mid-term foetus. Foetal bones are extremely rare; such fragile remains rarely survive. This unfortunate woman was pregnant and in her second trimester when she died. It is thought that she was cremated lying on her back and face upwards, because this would have allowed her soft tissue to have protected the foetus sufficiently to permit some of its skeletal material to survive.

The collar bone of another adult individual had also been placed in the urn with these bones. This was certainly not an accidental inclusion: it is possible that this bone held some particular significance for this woman and for Bronze Age people generally. A disproportionally high number of collar bones occurred amongst the human remains found in a Bronze Age context in Glencurran cave in the Burren, Co. Clare. Additional parts of human skeletons are occasionally found in burials or as finds at burnt mounds or on settlement sites and may have been retained as a memento of some event or as an ancestral keepsake. A piece of a femur of a young child was found with the skeleton of a teenager in a cist at Ballybrennan, Co. West-meath, for instance.

The Ballynacarriga burial probably dates from about 2000 BC. It was placed in the centre of a ring-ditch and the woman was clearly a person of some importance. The mouth of the urn must have been covered with some material to contain the bones when it was inverted in the pit. We do not know whether the bones had been placed in the vessel in any anatomical order (such as skull fragments first and hands or feet last). Since the vessel had been turned upside down, this might be an impossible analysis even if examined under laboratory conditions. The vessel is an encrusted urn, so called because it is decorated with applied strips of clay which in this instance may be an echo of the leather or rope straps used to suspend domestic containers made of some organic material.

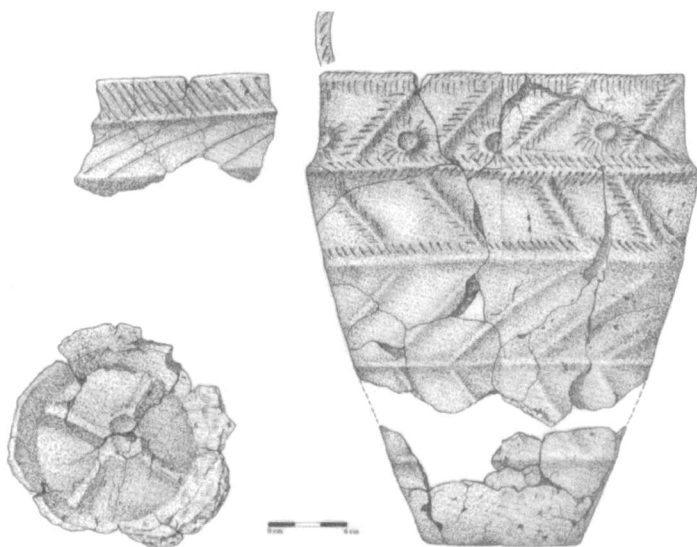

7.2—The Ballynacarriga encrusted urn.

The practice of inverting a burial urn is a remarkably widespread one in Ireland and Britain and thousands of examples have been recorded. It becomes popular shortly after 2000 BC and continues for several centuries. On occasion, smaller bowls or vases have also been placed upside down in graves in conjunction with unburnt or cremated burials.

Chris Lynn has speculated that inverted urns might be houses of the dead and replicate in some way the round houses of the living. In some cases decoration on the conical body contrasts with that on the rest of the vessel in the same way that walls differ from roofs in wooden or wicker structures—that is certainly true of the Ballynacarriga urn. It is also possible, as he notes, that urn-makers were attempting to illustrate a different sort of dwelling in the afterlife. Obviously, the urns can be seen

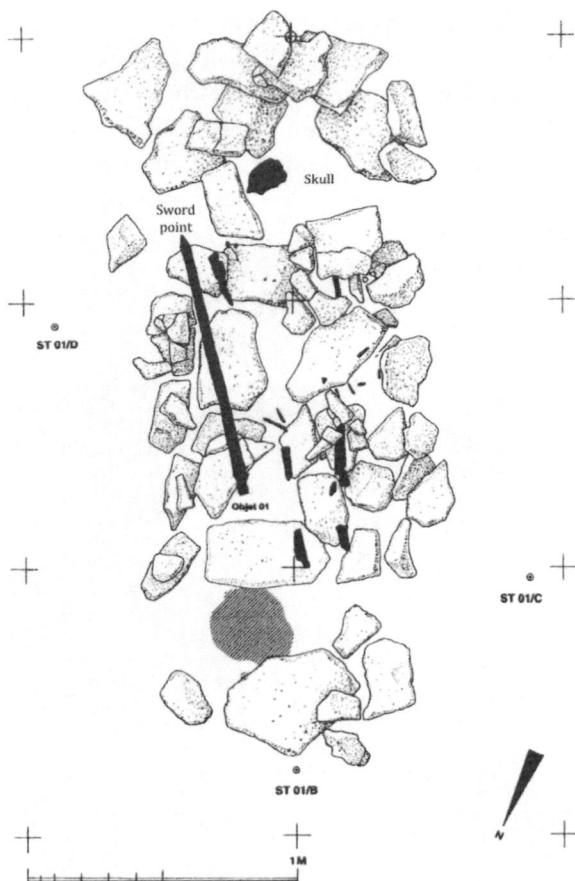

7.3—A warrior burial with inverted iron sword at Diarville, Meurthe-et-Moselle, France.

as protective coverings for the human remains, even as containers for the spirit of the deceased, but this could have been achieved by simply covering the upright vessel in some way, so there may be deeper and more potent symbolic meanings here.

Since cremation is such a destructive process it is not surprising that many details of ritual may not be recoverable, but some later prehistoric unburnt burials

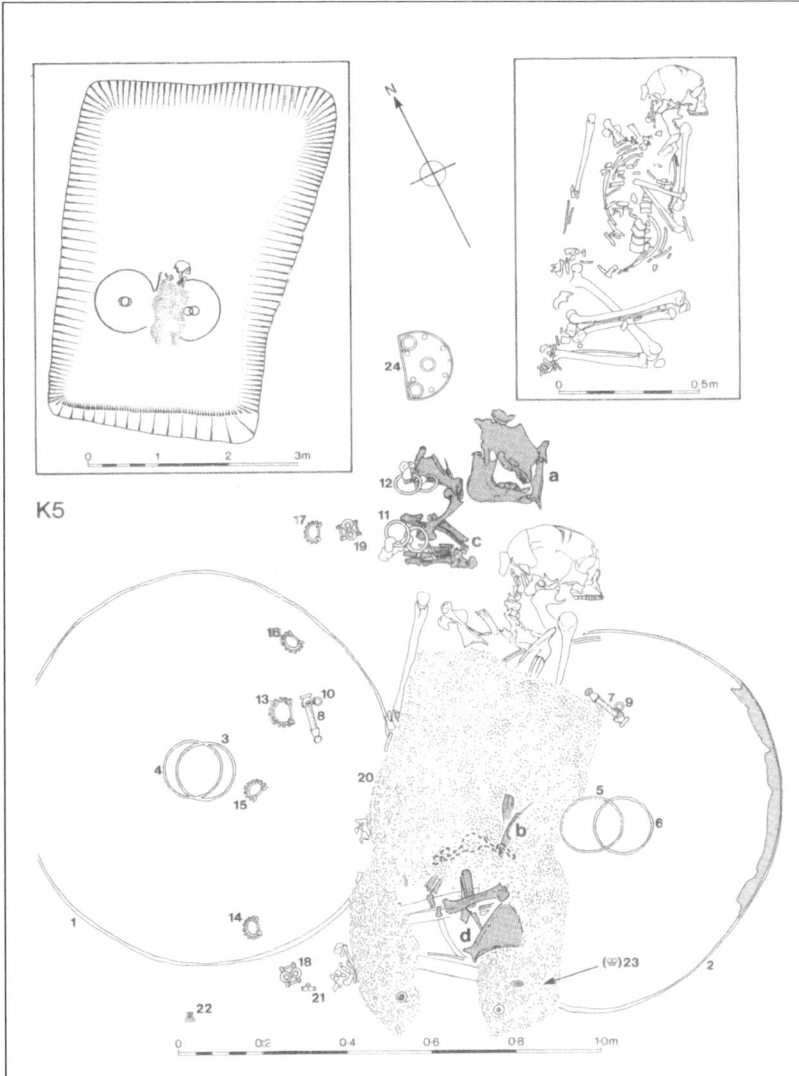

7.4—Chariot burial at Kirkburn, Yorkshire: pig bones are marked a–d and the reversed and inverted chain-mail tunic overlying the corpse is stippled.

offer a clue as to what inversion might actually mean in a funerary context. In two burial mounds of early Iron Age date in north-eastern France, one at Clayeures, the other at Diarville (Meurthe-et-Moselle), an iron sword, wrapped in cloth and without its scabbard, had been placed alongside the body of a warrior. The swords were inverted, the point towards the head, the hilt towards the feet. This practice has been recorded in other Iron Age burials: in one at Perrogney (Haute-Marne) a sword had been placed with its point towards the head and a spear had been deposited pointing downwards towards the feet.

A very different form of inversion is to be found in another Iron Age burial in northern England. A chariot burial at Kirkburn, Yorkshire, had been placed in a pit beneath a square mound. In addition to a dismantled two-wheeled vehicle with various fitments, it contained the flexed skeleton of a male 25–35 years old. He was accompanied by various grave-goods, including two deposits of pig bones at head and feet, two bridle bits and some bronze fittings possibly for the lid of a D-shaped box. The body lay beneath an iron chain-mail tunic. The coat of mail was upside down and inverted, the hem lying across the chest of the corpse and the shoulders across the legs.

Perhaps the most noteworthy instance of reversal in a burial is to be found in a famous Iron Age burial at Hochdorf (Baden-Württemberg, Germany). The dead man was laid on a bronze couch and accompanied by all the status symbols of an élite member of society at the time: a drinking set, a wagon and rich personal ornaments. Craftsmen were summoned to the burial site to make some of the ornaments, including strips of decorated sheet gold for the dead man's shoes. The shoes had perished but the decorative golden attachments indicated that the right shoe had been placed on the left foot and vice versa. This was not a mistake in the highly charged and complicated ceremonial associated with this important figure. The reversal represented the passing of a person from this world to the next, to a world that was a mirror image of this one.

7.5—A funeral scene on an eighth-century picture-stone at Tängelgårda in Gotland.

THE OFFICER'S FUNERAL,

7.6—A nineteenth-century depiction of reversed footwear published in 1849 in Philadelphia as the cover to a printed sentimental song for chorus and piano by Caroline Norton Sheridan entitled 'The Officer's Funeral'.

It might be argued that in some cases the reversal of weaponry was merely an indication of decommissioning—in much the same way that some graves may contain a broken sword. This is unlikely, however, as one powerful Scandinavian image would graphically suggest. There is a scene on an eighth-century picture-stone at Tängelgårda in Gotland that depicts a funeral procession. A horse with eight legs, easily identifiable as the god Odin's horse Sleipnir, is shown carrying a fallen warrior to Valhalla. Behind the horse the three men in a procession are walking backwards and carrying their swords reversed. Reversal and inversion were symbols of enduring importance over many thousands of years.

A belief in an afterlife very different to life in this world is an ancient concept. In the early Irish tale known as *Echtra Nerai* ('The Adventure of Nera') the warrior

Nera enters the Otherworld; when he leaves it and wants to convince the outside world that he has really been in the *síd*, he is instructed, in an important allusion to the inverted nature of the Otherworld, to bring with him the fruits of summer to the winter world outside as proof: 'Bring the fruits of summer with you', he was told. 'So he brought wild garlic with him, and primroses and buttercups ...'. It is summer in one world, winter in the other. Indeed, it was this memorable phrase about 'the fruits of summer' in a medieval story that inspired my suggestion, almost a decade ago, that inversion or reversal in a funerary context might be a reference to an Otherworld.

This inverted world, a realm without care or suffering, tears or pain, without darkness, sickness, old age or death, was part of Indo-European philosophy. In the great 3,000-year-old epic the Rig Veda it is the 'endless deathless world'. It is a world where things are totally other, completely opposed to all of this earth, so it is unsurprising that its reversed nature should be reflected in some of the rich symbolism associated with death and burial.

There is no connection, but an Iron Age warrior would appreciate the modern symbolism of the riderless horse with boots and stirrups reversed in military ceremonial—whether in the nineteenth century in 'The Officer's Funeral' or in the funeral cortège of John F. Kennedy.

8

A chosen few

8.1—Poulawack cairn in the Burren, Co. Clare.

Clusters of burials are a common occurrence in the earlier Bronze Age; though they are called cemeteries, many do not seem to have been formal cemeteries in the ordinary sense of the word. In short, they do not always seem to represent a continuous sequence of individual burial from generation to generation. They range greatly in size and, even though many have been poorly recorded, a majority seem to have contained a dozen graves or less. A few contain more than several dozen graves, and in later cemeteries these are often token deposits of cremated bone, as we saw at Templenoe. It is clear that the use of some spanned several centuries. There are two contrasting forms: flat cemeteries where the graves have no surviving superimposed monument, and cemetery mounds where a round mound or cairn may contain a number of graves.

The variation in numbers of burials, in types of grave and in the rituals practised is remarkable. Cist and pit graves occur, unburnt burial (both articulated and disarticulated) and cremation are found, and multiple burials in the one grave are recorded. There is a range of pottery traditions; bowl, vase and different sorts of urn were popular, and ceramic fashions clearly changed over time.

Some of the larger cemeteries could have been the communal burial place of a small community, the different pottery types perhaps reflecting changes in ceramic fashion through time, or different social caste or ancestry, or even family affiliation. A relatively small number of cemeteries have produced pottery of just one tradition but more commonly two or more pottery fashions are represented. Judging from the small size of many cemeteries, it seems that only a fraction of the members of a family or community were formally buried, others presumably being disposed of in other ways. The occasional presence of different pottery types, particularly in small burial groups, suggests that some such mixtures may have had some magico-religious, social or political significance.

While the evidence indicates that some people may have had special status, clear and persistent evidence of a social hierarchy or significant differences based on sex are still hard to discern. Some of the questions posed by these cemeteries are

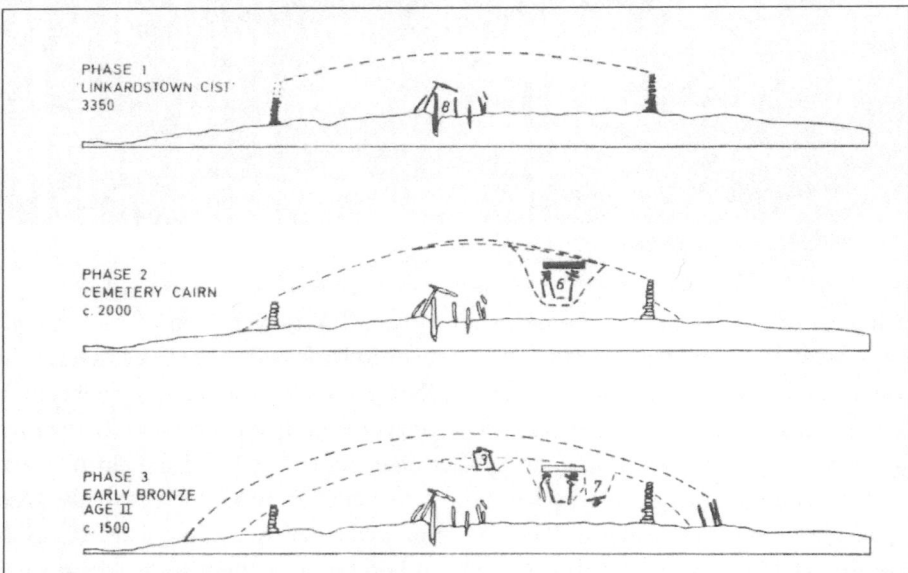

8.2—Simplified cross-sections of the Poulawack cairn, showing the location of some of the burials and the three major phases.

exemplified by the discoveries at Poulawack. This prominent cairn near Carron, in the Burren, Co. Clare, was excavated in 1934. It was found to contain a large, central slab-built grave at ground level, protected by a cairn of stones with a kerb of large slabs. This was a polygonal cist containing the disarticulated bones of an adult male, two females and a child, as well as a flint scraper, a boar's tusk and two fragments of unclassifiable pottery. Two other rectangular cists, built on the ground surface beneath the cairn, also contained unburnt bones. An unburnt crouched burial was found just outside the kerb, and four cists containing unburnt bones and one containing a cremation were discovered at various levels in the body of the cairn.

The excavator, Hugh Hencken, had no difficulty in identifying a sequence of burials at Poulawack. He noted the importance of the central primary grave and was struck by the fact that ten graves contained the remains of no less than sixteen people. While the sex of most of the poorly preserved skeletal remains could not be identified, the presence of five males and four females was thought to be fairly normal in what appeared to be a cemetery of a small community. However, the apparent absence of finds that would clearly date the burials was a disappointment. As he wrote, 'the scarcity of finds in this cairn makes any dating impossible except to say that it belongs to the Bronze Age'.

The advent of radiocarbon dating revolutionised the study of archaeology, and the first Irish dates materialised in the early 1950s. The development of accelerator mass spectrometry (AMS) dating that permits very small samples to be dated was a further important step some 30 years later. Another transformative development was a programme of radiocarbon dating of Irish material undertaken by Anna Brindley and Jan Lanting of the University of Groningen—and this in turn transformed our understanding of Poulawack.

The dating of a series of bone samples indicated that there were three major phases of burial activity. The primary burial on the site was indeed the central polygonal cist with its four occupants but it was now dated to the Neolithic, to 3614–3373 BC. A second phase centred on 2000 BC, when at least two cists were inserted into the cairn probably over several generations. A third phase, around 1500 BC, saw the enlargement of the cairn beyond the line of the kerb, with the addition of a minimum of two more burials.

Far from being a simple and relatively short-lived cemetery, this complex monument had a protracted ritual significance for at least 1,800 years, during which the remains of some dozen other individuals were placed in the cairn after the primary burial. This modest number over such a long timespan does not suggest regular usage but implies periodic episodes of burial activity, perhaps as little as one in every second or third generation.

This episodic and protracted funerary pattern has been identified elsewhere. The use of a cemetery at Carn More, north of Dundalk, comprising one unburnt burial and the cremated remains of sixteen individuals, is thought to have spanned at least 600 years. At a conservative estimate, a flat cemetery of some 27 individuals at Edmondstown, Co. Dublin, was in use for 400 years with—according to one possible assessment—one adult male being buried there per century.

A partly destroyed cairn in Carrig, on the slopes of Lugnagun, Co. Wicklow, was excavated in 1985. Four cist graves were found under what survived of the cairn. All the human remains were burnt, the bones being partly crushed after cremation. Two were accompanied by highly decorated vases dating from around 2000 BC; others were contained in cordoned urns generally dated to between 1700 BC and 1500 BC. One of the cists had been used on no less than six separate occasions. The final burial on site was dated to around 900 BC and consisted of a token deposit of cremated bone accompanied by sherds of some very coarse pottery. Another burial, contained in a small inverted urn, was found in a pit beside the socket for a standing stone, about 15m to the north of the cairn. Altogether some twenty individuals were represented and there was a wide age range, from newborn to over 50 years; the majority, however, were adults aged twenty years or more. Once again, it seems that this was a burial place used for around 900 years; even though some burials contained more than one person, it does seem that a grave was added just once every 90 years or so.

Why was formal burial restricted to a select few and how were some people chosen for burial in cemeteries like these? At Poulawack the reuse of an older monument may have been an expression of a need to connect with real or imagined ancestral associations. This might explain the long timespan between the first two periods of burial there. The subsequent periodic use might also denote a further particular concern with ancestry and lineage but there may have been other reasons too. The distinct phases of burial activity detected may have occurred in times of social stress or instability or at times deemed propitious for some other reason when there was a special need to express a sense of history and social continuity.

The selection of a particular person for burial may have been prompted by many factors. Many ethnographic studies tell us that infertility in crops or livestock, premature deaths or some other inauspicious event may have an impact on the customary treatment of the dead, perhaps demanding some special action at a special place. The sheer variety of ritual in some cemeteries, which is often one of their more striking features, might actually reflect the infrequent use of these monuments, with ceremonial details remembered imprecisely from one generation to the next.

The Poulawack cairn was probably built and used by a community for whom it was an enduring point of reference. In combining an ancestor cult with occasional selective burials, it reinforced their distinctiveness as a group and underpinned their history and identity. It became a monument that was a celebration of ancestral lineages. In time it may be possible to prove this because, as we have seen, the study of ancient DNA has the potential to clarify the kinship links in burial monuments like this.

What happened to the remains of the other members of this community? Of course, some may have been buried elsewhere but others may have been disposed of in a way that has left little or no archaeological trace. Again ethnographic evidence should alert us to how varied the response of the living may be in dealing with the social and emotional problems of death, and how some might be chosen for special funerary treatment and yet not survive in the archaeological record. Here the story of Okoulabari's bones is revealing.

In 1931 a French visitor published a short account of a funeral that he witnessed among the Mbere, a Bantu people in the central African Congo. A man named Okoulabari had died of sleeping sickness. He was an important person, having four wives, and in his time he had hunted elephants. He died on a Monday morning and the corpse had been laid out on a wooden bed padded with leaves in a half-open hut. The body was coated with a red powder taken from the sapwood of the coralwood tree, which has medicinal properties.

The face of the dead man was painted with white earth; the eyebrows and the mouth were strengthened and widened, and coiled thread-like designs were drawn on the cheeks. The entire body, including the feet, was covered up to the neck in strips of raffia. The arms were stretched out alongside the body. The wives of the dead man, their hair completely shaved, rolled in the dust wearing only banana leaves attached to a belt by a cord. The men took no part in these demonstrations, which they nevertheless attended with reverence.

At dusk the deceased's wives, assisted by their relatives, began to sing and dance in a circle. They recounted the qualities and exploits of the dead man; his hunting deeds were mentioned frequently in the lament. They also remembered the ivory he had sold and the European loincloths he had bought for his wives with the money he earned. On the following day the parents of the deceased had not arrived, and nothing happened on the Wednesday. It may have been thought an inauspicious day or at least a day of rest.

The songs resumed at dusk and continued the next day. At dawn on Thursday the parents arrived and it was time for the burial, for the smell from the corpse was becoming difficult to ignore. A pit was dug in the forest some 200m or 300m from the village; the width and the length were those of the body, the depth was approximately 1m. The corpse was simply attached to a long stick carried on the shoulders of two of the dead man's relatives without any special ceremony. It was preceded and followed by the funeral procession, and lamentations redoubled as the body was carried along the small track leading to the grave. The corpse was placed without great care on the floor of the grave, and the eldest son of the deceased, advancing to the edge, threw the first handful of earth on the corpse, whose head had remained uncovered, saying: 'You are well here; do not go back to the village'. Then all the assistants filled the pit, repeating the same words.

It seems that the funeral ceremonies of these people were dominated by the fear that the spirit of the dead might take harmful action against the living. For this reason the location of the village was changed frequently, every two or three years; because the spirits of the dead were supposed to know only the path to the huts where they lived, they were unable to roam around the new village, even if it was adjacent to the old one.

A monument was then built over the grave: wooden slats forming more or less geometric designs, diamonds and squares, with small stones in the centre, were placed on the ground. A light chair made of wooden sticks, so fragile that it could only be used by a spirit, was placed in the centre. The clothes, plates, bottles and copper dishes of the deceased were placed on the ground or on a structure made of branches. Multicoloured leaves or, sometimes, agaves were laid in front of these. Then all returned to the village, still singing and wailing; the wives of the dead kept their mourning attire for a few weeks, or even several years.

The hut in which the body of the dead man had been kept was destroyed and burnt. At the exact location where the corpse was kept pending burial, a mound of small stones was built, bounded by wooden sticks so that dogs and poultry, attracted by the smell, did not come scratching the soiled earth. After about a month and a half, when Okoulabari's corpse had decomposed, it was dug up. Some bones, parts of the skull, kneecaps, fragments of the ulna and the radius, were removed and brought back to the village. There they were carefully cleaned, covered with coralwood powder and placed in a sort of basket by his heir. A funerary mask was then affixed to the basket.

This was an important ceremony always attended by a great crowd of people. This rite of partial exhumation was only accorded to powerful men and was intended to dissuade them from exercising their power against the living after death. The bodies of women and people without influence were permanently left in place.

The basket of bones and the mask were put in a small hut about $1m^2$ by 1m high. The dead man's heir would leave an offering of part of the liver of the animals he hunted. If it was very cold, a fire might be lit in the hut. If bad luck befell the village or the heir, mainly in hunting, it was because the deceased pursued them in anger, even when involuntarily offended. Then propitiatory ceremonies were needed to appease the dead.

What is of interest here is that, despite his importance and the very elaborate and protracted funerary rites that took place, Okoulabari's body had no final resting-place. What finally happened to his fragmentary bones is not recorded, but for a time they were evidently a potent force in the daily lives of his people. Maybe they were eventually dispersed among his relatives or given an inconspicuous burial. This may have been the fate of those numerous Bronze Age folk, important though they may have been, whose remains were not placed in cemeteries like Poulawack.

9

Gifts to an Otherworld

9.1—Selection of objects in the Dowris Hoard.

What has been called the Dowris Hoard is the largest collection of bronze objects ever found in Ireland and originally it may have comprised over 200 items. This extraordinary discovery of 'at least a horse-load of gold-coloured bronze antiquities', as one early report described it, was made in the 1820s by two men digging potato beds in reclaimed bogland in a small field just over 500m south of a lake called Lough Coura and about 7km north-east of the modern town of Birr, Co. Offaly. Named after the adjacent townland of Doorosheath, this great find has given its name to the major phase of the late Bronze Age in Ireland.

Lough Coura no longer exists; the land has been drained and reclaimed, but in the early nineteenth century it formed an area of open water about 40ha in extent and some 56m deep. In late prehistoric times it was probably a much more extensive body of water located at the foot of several low glacial ridges encompassed by bog. It was certainly situated on the edge of a vast expanse of midland bog. This immense and hostile area stretched northwards and was broadly demarcated to the south and east by the higher, undulating good agricultural land that formed a broad arc at the foot of the Slieve Bloom Mountains.

The lake's liminal location in or by a bog—on the interface between the wild and the tamed—may have invested it with special meaning. The area of open water may have been perceived as an opening in the earth giving access to an other- or under-world. The bog would have been a place shaped by non-human forces, and both water and bog may have demanded a votive offering from time to time to placate the spirits or gods who lived there. To paraphrase Seamus Heaney, its wet centre may have seemed bottomless.

The term 'hoard' was applied to the Dowris find because it was assumed that it represented a collection of objects all buried at the one time. It has been considered as a collective dryland deposit placed on the margins of a bog in a single act by a group of people that reflected their shared kinship. Given the widespread popularity of deposition in watery contexts in the later Bronze Age, however, it does seem more likely that this was the situation here. This diverse set of objects may have been deposited in the ancient lake over a period of time, perhaps several centuries, by a number of different people. Indeed, some pieces may have been personal heirlooms when finally consigned to the depths of the greater Lough Coura. It seems probable that the watery rituals at Dowris began sometime before 1000 BC.

No precise details of the original contents of the find exist and some of the collection was dispersed. Today 110 bronze items are preserved in the National Museum and a further 67 in the British Museum (of which most, though not all, probably came from the find); the latter collection also contains two fragments of waste bronze and six sandstone rubbing or polishing stones. Of the surviving pieces, the most numerous are hollow-cast bronze pendants (48), spearheads (36), socketed axes (35), cast-bronze trumpets or horns (26), knives (7), swords (5), socketed gouges (5), buckets (3) and cauldrons (3) of sheet bronze, and razors (3). A socketed hammer and a scabbard chape—the metal tip—are also preserved.

Many of the surviving objects are complete or in a reasonably good condition. All of the swords are damaged or broken, but most of the axes are, like the spearheads, well preserved. A majority of the relatively small horns are complete or nearly so. The presence of just relatively small fragments of some objects is puzzling: in six cases only about half an axehead is present; three of the horns are represented by small tubular pieces and two others by small knobs. Two of the surviving buckets

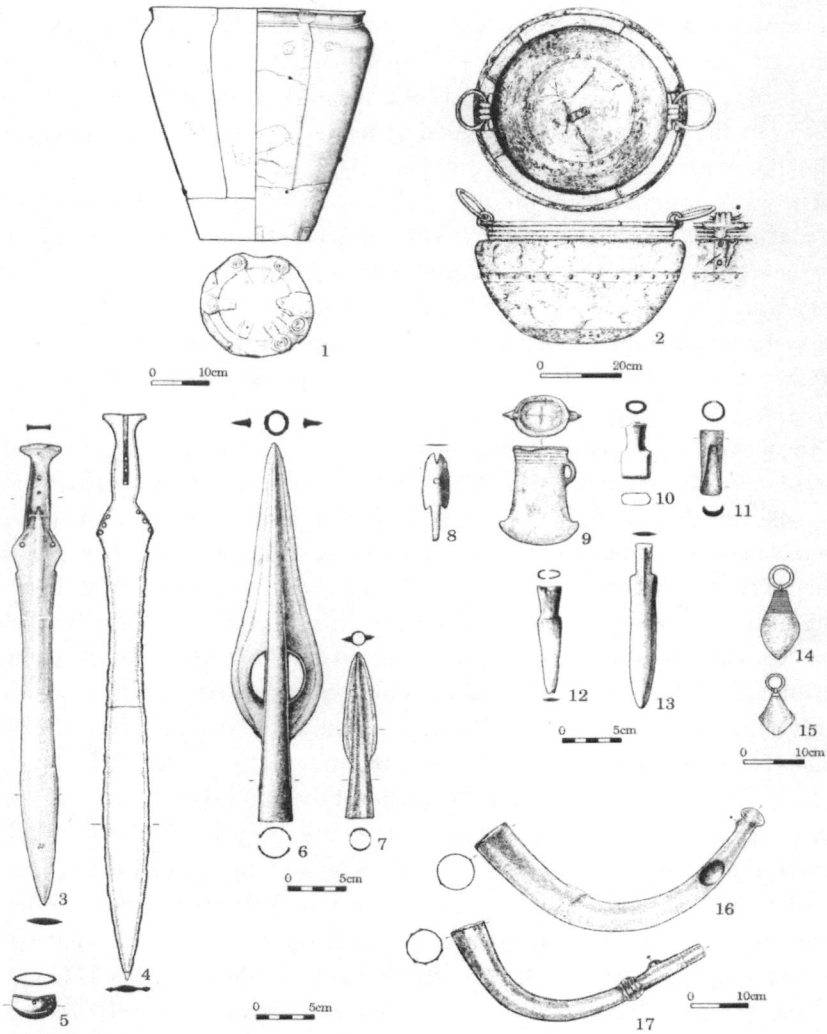

9.2—Some objects in the Dowris Hoard.

and two of the cauldrons are also represented by parts. There is part of the base of one bucket and two attachments for the base of another; two cauldrons are represented by parts of their rims. The fragmentary items must have had some special value in their own right to be part of ceremonies that also involved prestigious items like buckets, cauldrons and horns. Broken objects, especially weapons, may have been ceremonially decommissioned.

To dispose of a complete bronze bucket or cauldron, even one that had seen some use as the centrepiece of a long series of ceremonial feasts, must have been an act of particular significance Its submergence in the lake may have been part of a public ceremony officiated over by someone of religious or political importance. Some of the horns found may have been sounded on such special occasions. The deposition of a spear or sword, on the other hand, might conceivably have been a more private commemorative event coinciding with the death of its warrior owner. A woodworker's axe or gouge may have been a craftsman's tribute, and scrap bronze or polishing stone the offering of a metalworker. In short, the varied range of objects may denote a hierarchy of participants as well as a protracted series of different sorts of performance—some communal in the hope of benefiting a social group, some perhaps of a more individual nature.

The deposition of metalwork in watery contexts, in rivers, lakes or bog pools, is a particularly widespread phenomenon in the later Bronze Age in parts of western and northern Europe. In Ireland there is a high proportion of prehistoric weaponry from riverine contexts, and the open water of certain rivers like the Shannon, the Bann and the Barrow seems to have been particularly favoured. Some finds may reflect the proximity of settlements and others may be the result of loss, but the fact that so many river finds come from very particular places is probably an indication that returning to the same watery location to perform the same type of action was in itself an act of some ritual importance.

At least 148 Bronze Age and 33 Iron Age artefacts have been recorded from the River Shannon. Weapons of one sort or another, around 70%, dominate the collection. It is possible that many of these were offerings to a riverine goddess. While many river names refer to obvious features such as water or flow, a few do appear to allude to a divine female. In France, for example, the Marne was the personification of the mother goddess Matrona and the Seine was associated with the goddess Sequana. The ancient name of the River Dee in Scotland was Devona (goddess). According to medieval place-lore, the Shannon was named after a goddess called Sionainn, but this story is generally considered to be a copy of that of Boand, goddess of the River Boyne. Nevertheless, behind this scholarly inventiveness there may well lie a genuine ancient river deity once worthy of votive offerings.

Whatever the motivation behind river deposits, various writers now recognise that there is a difference between different kinds of water, notably between the flowing water of a river and the still water of a lake or bog pool. An enormous amount of prehistoric material has been found in Irish bogs and much of it is assumed to be ritual deposition. Bogs vary greatly in form and extent, and it is thought that about 16% of the country was once peatland. Irish raised bogs are generally far deeper than the blanket bogs common in mountain areas and in the west and may reach depths of 9–12m.

The great midland bogs in particular, like that north of Dowris, were probably seen as inhospitable and alien places, and human interaction therein was fraught with meanings quite foreign to us. Bog flows or bog bursts, when whole sections of bog move when layers of peat become semi-liquified, are relatively common. In prehistory they would probably have seemed to represent the action of some inherent subterranean power. Sudden shifts to dryer conditions detected in Littleton Bog near Thurles, Co. Tipperary, are taken to indicate bog bursts in the late Bronze Age, and a wooden trackway in nearby Derryville Bog was actually destroyed by a bog burst *c.* 600 BC.

Many have been recorded in historical times and one of the earliest known occurred in Cappanihane Bog, Co. Limerick, north-west of Charleville, in June 1697. Gerard Boate, in his seventeenth-century account of Ireland's natural history, describes it in dramatic terms:

'A greed [*sic*] noise was heard in the earth like thunder, attended with whirlwinds. Soon after, to the terror of the spectators, a bog stretching north and south began to move, as well as the pasture land, which lay on the side of it, separated by a very large ditch, and a small hill in the middle of the bog sunk flat. The ground fluctuated like a wave, the pasture land, rising very high and rolling on with great violence, covered a meadow sixteen feet deep. In this motion it drew after it a great part of the bog into the place where the pasture land stood before, and the chasms spurted out water and noxious vapours, and continued to do so.'

The occurrence of a strange light known as a 'will o' the wisp' hovering in the bog at night would surely add to the trepidation that these places might provoke. Caused by the spontaneous combustion of marsh gases, these not surprisingly figure in folklore as supernatural spirits or ghosts. The notion that this sort of ignition is an explanation for the will o' the wisp has been thought problematic because methane simply does not ignite in this way. For some writers this indicates that the will o' the wisp is possibly a figment of popular imagination. John Feehan notes, however, that the compound diphosphane, produced by micro-organisms in an anaerobic bog, does burn spontaneously when it meets the air and could ignite methane.

Seamus Heaney famously described Tollund Man, found in a Jutland bog in 1950, as a 'bridegroom to the goddess'. It may be that this bog body was indeed held in a feminised bog's dark embrace. In Nordic mythology the bogland hall of

Fensalir was supposedly the dwelling place of the goddess Frigg, but neither myth nor folklore have any significant clues to offer us about the supernatural inhabitants of Irish bogs.

Katherine Leonard has noted the particular importance of bog pools in the depositional practices in this environment. In the relatively few cases where the depths of discoveries have been recorded, it is clear that some bronze finds come from midway in a bog or from near the base—even to a depth of 3m or more. For instance, a deposit of bronze objects from a bog at Ballykeaghra, near Tuam, Co. Galway, was found about 3m below the surface and 1.5m from the basal sand layer of the bog. It comprised 35 small rings, a bracelet, a neck-ring and a tweezer-like object. Presumably it had been placed in a pool, perhaps in an organic bag that was not preserved, and allowed to sink to the bottom. The same may be said of two bronze horse bits and two pendants from Attymon, Co. Galway. These prestigious Iron Age objects were found 'on hard turf bottom of a bog at a depth of 24 feet' (c. 7.2m) and were probably part of the equipment of a pair of chariot horses. They too must have been placed in a pool whose still, dark waters may have had a very special significance and may have been seen as portals to the Otherworld.

A votive offering of exceptional importance was found in marshy ground in 2004 in the townland of Tamlaght, Co. Armagh. The site lies about 800m southwest of the hillfort called Haughey's Fort and just under 2km from the celebrated Navan Fort. In ancient times it was probably a small bog set in a drumlin landscape. On discovery the find looked just like a rather miserable collection of scrap metal, but it is in fact one of the most important prehistoric finds of recent times in Ireland.

It comprised a bronze leaf-shaped sword and a small bronze bowl that was placed near its hilt. The bowl contained fragments of a decorated bronze cup and a small bronze ring. All had been damaged to a greater or lesser degree and this may have been due to relatively recent plough or spade cultivation. The sword is of native manufacture but the bowl, cup and possibly the ring are imports from the European continent, where they date from approximately 1000 BC.

The bowl is a Fuchsstadt-type vessel, named after a Bavarian find, a variety found over much of central Europe, especially in the region of the rivers Danube, Rhine and Maine. They are highly prized objects often found with weaponry in warrior graves or in hoards with feasting equipment. The cup with embossed decoration is named after a hoard of these vessels from Jenišovice in Bohemia, and it too is a significant item often associated with feasting cauldrons in eastern Europe.

Both bowl and cup from Tamlaght were probably part of a ceremonial drinking set that might have included a bucket like the one from Dowris. These high-status

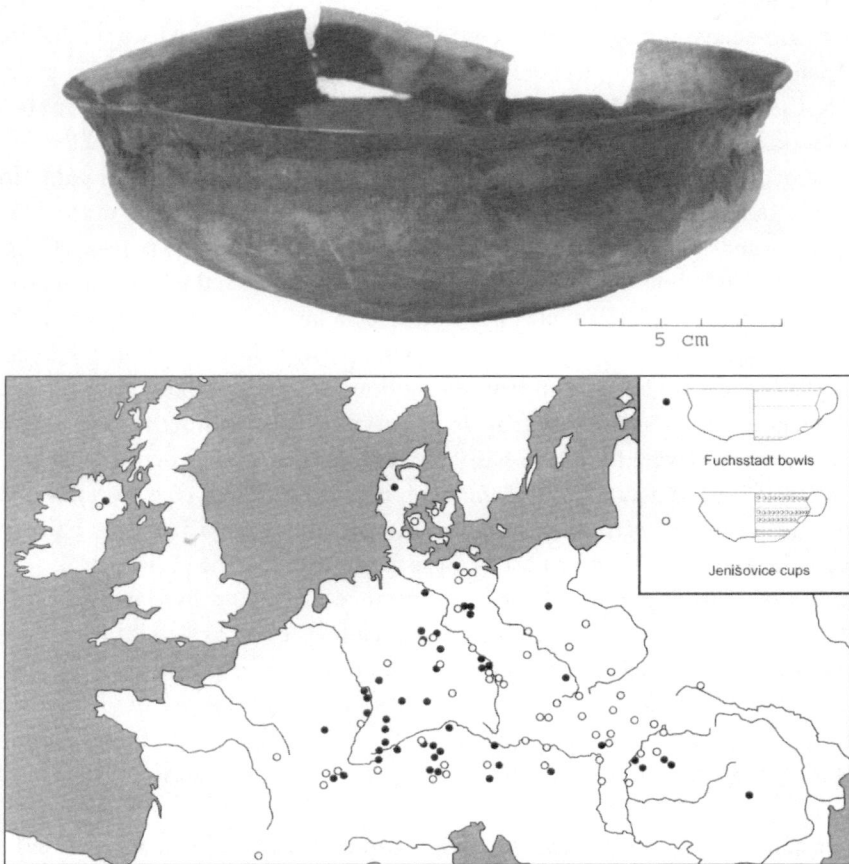

9.3—Above: the Fuchsstadt bowl from the Tamlaght hoard. Below: distribution of Jenišovice and Fuchsstadt vessels.

objects illustrate the complex networks of contact and exchange that were the norm in late Bronze Age Europe. The presence of a sword indicates an unsurprising link between drinking ceremonial and a warrior class. The bowl and cup are types otherwise unknown in these islands and their rarity would suggest that this was quite an exceptional gift to the Otherworld. It is also a telling indication, like the swords and spears in the Dowris find and innumerable other discoveries, of an intimate connection between a warrior ideology and that wetland realm.

In one case at least it is possible to make a passable guess as to which otherworldly entity might have been the object of an offering of fine metalwork. The famous Broighter gold hoard comprises a richly decorated tubular torc, a model boat, a miniature cauldron and several neck ornaments. It had been deposited on the shore of Lough Foyle, Co. Derry. When found in 1896, the objects were surrounded by a sticky dark substance, probably the remains of a container of some organic material. Richard Warner has argued that they represented a prestigious votive offering to Manannán, god of the sea, whose otherworldly realm was said, in some accounts, to lie beneath that body of water. Manannán is famous as the creator of the *corrbolg* or crane-bag to hold his treasured possessions. Since the container that once held the Broighter gold has not survived, we will never know whether it was made from the skin of a crane in honour of the god.

10

The puzzle of fragments

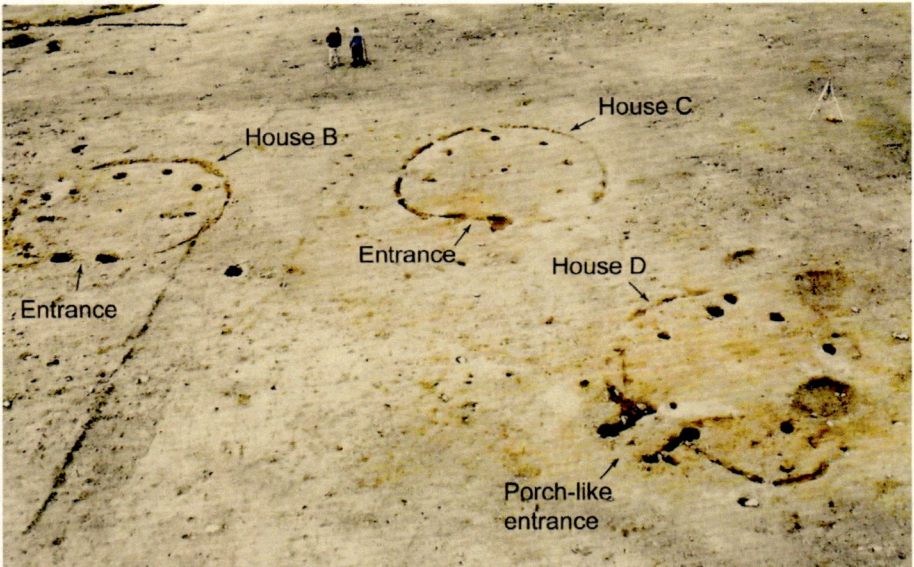

10.1—Excavation of three house sites at Ballybrowney, Co. Cork, where entrances were marked by fragmentary deposits.

Many a fictional detective has expressed a disbelief in coincidence, and the psychologist Carl Jung called it synchronicity when he asserted that there were circumstances that were meaningful even if they displayed no obvious common cause. Many archaeologists would now agree. It is a challenge to explain some fragmentary and partial human remains, for instance, but they occur again and again in both burial and settlement contexts. The extra collar bone in the Ballynacarriga urn and the piece of a femur found in a cist at Ballybrennan, Co. Westmeath, are just two burial examples.

The list of additional body parts identified in burials can be greatly extended. For example, a grave in that Keenoge cemetery contained a young female in a crouched position accompanied by several pieces of the skull of an older adult male, while another grave with the crouched burial of an adult male also contained part of a woman's pelvis. Like Okoulabari's bones, all of these fragments were probably endowed with distinctive meaning. This reciprocity between the living and the dead was a form of communication that had far-reaching effects beyond the grave. In fact, in the retention and redistribution of body parts the dead were reincorporated into the community.

Identifying such singular additions in a cremation is often a more difficult exercise, given the frequent presence of multiple burials and the selective collection of bones. At Carmanhall, Co. Dublin, where animals may have been added to the funeral pyre, the analysis of the cremation in one of the burials revealed that the bones were those of an adult of indeterminate sex along with some animal bones. However, a single bone fragment, possibly that of an infant, was added to the deposit.

Kerri Cleary has studied the deposition of human remains and broken quernstones on Bronze Age settlement sites and she has identified over a dozen where fragmented unburnt or cremated human bones have been found. Skull fragments are well represented, and some cremation deposits were placed in pits, ditches and the structural post-holes of houses. At Cloghers, near Tralee, Co. Kerry, fragments of cremated bone, including parts of a rib, two long bones and a shoulder bone from at least two individuals, were found in a post-hole at the entrance to a round house. Fragments of saddle querns get similar treatment at an even greater number of sites, some being placed in pits, others in post-holes.

Part of a Bronze Age village settlement was excavated at Ballybrowney, south of Fermoy, Co. Cork. An enclosure about 20m in diameter, formed by a wall of timber planks, had an oval house at its centre, and three circular houses lay to the north (B, C and D). One post-hole of the entrance to the oval house in the enclosure contained four sherds of pottery and a saddle quern fragment, and the opposite post-hole contained a sherd of pottery. In one of the other houses (B) the southern post-hole of the entrance produced a worked stone, possibly an anvil, and the opposite northern post-hole contained a saddle quern fragment. The southern post-hole of the entrance to another house (C) contained pottery, and pottery was also found in the entrance to the third house (D). Curiously, in this case it was the inner western post-hole of the porch-like entrance and the outermost post-hole on the eastern side that produced the pottery fragments. It is possible that some of these finds, particularly single sherds of pottery, may be entirely coincidental, but there were patterns here that would seem to be more than mere coincidence. Even fragments of pottery may be significant, perhaps representing their makers or owners.

The quern-stones, important in another way because of their role in food production, probably symbolised life and fertility.

Context is obviously one important factor in interpreting such remains. Some fragments were possibly foundation deposits linked to the establishment of the settlement or to the construction of a house. The wooden posts they marked may have been ancestral timbers from an older structure. The purpose of the offerings may have been to placate new local spirits and to bring good fortune. Some may have been placed in liminal locations like a boundary ditch or entranceway, as at Ballybrowney and Cloghers. Others were closing deposits marking significant moments in the life of a community, such as the abandonment of a settlement or the dismantling or destruction of a house.

Puzzling pottery fragments are found in burials too, though identifying them is sometimes challenging, given practices such as multiple burial and reuse of the one grave. For example, a pit burial at Glenlary, near Galbally, Co. Limerick, held an inverted collared urn that contained the cremated bones of two adults. A miniature vase had been placed beside the urn. A flint blade and just the one sherd of another urn were also recovered.

In another example, a cist grave at Kilgraney, south of Bagenalstown, Co. Carlow, contained the cremated remains of two adults and a juvenile. A complete bowl and sherds of a second bowl were also found. Only five small fragments of the second vessel had been placed in the cist and the surface of these was quite badly worn. Presumably this pot had been used for a time elsewhere before its pieces were deposited. While fragments like these had a symbolic meaning, perhaps the actual act of breaking a pot was a significant feature of the burial rite. Maybe it was destroyed and symbolically killed to prevent its being used again.

Accumulations of heavily fragmented metalwork and raw materials have often been considered—with some justification at times—as hoards of scrap metal, perhaps the materials of a bronzesmith retained for recycling. While this might be the explanation for very large collections of bronze waste, it seems a particularly unlikely explanation for the fragmented pieces in the Dowris deposit and in some miniature hoards as well.

A good example of the latter is a small hoard found in 1941 under a rock on the site of a cutaway bog at Cooga, south-west of Easkey, Co. Sligo. It contained a small portion of a bronze sword, two damaged socketed bronze axes and a small lump of bronze. Because of their fragmentary nature it was assumed that this was probably a collection of waste material, perhaps the possession of a bronzesmith. Indeed, it has been called a 'founder's hoard'. Now, such a functional description may not always be the explanation, and such fragments may be more than they

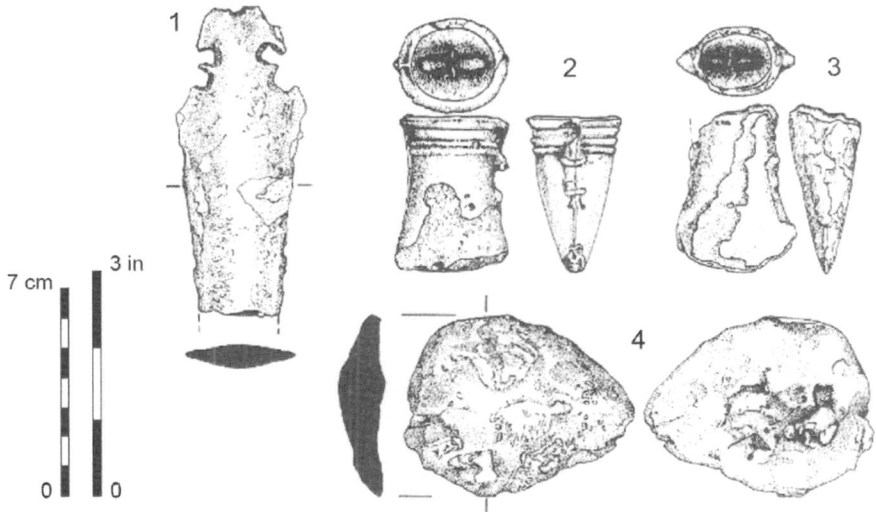

10.2—The Cooga hoard.

seem. The deliberate practice of selective fragmentation that we have seen in the case of both human bodies and quern-stones may apply here too.

Pieces of bronze may have been carefully preserved and then circulated among some members of the community as valued items and, perhaps like relics, created preternatural ties and sustained social connections. Some artefacts may have been deliberately fragmented and then dispersed in a network of places across the landscape, forming a link between individuals or communities. By selecting an object, breaking it and distributing the parts, a number of individuals may symbolically proclaim a new or renewed social relationship. Far from being mere pieces of waste material just suitable for recycling, it is worth considering that different stories may have been attached to some fragmentary components of both the Dowris deposit and the Cooga hoard. Fragmentation simply changed the meaning of the artefact and its missing parts.

The waste metal explanation can hardly be applied to another miniature hoard from Derryniggin in north County Leitrim. Of earlier date, it comprised two decorated bronze axeheads and two flint knives. They were found in a bog in the course of turf-cutting. Both flint knives are complete but the butts of both axeheads are missing and the smaller was fractured at a possible casting flaw. Clearly there was some important difference in the properties of metal and stone. The axeheads may once have possessed powerful magic, like other fractured objects, and may have

85

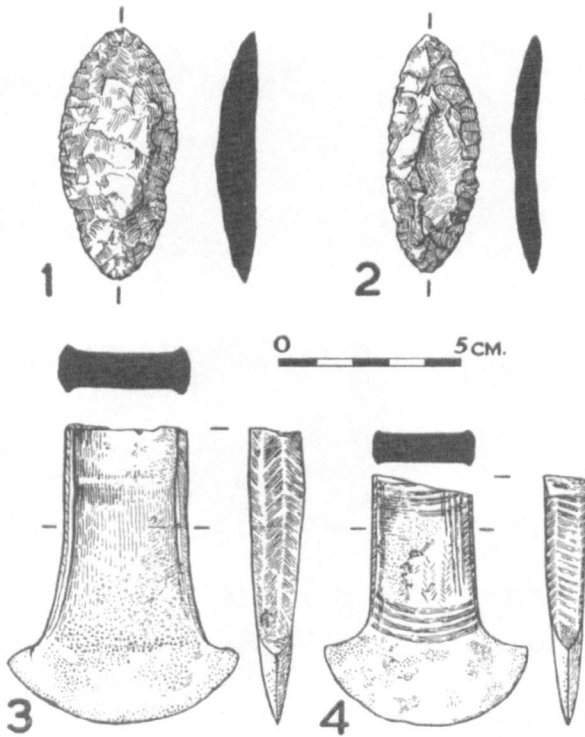

10.3—The Derryniggin hoard.

been broken on the death of their owner or at some other transformative moment that rendered them polluted in some way. In contrast, the two flint knives are intact and finely worked.

There are interesting differences between the Cooga and Derryniggin hoards, and not just in content and date: one was a dryland discovery, the other a wetland find. In both, however, pieces of some of the objects were dispersed elsewhere, rather like some of the human body parts already mentioned. Fragments of human bodies and artefacts both seem to have been part of a cult of relics, and this is a pattern that does blur the distinction between people and objects that is such a feature of the modern world.

Of course, not all fragmented objects were necessarily relics or talismans of some description. A hoard of five gold lunulae of early Bronze Age date was found in 1859 in boggy ground in Ballinderry townland, north of Carbury Hill, Co. Kildare, and suggests another possibility. Precise details are scant but, thanks to careful

10.4—The Ballinderry lunula hoard, Co. Kildare.

scrutiny of a variety of early sources, Mary Cahill has determined that all five had been originally deposited in two or more pieces. The two complete lunulae were originally broken in two and were repaired in modern times. One of these, sometime after its discovery in modern times, had a piece cut out of it to be placed as a ring in a pig's snout. The three others are represented by substantial fragments. These finely made sheet-gold objects are thought to have been neck ornaments, but they could well have had a mystical, even a solar, significance like the Coggalbeg piece. In this case, if the items had this sacred meaning, their fragmentation may have been a form of deconsecration.

Magical fragments may be identifiable in another gold hoard too. Simple penannular bracelets in this precious metal are well known in the later Bronze Age. Fifteen come from two hoards found on Cathedral Hill, Downpatrick, Co. Down. Both are well-documented discoveries found in the course of grave-digging in the 1950s. One hoard had been carefully deposited in a very small pit, 20cm in greatest diameter and covered by some stones. It consisted of eleven bracelets and part of a neck-ring which had been carefully stacked one upon the other, the smaller ones at the bottom, the three largest at the top and separated from the rest by an inch of clay filling. One of these, a large bracelet several times heavier than the others, was represented by just one half, and a chisel mark clearly showed that it had been partly cut by such an implement. Another bracelet, also more massive than the rest, had some engraved geometric decoration. Only about half of the neck-ring had been deposited and it too had been partly cut with a chisel.

Metal analyses showed that these three objects, the two bracelets and the neck-ring, had different trace elements to the others and confirmed that they were imports probably from south-western Iberia. The decorated neck-ring was of a type usually dated to around 1200 BC. These imported pieces were undoubtedly highly valued and perhaps kept as treasured heirlooms for several centuries before two of them were fragmented to serve a new and surprising purpose.

The simple bracelets in the hoard contained different trace elements and were of a common Irish type usually dated to 1000 BC or somewhat later. A quite unexpected result of their analysis was the revelation that they had been surfaced with gold from the older exotic imports. This, it seems, would not have significantly improved their appearance, so there was no compelling aesthetic reason for this puzzling treatment. It is distinctly possible that the imported gold had some transformative quality that had to be imparted to the native objects. In this instance gold fragments were used in a process of magical alchemy to produce bracelets of unusual distinction. These were something more or something other than simple personal ornaments.

11

What's in a name?

11.1—Standing stone at Garraunbaun, Co. Galway.

Brian Friel's play *Translations* was an evocative drama about dispossession and the loss of the Irish language, and it depicted the activities of the Ordnance Survey in Donegal in the 1830s as a military and Anglicising operation. Even though the Survey was first and foremost a detailed mapping exercise and a record of land and buildings to allow the reform of the country's local taxation system, the many hundreds of six-inch sheets produced furnish an enormous amount of archaeological information. *Translations*, however, has coloured popular and academic perceptions of the Survey ever since. The surveyors did not translate place-names but for the most part standardised already Anglicised names or offered phonetic versions of them, and after careful research adopted, as a rule, the version closest to the original Irish form. Thus *An Dún Mór* became Dunmore, not 'The Big Fort'.

This was probably not the best way to proceed, and daft mistakes were of course made. Some of these have been identified by the writer and cartographer Tim Robinson. In his brilliant study of the Aran Islands, for example, he noted the name Illaunanaur, an Anglicised version of *Oileán na nDeor*, the 'island of tears', a name documented at the south-eastern end of Inis Mór. There is no inland island there, however, and the name was misrecorded. It should have been rendered as *Gleann na nDeor*, a narrow valley near the coast. This 'valley of tears' was a spot where islanders could wave a final farewell to relatives and friends on ships awaiting a fair wind in Sunda Ghrióra or Gregory's Sound before sailing from Galway to America. Here the original place-name retains the memory of a bitter truth.

Sheeauns is a large townland between Cleggan and Ballynakill Bay. It is rich in archaeological monuments and its name in Irish, as Robinson pointed out as he traversed this part of north Connemara, is *Na Siáin*, the 'fairy mounds'. A short distance to the east is Garraunbaun, and there on a hilltop overlooking Ballynakill Bay he came across a standing stone: 'It was a stumpy boulder set on end, about five feet high, of milk-white quartz dappled with grey lichen, and in the twilight it looked exactly like the rump of an old white horse, peacefully grazing'.

The townland name Garraunbaun had been assumed to be an Anglicisation of *An Garrán Bán*, 'the white thicket or shrubbery', but Robinson's research revealed that one surveyor in 1839 had noted the name as *An Gearrán Bán*, meaning 'the white gelding or small horse'. The additional vowel was important, for Robinson had also recorded a local story about a legendary horse that used to emerge from nearby Garraunbaun Lake. A man once saddled the horse but when he removed the saddle and hung it on the standing stone the horse galloped away and returned to the lake. The mark of the saddle was supposed to remain on the stone. Robinson thought that the standing stone could now be seen as the mythical white horse itself and that this was a legend fossilised in a place-name that was, as he wrote, mis-understood and gelded by later officialdom.

Allusions to white horses or mares in the Irish landscape are commoner than one might think. While medieval creativity cannot be ruled out and some place-names linked to prehistoric sites may be scholarly inventions, others could well have more ancient pedigrees. This is the case in the Tara landscape. The Hill of Tara, with its exceptional history and mythology, is rightly considered to be one of the pre-eminent cult sites in ancient Ireland. A host of monuments and natural features on the hill and in its vicinity are noticed in numerous early tales and testify to their former importance.

As Conor Newman has shown, the Gabhra River flows through the Tara land-scape and its route is marked by a whole series of significant archaeological sites.

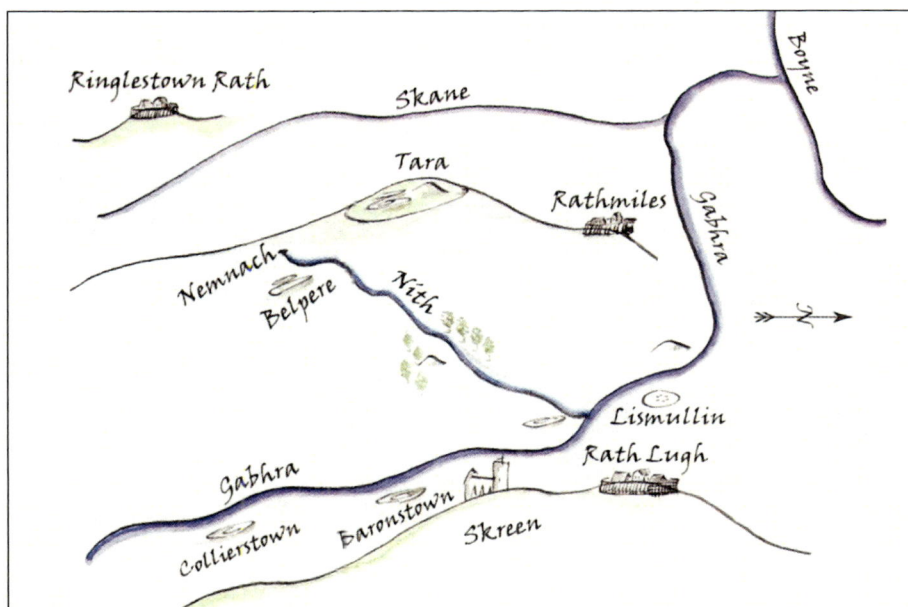

11.2—A sketch-map of the Tara landscape, showing the Gabhra River and some major monuments.

Now little more than a stream in places, its flood-plain shows that it was once a more substantial feature. The major sites that flank its course and are a measure of its significance include an Iron Age circular timber temple at Lismullin, an earthwork called Rath Lugh, named after the great Celtic god, an Iron Age and early medieval settlement at Baronstown and a medieval cemetery at Collierstown. A large burial mound is located at the junction with the Níth River, which flows from the sacred well called Nemnach on the Hill of Tara and whose route is also tracked by monuments.

The name of the Gabhra is laden with meaning. In Old Irish *gabor* may mean a white horse or mare. This, then, is the 'river of the white mare'; not only has it a physical connection to Tara but also its equine character links it to the horse rituals that were an integral part of the prehistoric rites of sacral kingship on that hilltop.

This equine motif is incorporated in other place-names associated with significant sites. These include the large mound called *Sgiath Gabhra*, the 'shield or defence of the white mare', that was a part of the inauguration landscape of the Maguire lordship in Cornashee, near Lisnaskea, Co. Fermanagh. This prehistoric mound lies in the centre of a large enclosure that contains a smaller oval monument. The impressive site appears to be approached by a wide avenue on the southeast, but the antiquity of this feature is uncertain. The *sciath* in *Sgiath Gabhra*,

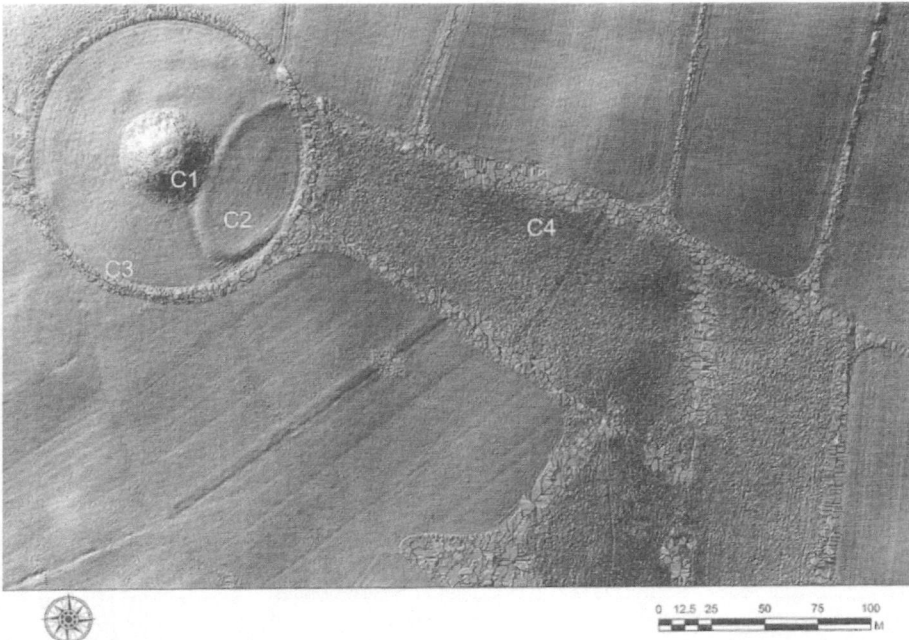

11.3—Aerial digital image of Cornashee: visible monuments at Sgiath Gabhra include the large mound (C1), oval enclosure (C2), large enclosure (C3) and possible processional avenue (C4).

meaning a shield, may be a reference to the protection provided by the enclosing rampart, and the white mare may be an evocative allusion to ancient king-making rituals in which horses played an important role, as we shall see.

Lagore, Co. Meath, the royal lake-dwelling of the medieval kings of Brega, has equine associations too. It is known in Irish as *Loch nGabor* ('the lake of the white mare') or *Loch Da Gabor* ('the lake of the two white mares') and is where, according to *dindshenchas* tradition, two horses named *Gáeth* and *Grían* (Wind and Sun) were drowned.

The sacralisation of a landscape occurs and operates at different scales, as Newman reminds us. At Tara it is on a grand scale: the twin hills of Tara and Skreen, separated and linked by the Gabhra, are cosmological opposites. Skreen or Achall was the counterpart of Tara and is associated with failed kingship. The same impressive scale is true of other great royal sites like Rathcroghan or Navan.

Numerous clusters of archaeological monuments hint at the former existence of many smaller sacred landscapes. The area between Cong and Ballinrobe in County Mayo is a good example. A concentration of megalithic tombs, cairns and stone circles in *Mag Tuired* of Cong, now called Moytura, is evidence of its importance in the Neolithic and Bronze Age. We have no idea what myths and legends may have been originally attached to these monuments but in medieval times it was decided that this had been the location of a great battle between the Tuatha Dé Danann and the Fir Bolg. Since even mythical battles should have a battlefield, learned storytellers placed this event in the monument-rich Cong area. They situated a second Battle of Moytura or *Cath Maige Tuired* in County Sligo at Moytirra. The full meaning of *Magh Tuireadh* (in modern spelling) is uncertain but perhaps it was the 'Plain of Pillars'. This second conflict was between the Tuatha Dé Danann and the Fomoiri (a name that may mean 'the people from beneath the sea'). Given its archaic content, this is thought to be the original battle and was an Irish variation on the theme of the war of the gods well known in Nordic and Greek myth. It has been compared to the combat between the Asuras and Devas in Vedic India and that between the Aesir and Vanir in Scandinavian mythology.

The account of a Cong battle fascinated William Wilde, who lived for a time in the area. He was familiar with the great concentration of ancient remains there and walked the locality, with a translation of the medieval tale in his hand, happily identifying individual monuments with particular people and events. For example, one young Fir Bolg warrior slain in combat was said to have been buried in 'the Carn of the One Man'. The enthusiastic Wilde, on digging into a likely burial mound and discovering a small cist holding a vase containing some cremated bone, was fully persuaded that he had found the warrior's grave. He exclaimed that 'perhaps a more convincing proof of the authenticity of ancient Irish or any other history has never been afforded'. Today the many burials of this sort can be accurately if prosaically dated to about 2000 BC, so it is not easy to recapture the romantic colour that an epic legend could once apply to a simple burial cairn. Even though the battle is the stuff of myth, the tombs and cairns and circles mark the area as a special place.

In nearby Connemara we may never recapture the ancient meaning of the stumpy stone in Garraunbaun, but it was probably an important marker in a landscape filled with supernatural connotations. The names *Na Siáin* and *An Gearrán Bán* are the last remnants of a lost mythology.

12

Mountains of the mind

12.1—Slieve Donard, with the Dundrum sand-hills in the foreground.

Mount Meru is celebrated in Hindu mythology as the centre of the universe. This mythical place, replicated in the form of many eastern temples, is probably the best-known mountain in Indo-European mythology. There are many other celebrated mountains but they are not all perceived as the *axis mundi*, the centre of the universe. Like Himinbjörg in Scandinavian myth and Mount Olympus in Greece, some other mountains are the dwelling places of the gods. This cosmic association of mountain peaks has persisted through the ages. St Augustine in one of his sermons condemns those who climb mountains to be closer to their god. A belief in a link to celestial divinities and supernatural powers may be one reason for the presence of so many prehistoric burial mounds on hilltops in Ireland, where high places are an important element in the island's sacred geography. Their importance is often reflected in their numerous mythological associations.

Stefan Bergh has written:

'Among the unlimited number of places present in a natural landscape, the mountain or high ground has always had a special role as a place of significance. This applies not only to well-known and conspicuous mountains like Kilimanjaro in Kenya or Uluru in Australia, or, closer to home, Croagh Patrick in Co. Mayo, but also to the more insignificant hills or high ground that might not catch the eye immediately. ... Mountains have a visible presence in the landscape and have a strong identity. Among the Saamis, each family has a special relationship with a certain mountain. This mountain provides the focal point for offerings and rituals. A second aspect of the role that mountains can assume is that of authority, since a place on the summit inevitably dominates its surroundings and—perhaps significantly—the activities that may not be visible from the land below. So while the presence of the mountain is collectively felt, only a few might have access to detailed knowledge of the topography and its content. This concealment of knowledge is a common way of achieving authority as it creates uncertainty among those not allowed to participate and thereby mystifies the place as such.'

Slieve Donard, on the eastern coast of County Down, at 849m is the highest peak in the Mourne Mountains. It has two prehistoric cairns on its prominent summit. Its name derives from St Domangart, who founded a monastic site at nearby Maghera but is said to have lived as a hermit in one of the cairns. Little is known of this early saint. He was said to have been the son of Echu, the last pagan king of the region, and his mother was a woman named Derinell Chethar Chichech—Derinell of the Four Breasts. A couple of other multi-breasted women are known, and this may be an echo of a female fertility figure like the famous many-breasted Artemis of Ephesus. Intriguing as this saint's pagan pedigree may be, however, the older mythology of the mountain is even more curious. Its original name was Sliabh Slánga and it was named after one of the sons of Partholón, the mythical leader of the first invasion of Ireland after the biblical Flood. Slánga was supposedly buried in the great cairn on the summit later occupied by Donard, who had been named by St Patrick as the ever-living guardian of the place.

In time Slieve Donard became the focus of a pilgrimage towards the end of July, and historical evidence indicates that this lasted for several centuries at least. The tradition seems to have continued until the early nineteenth century but, given the pagan associations of the mountaintop, it may have been a very ancient practice.

Croagh Patrick in Mayo is probably the best-known pilgrimage mountain, with a long history of religious activity. As early as the seventh century St Patrick is

12.2—Croagh Patrick, Co. Mayo, with the pilgrimage route clearly visible.

recorded as fasting on the mountain for 40 days and nights. An old routeway, known as Tóchar Phádraig, approaches the summit from the east, and in the past pilgrimages took place at various dates in the year. In modern times the main pilgrimage occurs on the last Sunday in July. A small church, built in 1905, now crowns the summit, but limited excavation in 1994 revealed the remains of a small early oratory nearby and confirmed the existence of an enclosing stone rampart. No certain traces of prehistoric activity survive on the summit, but the mountain's pagan associations

12.3—The Paps, Co. Kerry

were important enough for St Patrick to install one of his followers, name unknown, as another immortal guardian there, as he had on Slieve Donard.

While prehistoric monuments may have marked some mountains as special places, in one instance a land form may have been an additional causative factor. An impressive pair of hills, each about 690m high, south-east of Killarney, Co. Kerry, are known as the Paps. There is a large prehistoric cairn on the summit of each hill. In Irish they are named *Dá Chích Anann*, 'the breasts of Ana', and are frequently described as the breasts of a goddess who in a tenth-century text, 'Cormac's Glossary', is called 'mother of the Irish gods'. The name Ana (Anu in Old Irish) seems to have been sometimes confused or conflated with Danu of the Tuatha Dé Danann but, whatever her status, at the very least Ana may be considered a local deity associated with the land. That the land was female was a part of Indo-European belief systems and the cairn-builders—and, indeed, any pagan visitor to Kerry—would have had to be particularly dim not to have recognised the resemblance of this pair of hills to a part of the female body.

The cairns on the Paps are probably Neolithic passage tombs, though in the absence of excavation no certainty is possible. We can be sure, however, that Queen Maeve's cairn, or *Miosgan Meva*, on the summit of Knocknarea is one such monu-

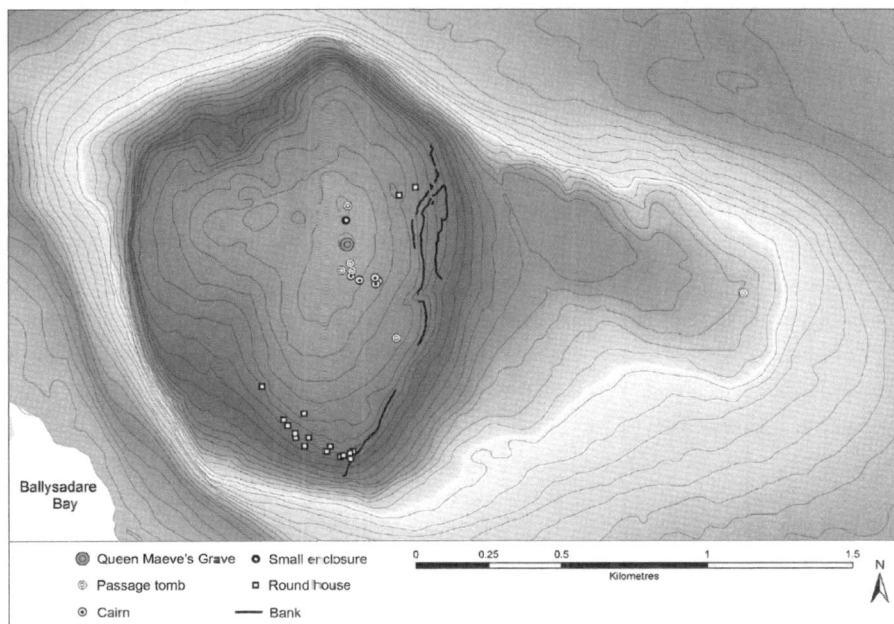

12.4—Knocknarea, Co. Sligo.

12.5—Two of the four cairns on Knockma, Co. Galway.

ment, even though it has not been excavated. This conspicuous mountain in County Sligo is a very characteristic landmark, its visual impact enhanced by the huge cairn on its flat summit. There are some five small tombs in its immediate vicinity, this characteristic clustering being an indication that this was a small passage tomb cemetery.

Survey and excavation have shown that the eastern side of the mountain was demarcated by a complex system of stone-built walls more or less following the 250–260m contours about 100m downhill from the 327m-high summit. The bank complex has a total length of *c.* 2.4km and several hut sites are linked to it. They probably represent occupation associated with summit ceremonials. The banks demonstrate that the ritual space was demarcated on the ground. The whole mountain of Knocknarea was thus transformed into a monument.

Such a hilltop cluster of passage tombs is reminiscent of a small group of four cairns on the summit of Knockma, near Tuam, Co. Galway. They too probably represent a passage tomb cemetery. Two are large, one remodelled in the nineteenth century as a folly, while two are damaged but still visible on the ground. Knockma stands apart in possessing the folkloric remnants of a rich mythology. It is associated with a certain Finnbheara, who figures briefly in several medieval tales. He is one of the Tuatha Dé Danann and brother of Óengus, who inhabits Brug na Bóinne (Newgrange). In one text he pays a visit to the Brug to see the womenfolk there and insults the beautiful Eithne. In later folklore he becomes lord of the *síd* of Knockma and king of the Connacht fairies. He seems to have specialised in enticing young women to his otherworldly realm.

Though we have no idea of the rituals once practised in these high places, in the pagan past these landscapes were metaphysically charged and reflected mythic history. They had an emotional impact quite foreign to modern ways of rational thinking, forever seeking understanding and elucidation. Summit tombs contained the bones of ancestors and they or the hills themselves were links to another world that demanded no explanation. Touching the sky, they were a part of a tripartite division of the cosmos with earth and underworld below. Then as now, they were perceived as special places.

13

On the edge of the world

13.1—Dún Aonghasa, Aran.

If mountains were a liminal space between earth and sky, so too were places situated on a threshold between land and sea. Dún Aonghasa is located in a commanding coastal position, almost at the highest point of the southern end of a north–south ridge on Inis Mór, Aran. This high ground dominates the lower lands of Kilmurvey to the north-east.

Today this well-known monument stands dramatically on the edge of a sheer sea cliff 87m high. Its earliest stone ramparts were probably built around 1100 BC and the wall of its early central enclosure is now entombed in the great inner rampart visible today. In the late Bronze Age this was probably a hillfort with a central enclosure and two outer ramparts. It was remodelled, possibly in the Iron Age, when the inner enclosure was augmented and heightened and a stone *chevaux-de-*

frise constructed outside the middle enclosure. The latter was a term used to describe wooden stakes or upright pointed stones placed in the ground to hinder attackers and is said to derive from spikes used by Frisians to impede enemy cavalry in the seventeenth century.

Examples of this stony defence are known in prehistoric times, from Iberia to Scotland. They could have been an effective method of impeding an attack, but they also served to control access. Greek mythology, however, invites us to think that such stones may have had a noteworthy symbolic purpose too. The myth of the foundation of Thebes tells of a certain Cadmus who, instructed by the oracle at Delphi to found a town, encountered a dragon guarding a spring. When the hero killed the dragon, Athena appeared and told him to sow the dragon's teeth. He did so, and a group of fully armed men sprang from the ground. Five of these supernatural *Spartoi*, the fierce 'sown men', helped him found the city. It is a fascinating thought that the prehistoric significance of Dún Aonghasa was enhanced by the presence of dragon's teeth—in other words, by a phalanx of formidable symbolic stone warriors.

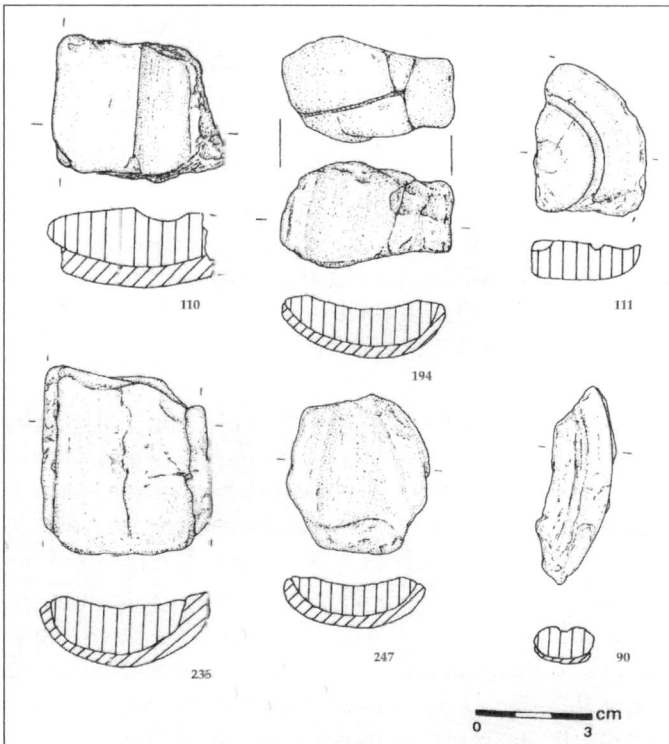

13.2—Dún Aonghasa: fragments of clay moulds for casting bronze swords (236, 194, 247), a spearhead (110), the head of a disc-headed pin (111) and a bracelet (90).

Traces of settlement were found within the inner enclosure and in the middle enclosure. The remains of a number of circular huts and other structures were identified in the inner area. Finds included fragments of coarse pottery, crucibles, clay moulds, bone pins, amber beads ultimately of Baltic origin, bronze chisels, rings, an axe fragment, and a small hoard of four hollow bronze rings. Fish bones, sea shells and animal bones, notably of sheep, were recovered too.

The discovery of evidence for metalworking is particularly interesting because this is relatively rare on settlements of the period. The clay moulds indicate the casting of bronze swords, spearheads, bracelets and pins on or near the site. At first glance a hilltop location on the edge of the Atlantic might seem to be an unlikely setting for this sort of work, for most (if not all) of the resources needed for metal production must have been imported. These would have included the necessary metals, the clay for the moulds and possibly the wood for charcoal as well. This was a prestigious technology and a transformative craft. It was probably a magical enterprise, and it may be that the location on the edge of the known world gave added supernatural value to the swords and other high-status objects made here.

Status, prominence and possibly defence were in all likelihood intertwining factors in the choice of location for Dún Aonghasa. Other triple-ramparted forts of Bronze Age date were built on similar heights, but Aran would have offered one other exceptional reason. The alchemy of metalworking here may have been particularly special.

The inhabitants of Dún Aonghasa would have witnessed sunrise and sunset in a remarkable way. In its daytime journey the sun would rise on the landward horizon and sink beneath the limitless ocean to the west. There it would begin its nighttime journey through the Otherworld to rise again in the east. This cosmic story was certainly a Bronze Age concern, for it is depicted in various ways on Scandinavian metalwork.

Most famously it is represented on the Trundholm sun chariot, where the gold-plated bronze disc, mounted on a wheeled vehicle, is drawn by a horse from left to right and depicts the sun's westward route across the heavens. When reversed, the back of the bronze disc, never gold-covered, is pulled by the horse from right to left, representing the sun's nocturnal journey under the land or under the sea towards the dawn in the east. A bronze disc now in the British Museum was once in the collection of Thomas Cooke of Birr, Co. Offaly, and is presumably of Irish origin. It bears a remarkable similarity to the Trundholm piece and is an indication that this solar symbolism was part of later Bronze Age ideology in Ireland too. We have no idea how this Irish sun symbol was displayed but it could have been attached to a small replica of a wagon or even mounted in a model boat.

13.3—(1) The Trundholm 'chariot of the sun'. The gilded face of the bronze sun disc is mainly decorated with concentric circle motifs and is drawn by the horse from left to right. The bronze face (below) bearing concentric circle motifs and a design of linked spirals is to the fore when the vehicle is drawn from right to left. (2) Bronze disc with no recorded provenance but probably from Ireland. Various scales.

As we saw when considering the veneration of the sun, in Bronze Age iconography elsewhere in Europe the sun was usually transported in a solar boat, and Aran folk might well have believed that it made its daytime and night-time journeys in a great currach. Because of its coastal setting, and particularly because of its exceptional solar vantage point, bronze objects made in Dún Aonghasa may have had a special cosmic charge.

A small promontory fort on a rocky peninsula in Galicia in north-western Spain appears to have been associated with solar orientation. Like Dún Aonghasa, the isolated Castro de Baroña is located on the Atlantic coast. It is defended by several stone walls and contains a number of hut sites. It has been argued that this location was chosen because it was situated between the sky, the land and the sea. A rocky hillock beside the fort offers several possible solar alignments, including a pathway or corridor through the rocks that points in a dramatic fashion towards sunset at the winter solstice. It is very possible that the dwellers in Dún Aonghasa were similarly focused on the profoundly moving spectacle of the setting sun.

Today it is easy to forget how awe-inspiring this may have been. A Roman writer records that in 137 BC an early Roman expedition in north-western Spain under the command of Decimus Junius Brutus halted its advance on the banks of the River Minho, south of Vigo. There the soldiers watched in horror as the sun set in the sea, setting its waters ablaze and appearing to grow in size, causing panic among them and leading them to flee homewards.

We know that the mystery of the sun's nocturnal journey beneath the earth was a real concern in medieval times. The question was asked in the early twelfth-century text *Immram Úa Corra* ('The Voyage of the Huí Corra'), a story of the sea voyage of three brothers who, when looking at the setting sun on the Atlantic coast in the west of Ireland, demanded: *Cia leth i teit an grian o thét fon fairrciu?* ('Where does the sun go when it goes under the sea?'). It figures, too, in a section of the ninth-century Old Irish text *In Tenga Bithnua* ('The Evernew Tongue'), in which the spirit of the Apostle Philip (whose tongue was cut out nine times and nine times miraculously regenerated) addresses the wise men of Jerusalem to explain the creation of the world to them. Here we are told that on the fourth day of Creation God made 'the fiery circuit of the sun which … illuminates twelve plains beneath the edges of the world in its shining every night'. Parts of the message of St Philip, the Evernew Tongue, explaining what happened to the sun at night, ran as follows:

'It is thus that the sun goes every evening:
First it shines on the stream beyond the sea, bringing it news of the
waters in the east.
Then it shines at night upon the lofty sea of fire, and upon the seas of
sulphurous flame which surround the red peoples.
Then it shines upon the hosts of youths in the pleasant fields, who utter
a cry to heaven for fear of the beast which kills many thousands of hosts
beneath the waves to the south …
It shines in the black valleys with melancholy streams across their faces
…
Then it shines upon the flocks of birds who sing many songs together
in the valley of the flowers …

Then it shines upon Adam's Paradise until it rises from the east in the morning ...'

Three thousand years ago the Dún Aonghasa enclosure may not have been quite so open to the elements. Some coastal erosion has certainly taken place and, while limestone collapse may have been episodic, one study has estimated an average loss rate of 0.4m per annum. This may be excessive, but it is likely that in the Bronze Age Dún Aonghasa stood on high ground a few hundred metres from the shore.

Its coastal location was important for other reasons. The Aran Islands were not isolated in the Bronze Age. The Atlantic seaways allowed the transmission of materials—such as copper, tin, Baltic amber and finished bronze objects—over great distances. In the centuries around and before 1500 BC, an urn burial on Inis Oírr and several megalithic tombs definitely indicate contact with the wider world. In the later Bronze Age, Aran may have been part of a coastal network that included settlement on Inishark, Inishbofin, Omey and Clare Island. It is conceivable that some of these islands may have been strategic contact points in a pattern of littoral communication over long distances. For the dwellers in and below Dún Aonghasa, boats would have found a safe haven and a convenient beaching ground on the sheltered sandy shore of Kilmurvey Bay beneath the great fort.

While currachs may well have been in common use at this time, there is as yet no Irish evidence for more substantial craft—but they may have existed. In England and Wales fragments of large boats constructed of sewn planks are known. They are considered to have been seaworthy, and one, a large, flat-bottomed craft found at Dover and dated to 1500 BC, was thought to have been quite capable of crossing the English Channel at a speed of 4.5–5 knots.

The use of sail is hard to identify in the archaeological record. In Ireland the first clear evidence is the model gold boat found at Broighter, Co. Derry, and dated to around the first century BC. With a sail and nine benches for rowers, it may represent a hide-built currach or a plank-built craft about 15m in length. The use of sailing currachs at an earlier date is entirely plausible, and a seventeenth-century drawing gives us an idea of what these may have been like. This was produced by one Thomas Phillips, a sea captain and engineer in the British Admiralty, in 1685. It shows a sturdy seagoing 'portable vessel of wicker', about 9m in length, as 'ordinarily used by the Wild Irish.'

It is possible, given the wide expanse of sea visible from Dún Aonghasa, that its Bronze Age inhabitants exercised a measure of control over the neighbouring seaways, just like the Barbary pirates of the North African coast of a later age. Trade was a probability: sea salt, clothing, dried fish, cured meat and, of course, magical

Cap.ᵗ Thomas Phillips, Seaman, & One of his Ma.ᵗⁱ Tower Engineers, his Draught of a Portable Vessell of Wicker, ordinarily used by the Wild Irish.

13.4—A seventeenth-century currach with sail.

metal were all valuable commodities. The importance of salt is often overlooked: a king of Cashel imposed a salt tax (*salanngabal*) on Aran. The ashes of burnt seaweed (*murlúaith*), used as an unrectified salt, could also be used to cure meat and fish.

Most trade and exchange were probably relatively localised and coastal—but longer voyages were probably attempted too. In examining the social structures that might underpin extended contacts and seafaring in the later Bronze Age, Robert Van de Noort has instanced the long-distance and highly ritualised exchange undertaken by the Trobriand Islanders, as described by Bronislaw Malinowski in his famous *Argonauts of the western Pacific* in 1922, in which the acquisition of prestige goods was key.

Reciprocal exchange, as a part of a *kula* ring or circuit between islands, included particular valuables used as payments in certain social contexts within the *kula* network. The political status of local leaders was directly related to the ownership and ceremonial display of these objects. Certain items, such as a type of reddish shell (*kula*), were especially prized. These shells, in the form of armlets and necklaces, circulated in prescribed directions among these island communities and were constantly exchanged. Every movement of the *kula* articles was fixed and regulated by a set of traditional rules and conventions. As a rule, they took two to ten years to make the round. Some exchanges were accompanied by elaborate magical rites and public ceremonies. On every island and in every village a limited number of men took part in the formalities, to receive the goods, to keep them for a short time and then to pass them on. These exchanges created a personal and lifelong bond between individuals.

The number of exchange partners that a man might have varied with his rank and importance. The passing from hand to hand of often ostensibly valueless and quite useless objects was effectively the foundation for a complex inter-tribal institution, for ordinary trade and barter took place, along with inter-tribal gatherings, with the ritual exchange of shells. The building of large seagoing canoes, accompanied by magical rites and tribal customs, was another important part of *kula* expeditions. This was a large inter-tribal network of relations consisting of thousands of men all bound together by a common passion for *kula* exchange and by many other minor ties and interests.

Bronze Age seafarers on Aran may have been equally adventurous and their seafaring links may have been equally complex and extensive. Their voyages, whether long or short, may have been circumscribed by ritual to secure safety and success. That urn burial on Inis Oírr, dating from around 1500 BC, was a cordoned urn and is an important discovery because pottery of this type is well represented in the north of Ireland and in Scotland. It has been found on Rathlin Island off the north Antrim coast, indicating that islands as well as sandy beaching places were important links in chains of maritime connectivity. Cordoned urn sherds have been found in the sand-hills at Portstewart, Co. Derry, and at Whitepark Bay on the Antrim coast. Settlements like the Bronze Age village at Corrstown, on the coast near Portrush, only 29km from Rathlin, must have had an important role too. The pottery found here was of the cordoned urn tradition.

The amber beads found in Dún Aonghasa are small but significant items. Over a dozen were recovered and they are almost certainly of Baltic amber. They would have been exotic and prestigious objects in any pattern of contact. A route from Denmark across the North Sea to Scotland and then to northern Ireland is one possibility. The bronze items made at Dún Aonghasa, with their magical value, may have been just as sought-after in any exchange pattern. Perishable goods, such as fish, meat and salt, may have been part of these contacts too. Ros Ó Maoldúin has pointed out that the provision of hospitality may have been an important component of such reciprocal engagements. Poets and musicians may have travelled, and myths and stories may have been shared.

Voyaging on an unpredictable ocean could well have been a means of winning fame and prestige. Some intrepid Dún Aonghasa argonauts may have engaged in this sort of travel to prove themselves. Some may even have ventured westwards in a heroic pursuit of the setting sun.

14

Aristocratic feasts

14.1—The Castlederg cauldron.

The bronze cauldron from Castlederg, Co. Tyrone, was found near the village of that name some time before 1840. Like so many others, it was discovered deep in a bog, but nothing more is known about its find circumstances. It is in splendid condition and stands just over 42cm in height. The body is formed of fifteen sheets of beaten bronze, including a bowl-shaped base, all riveted together with conical rivets. It has a capacity of fourteen litres. Some rivets form purely decorative seams with a reinforcing bronze strip on the interior. Two stout handles are cast on to the rim, each consisting of a ring in a tubular attachment.

14.2—Making a replica of the Castlederg cauldron.

Cauldrons like this are remarkable products of the bronzesmith's craft, displaying familiarity with sophisticated casting techniques, using lead-alloyed bronze for handle fitments and unleaded bronze for the carefully beaten sheet work and rivets. It would take a considerable investment in a craftsman's time to produce a cauldron like this.

A successful attempt to make a replica of the Castlederg cauldron demonstrated just how complex the task was and how it may have needed a team of expert craftsmen. One result of the experimental exercise reminds us of the lustrous appearance of newly minted and polished bronze. The amount of labour and sophisticated craftsmanship is one indication of the singular value of these objects. The patrons who commissioned them must have been people of considerable power and status.

It is generally believed that these were ceremonial vessels that served as centrepieces at communal feasts. These were probably occasions when special foodstuffs, especially meat, were consumed, and drink was probably important too. Such feasts were distinct from daily meals and probably included persons outside the usual social circle. In accepting this hospitality, these guests in turn were placed in a reciprocal relationship with their host. Thus social relationships were established or reinforced.

Cauldron use may have been highly ritualised and, much later in time, these vessels certainly have a magical character in medieval Welsh and Irish literature. In Homeric Greece they figure among the prestigious belongings of Bronze Age kings and heroes. In the *Odyssey* they were part of the precious possessions of Odysseus, for instance, and it is clear in the *Iliad* that the present of a cauldron was a mark of high esteem. Four cauldrons are among the gifts that Priam offers to Achilles.

Like the Castlederg example, many of these Irish cauldrons seem to have been isolated finds in watery places. Of course, they may have been accompanied by organic offerings that have left no trace but, in general, details about find-spots are non-existent. One example found in a bog at a depth of about 1m in the course of turf-cutting in Barnacurragh townland, near Tuam, Co. Galway, had been ritually deposited in an inverted position. Nothing else was found and nothing was noted in the vicinity when more of the bog was cut away. Nonetheless, it is probable that their deposition was accompanied by elaborate ceremonies. In ancient Greece cauldrons were used as votive offerings to gods and goddesses, and large numbers have been found in religious sanctuaries.

We know little about their actual usage. Lipid analysis of the contents of an early cauldron found during ploughing of a field at Feltwell Fen, Norfolk, confirmed the presence of carbonised food residue containing animal fat. The vessel also contained a bronze flesh-hook for extracting pieces of meat.

A number of these hooks have been found in Ireland. An example found in a bog at Dunaverney, near Ballymoney, Co. Antrim, is decorated with small model swans and ravens and must have been a very special piece indeed. The unique imagery in which birds of air and water are opposed does suggest that it had some particular symbolic significance. When it was used to pick up a portion of meat, the swans would have been in or near the liquid while the ravens would have been in the air above. This perhaps reflected some noteworthy narrative and suggests that the recounting of ancient myths may have been part of the proceedings.

If bronze cauldrons were a focal point at aristocratic feasts, the food they contained was probably shared by persons of similar rank and status. This was the case in Homeric epic, where the purpose of some feasts was to propitiate the gods, but invariably they also served to confirm the value of companionship and commen-

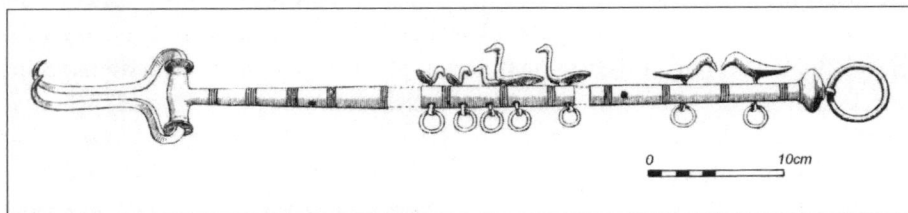

14.3—The Dunaverney flesh-hook.

sality, of equal sharing and equal esteem. Individual heroic participants might bathe or be bathed before a banquet. Although the heroes of Homer's tales had a clear preference for the roasted meat of animals of the hunt, the fashion of communal eating of meat boiled or stewed in bronze cauldrons was an élite practice in Mycenaean Greece. Cauldrons were also used to heat water for washing in the epic literature. Wine vessels and drinking cups formed part of the feasting equipment, and these events formed the setting for the telling or singing of stories.

Animals were ceremonially slaughtered and dismembered on these occasions and selected bones were burnt afterwards. Feasts were ritually intricate. While heroic Greek epic may not be a sure guide to ancient Irish practice, the *Iliad* does illustrate how complex such gatherings may have been. On these occasions animals were assembled, the participants' hands were washed and then barley was thrown at the animal to be sacrificed. Its head was raised and its throat was cut; it was then flayed and strips of raw pieces of flesh were burned over split wood, and then wine was poured over them. In some sacrificial feasts there is a reference to bread being laid out in baskets and meat being served. The feast might end with singing and drinking in honour of the god Apollo.

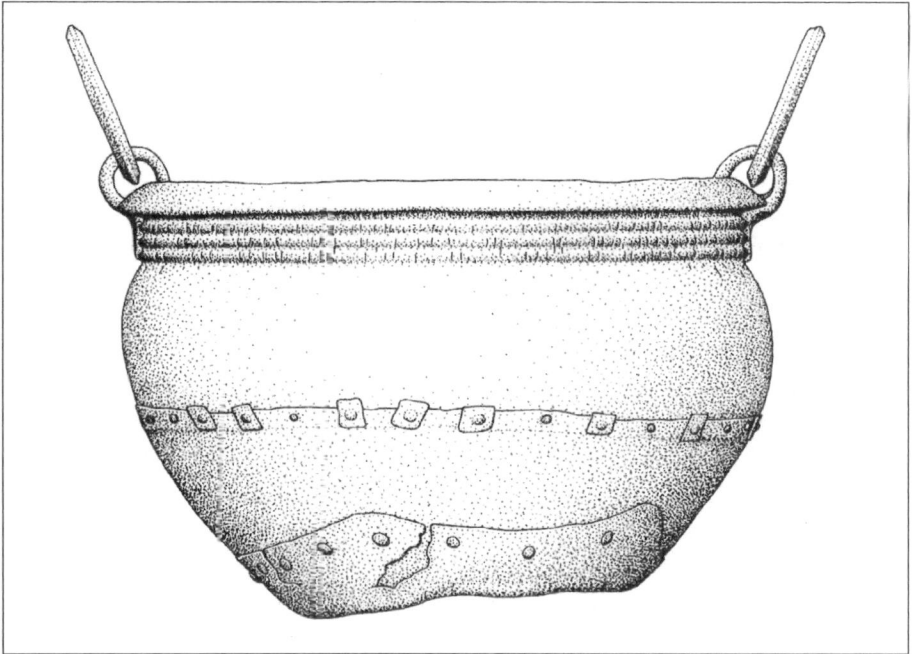

14.4—The Derreen cauldron.

A small cauldron from Derreen townland, near Castlerea, Co. Roscommon, was found many years ago in the course of turf-cutting. It had been placed in the still waters of a pool that was in time enveloped by the peat of Askey Bog or *Portach na hEasca* ('the marsh bog') around 1200 BC. It is an early type of cauldron made of three pieces of sheet bronze riveted together, and its pair of ring-shaped handle attachments are expertly cast on to the slightly in-turned rim. It was obviously put to good use, for its round base has been repaired with a large, irregularly shaped bronze patch. The repair work looks remarkably crude, but the nature of the rivets used suggests that it was undertaken by someone skilled in cauldron production. Why deliberately undertake an obviously poor piece of repair work? Some other early cauldrons are heavily repaired too, and these repairs often seem to take the form of deliberate and highly visible patching. This seems to have been an intentional act. It may have been meant to mark a particularly noteworthy feasting event or to give the vessel the appearance of an ancient and esteemed pedigree.

The memory of great feasts might survive for many generations. Witness Aodh Mac Gabhráin's contemporary poem *Pléaráca na Ruarcach*, which celebrates the Christmas festivities held in the castle at Dromahaire, Co. Leitrim, by the chieftain Brian na Múrtha Ó Ruairc in 1589. The poem was set to music by Turlough O'Carolan and translated into English for Jonathan Swift. It is a feast remembered to this day: 'O'Rourke's noble fare will ne'er be forgot, by those who were there, or those who were not. His revels to keep, we sup and we dine on seven score sheep, fat bullocks, and swine …'.

Feasting is a universal activity across the world and throughout human history. There is now a very large body of literature on the subject and on its social significance. Its study has become a complex interpretive process. The most popular explanation sees it as an action that reinforces community solidarity or social identity. It has also been presented as a strategy used by ambitious individuals to achieve social or political ends. It is not always easy to identify feasting behaviour in the archaeological record but, in general, it has often been inferred from the quantity and types of animal remains recovered. Funeral feasts and work feasts linked to building episodes have been identified from time to time. In an Irish context it is reasonable to assume that cauldrons and flesh-hooks are evidence of this sort of communal activity, but in themselves they tell us very little about the events in question.

It is easily forgotten that, while the feast itself may have been important, the preparations for such an event may have been a prolonged and equally significant process. There is some interesting Irish evidence from Navan Fort, ancient Emain Macha, Co. Armagh. As we shall see, excavations here revealed a remarkable picture of ritual continuity over many prehistoric centuries, culminating in the construction of a great circular timber temple around 95 BC. Before this a succession of circular timber structures were built on the same place over several centuries. It has been claimed that these may have been great feasting halls. Special feasts may have been held in special places.

Ceremonial feasting is a likely explanation because the bones of some animal species were present in unusual proportions and did not seem to represent an ordinary domestic assemblage. Pig was commonest (about 63%), cattle less so (30%), and sheep or goat less well represented (8%). All showed a high proportion of butchery marks, and some of the relatively small number of horse bones found were butchered or broken, suggesting the consumption of some horseflesh. Such a high proportion of pig bones is very rare on Iron Age sites in Britain and Ireland. Pigs were highly prized as feasting animals and were the preferred food in early Irish literature.

Strontium isotope analysis has become a common method for investigating the early geographical origins of humans and animals because it can determine the underlying characteristics of the rocks in the area from where an individual's food derives. The strontium isotope values in 35 animals from Navan Fort, of which 24 were pigs, proved to be exceptionally diverse. Two sheep and a pig with very low strontium values are very likely to have been raised in the basalt area of northern Ulster. The very high values are more difficult to pin to a location with confidence. These animals must have been transported from some distance away. They could have been raised in a restricted northerly area, but it is more likely that they derived from areas of older geology elsewhere, such as some limited areas of the north such as Donegal, the south-east in Wexford or the west in Galway. One of the animals had a high signature consistent with a coastal origin somewhere in the west, probably Donegal or Galway.

It thus seems probable that some of the materials for feasts at Navan came from a substantial distance. Since people must have come with the animals, perhaps as participants at the feast, these journeys may have been ceremonial events too. The same may have been the case with the delivery of other feasting goods and with the slaughtering of animals. While the ceremonial killing of animals may have been a highly ritualised task and assumed by a select few, much of the preparatory work and the serving on these occasions was probably undertaken by slaves.

The Navan evidence raises the possibility that the mass slaughter of animals could have been a general element in feasting rituals. While it is widely accepted that such feasts were important social communal occasions, they may have been inspired for many different reasons. The inverted Derreen cauldron, so reminiscent of an urn burial like Ballynacarriga, is a reminder that some may have been funeral feasts. The association of sword, bowl and drinking cup at Tamlaght should alert us to the possibility that drinking and feasting may have been part of the aristocratic ethos of a warrior élite. It is conceivable that cauldrons and flesh-hooks, and the ostentatious consumption of food and drink, had a role in communal banquets after battle. Whatever their inspiration, great feasts were probably remembered for many years 'by those who were there, or those who were not'.

15

The power of skulls

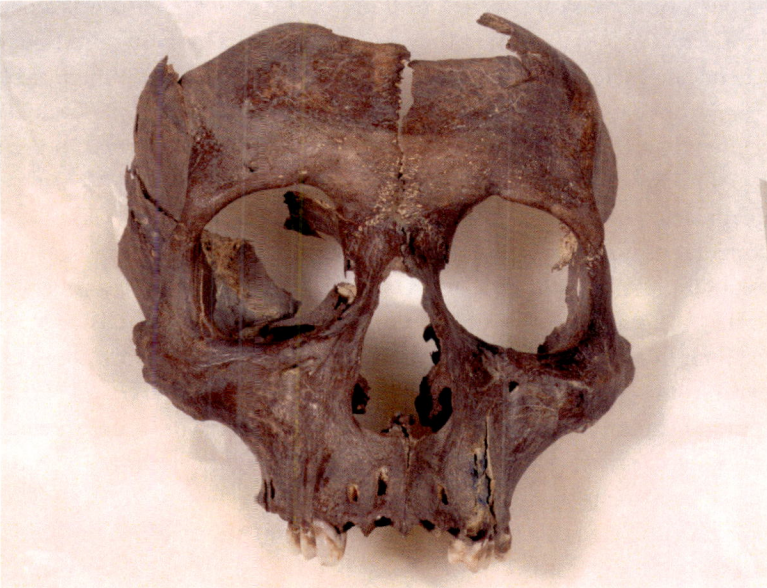

15.1—Portion of a skull from the King's Stables, Co. Armagh.

Practices expressing an interest in the human head are widespread in time and space, and there is a rich comparative ethnographic literature on this near-universal topic. There is abundant evidence testifying to the importance of the head in ritual and cultic practice throughout prehistory, and in more recent times, around the world. It is well documented in various parts of Iron Age Europe, for instance—and not just in the Celtic world. The head was often considered the central part of the human body, containing the essence of the individual. To possess a head or a skull—or even a part thereof, such as the skullcap or the jaw—was to appropriate the power of that person. This part of the human frame often figures prominently in fertility rites, cults of the dead and other rituals.

The special treatment of the skull is well documented in archaeology and has generally been understood as evidence of either ancestor worship or trophy-hunting. One obvious problem is the difficulty in distinguishing between the heads of revered ancestors and those of vanquished enemies. Moreover, the meaning of these social practices has evolved and changed over time. The innumerable saints' skulls preserved in part or in whole in reliquaries around Europe, their power now much diminished, are testimony to this. At least three skulls of St Brigid, whom we will meet in due course, are recorded in locations as far apart as Lisbon, Strasbourg and Neustadt in Germany.

Just parts of three skulls were found in the late Bronze Age levels at a crannog at Ballinderry, Co. Offaly, where they were thought to be foundation deposits. In the case of one male and one female skull, each had been modified: the face cut away from above the nose, leaving just the upper part. A third male skull was just represented by a fragment cut from the cranium. What happened to the missing pieces is not known. Part of a skull found at another crannog at Moynagh Lough, Co. Meath, also consisted of just the top half of the cranium.

The facial part of a skull was found in an artificial pond known as the King's Stables about 500m north-west of Navan Fort, Co. Armagh. This monument was popularly thought to be the site where the ancient kings of Ulster stabled and watered their horses. It is an approximately circular sunken hollow, about 2m below the surrounding ground surface, and is surrounded by a low, broad earthen bank with a broad gap on its western side. The interior filled with water in wet weather but normally the surface appeared as a soft moss. Only about 5% was excavated but with interesting results.

The limited excavation produced eighteen fragments of clay moulds for the manufacture of bronze swords, two sherds of coarse pottery, a small plank of alder, two items of worked bone, some animal bones (mostly cattle, deer antler, dog and pig) and a cut portion of the skull of a young adult human, probably male. It is in poor condition, in contrast to the animal bones from the same context, suggesting that it had been redeposited. Perhaps it had been publicly displayed elsewhere before being placed in the pond. Radiocarbon dates suggest usage sometime shortly after 1000 BC. The King's Stables seems to have been an artificial pool deliberately constructed for cult purposes that included offerings of animal and human remains as well as material associated with bronze-working.

Fragments of an adult skull found in the ditch of a ring-barrow at Kilmahuddrick, near Clondalkin, Co. Dublin, were of broadly similar date and showed signs of weathering on the outer surface, also suggesting exposure to the elements at some point. Parts of human skulls of later Bronze Age date come from other

15.2—A pit in the centre of an oval house at Lough Gur, Co. Limerick, containing fragments of a child's skull placed beside the large stone in the centre.

contexts too. Parts of a skull were found in the upper levels of a burnt mound at Cragbrien, Co. Clare, and a complete skull had been placed beside a natural spring near another burnt mound at Inchagreenoge, Co. Limerick.

Human bones are occasionally found on settlement sites. Three skull fragments, in good condition, come from the fill of a ditch of an enclosure at Chancellorsland, Co. Tipperary. Human bones and skull fragments have also been found on various sites on Knockadoon at Lough Gur, Co. Limerick. Pieces of the upper part of a child's skull were found in a pit in the centre of an oval house there—probably a good indication that skulls should not be automatically considered as the remains of ancestors or trophy objects. This may have been a foundation deposit carefully placed beneath the floor of the dwelling to celebrate its construction and to bring good fortune.

Iron Age examples include an important find at Raffin, south of Nobber, Co. Meath, where a circular enclosure some 65m in diameter, formed by a bank with internal ditch, had at its centre a circular structure surrounded by a ring of timber posts. A small pit marked by a pillar stone was found in the northern part of the enclosure. It contained successive layers of charcoal and soil, and the reddish colour of its sides indicated a series of burning episodes. Part of the frontal cranium of an adult human lay on the uppermost layer. The burning episodes were contemporary

15.3—(A) The re-erected standing stone that originally sealed the ritual pit at Raffin. (B) The ritual pit during excavation, with traces of burnt soil (stained red) visible on the sides and bottom.

and took place between the third and fifth centuries AD. The bone was dated to 110–140 BC and was at least 100 years old when placed on the upper layer beneath the pillar stone. The skull portion was worn smooth, suggesting frequent handling, and evidently this was an offering that had a long history and some very special meaning.

Skull fragments and a large quantity of teeth were found as secondary deposits in passage tomb no. 27 at Carrowmore, Co. Sligo, and the excavator noted the possibility that these might be the remnants of an Iron Age tradition of skull deposition. During drainage works in Loughnashade, north-west of Navan Fort, Co. Armagh, in 1798 four large bronze horns were discovered along with some human skulls and other bones. No precise details have been recorded and the bones and three of the horns have disappeared. The surviving horn is a great curving piece made of riveted sheet bronze with a decorative disc at the bell end with skilled repoussé ornament. The discovery of such fine bronzework and human bones suggests that the site was the focus of ritual depositions all contemporary with the activities in the nearby Navan enclosure.

The special treatment of the skull is occasionally recorded in the early medieval period. In many cases of decapitation the severed head was placed in the grave in an anatomically correct position. These people may well have been executed but their heads were not perceived as relics or objects of particular significance. Such disarticulated skulls are relatively rare, however. Some isolated later medieval skulls found in urban contexts may have been openly displayed.

One skull, that of a man in his early 50s, was found in a souterrain in the stone fort of Cahercommaun, in the Burren, Co. Clare. An iron hook with a suspension ring and two iron knives lay beneath it. The hook suggested that the skull may once have been publicly exhibited. It had been buried in the floor of the chamber near its end and was assumed to be a foundation deposit. Sixteen skull fragments found at the crannog at Lagore, Co. Meath, display evidence of violent decapitation and are thought to represent judicial executions, although the fact that just the occipital part of the cranium was deposited at this site is an indication that some ritual imperative was in play here too.

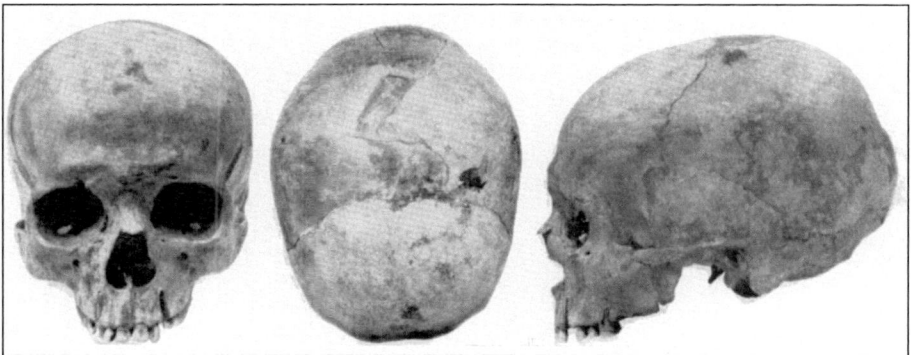

15.4—The Cahercommaun skull.

The finds from the King's Stables and from Kilmahuddrick are probable examples of prehistoric skulls that may have been exposed as trophies or venerated as ancestral figures. In some instances the intention may have been to keep such ancestors alive, considering them as members of the community even after their death. Their skulls may have been periodically displayed on ceremonial occasions. The worn fragment from Raffin probably had some supernatural quality. They all raise many questions—not least who they were and, more generally, what was the social status or position of such Bronze Age or Iron Age people who had their skulls removed. Of course, the bones of certain important people may have had a special significance and carried magical powers. Their dates span 1,000 years or so and are testimony to the continuing importance of the skull in later prehistory.

A cult of ancestors may be a reasonable explanation for some remains—bones and skulls—and they may have acted as a tangible sign of ancestral approbation, justifying both political continuity and legitimacy. Obviously, they could take on different meanings in different communities. Their presence could be an effective way of increasing personal prestige, and their highly charged associations may have offered an important means of exercising power. On a simpler level, some may have been family heirlooms encapsulating history and identity. Some may have had healing properties or offered protection against malevolent forces. Most were powerful objects in ways we can only dimly comprehend.

16

The language of the stones

16.1—A decorated kerbstone at Newgrange.

Carved decoration on the stones of some passage tombs is a remarkable feature of this category of megalithic monument. The decorated tombs, about 50 in number, are mainly found in the north and east of the country, and the greatest concentration occurs in County Meath in the great cemeteries at Loughcrew and in the Boyne Valley. Ornament has been found on kerbstones, roof-stones and orthostats. In some instances it is clear that it was carved after the stones had been put in place; in other cases designs were hidden or inaccessible and must have been carved prior to placing or replacing the stone in position.

The designs were executed by incision or by picking with a sharply pointed implement. A flint point or chisel was probably hammered with a wooden mallet to

16.2—A radial design and other motifs on a decorated kerbstone at Knowth, Co. Meath.

produce the motifs. No evidence of painting has ever been found in an Irish tomb though this technique is known in megalithic tombs in the Iberian Peninsula and in Brittany.

The art varies from the seemingly haphazard to the remarkably formal. Although some of the more haphazard designs cannot be readily classified, it is still possible to identify about a dozen general motif types. Single and concentric circles are common, and they are sometimes penannular as on some stones at the great mound at Knowth. Similar circles with central dots are particularly frequent at some sites. Semicircular or multiple arcs are also common. Radial designs, meanders or undulating linear motifs, and angular zigzags or chevron motifs occur. Angular motifs, including lozenges and triangles, sometimes form panels of ornament. Spirals, double spirals and linked spirals are also found. Other motifs include parallel lines, dots and so-called cup marks.

Some of this art is boldly displayed in visually impressive patterns. The famous entrance stone at Newgrange is a classic example. These compositions almost certainly had some special meaning. Numerous explanations have been offered for particular designs over the years. Radial motifs, for instance, have plausibly been seen as sun symbols. Some elongated U-shaped or broad arc-shaped designs have been claimed to be boats. Pairs of spirals have been considered to be stylised human eyes or faces ultimately inspired by vaguely humanoid Iberian plaques and idols.

0   50cm

16.3—The entrance stone at Newgrange.

A few Irish carvings have been thought to be stylised representations of human figures, and face-like designs have been seen in pairs of spirals, as on a decorated flint
macehead from Knowth.

It was once believed that some such designs might be evidence that a goddess
with human characteristics was worshipped by the builders of passage tombs and,
since anthropomorphic designs and human faces are recorded in passage tomb
contexts on the Continent, both in Brittany and in Iberia, highly stylised representations of this sort are not an impossibility in the Irish material. Mythic themes
may be encoded in some designs. For instance, it has been suggested that triple spirals might be a representation of the foundation myth of the sacred River Boyne—
for it was formed by three waves that sprang from a well at Carbury, Co. Kildare.

It is easy to see why some might see a human face on a macehead from Knowth
or a solar symbol in the rays carved on a basin stone. The study of compositional
groups and of the locational patterns of these compositions may advance our
understanding of this enigmatic phenomenon. It is clear that some stones and their
art mark key areas where specific rituals may have taken place both inside and outside some tombs: the decorated stone above the Newgrange roof-box is an obvious
example, as are the highly decorated kerbstones at tomb entrances. Some motifs
recur repeatedly at particular locations in and around some monuments. The decorated kerbstones around the great mound at Knowth, like some adjacent settings
of stones revealed by excavation, may denote important points on a processional
circuit around the site. Here some groups of adjacent stones appear to share similar
overall designs.

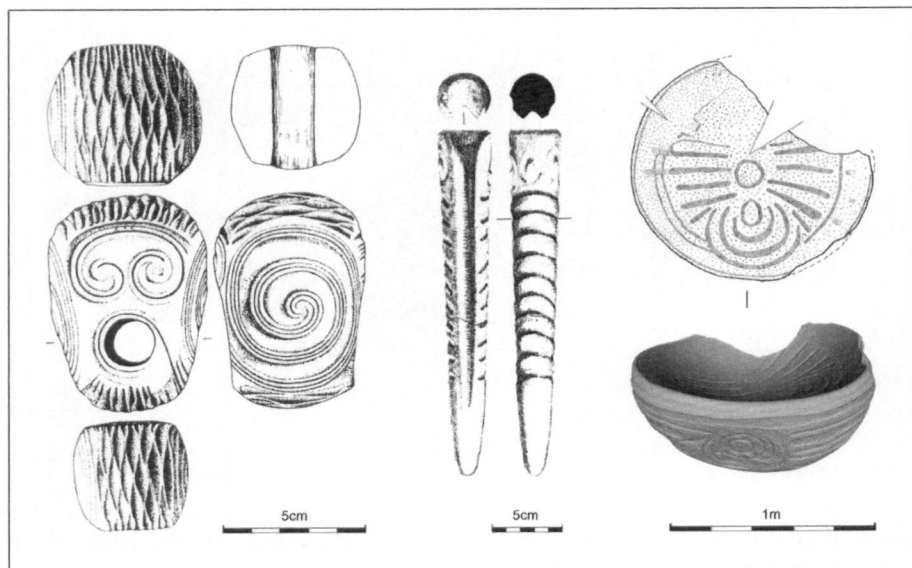

16.4—Decorated finds from Knowth: carved flint macehead, grooved sandstone object and stone basin.

Decorative motifs are used in varying combinations and sometimes there appears to be no attempt to achieve an overall composition, with many stones having just one or two motifs apparently placed at random. Some are hidden, occurring mainly on the upper surfaces of roof-stones of the tomb and on the backs of kerbstones. Such hidden art was not meant for display and the very act of inscribing it was probably its most essential aspect—perhaps even a mystical experience. The great stones employed may have had magical significance as well, and their size, shape, colour and texture may have been important. In choosing to use large and often unmodified blocks, rather than smaller dry masonry, the builders of these monuments were expressing a belief that great stones had a meaning in their own right.

The claim that the origin of some motifs may be entoptic (from the Greek *entos* 'within', *optikos* 'vision'), namely sensory visual images produced in states of altered consciousness and induced by hallucinatory drugs or by sensory deprivation in shamanic rites, is not generally accepted. It may well be that individual motifs and combinations of motifs had multiple meanings, and meanings may have changed over time. In short, individual motifs may be multivocal—they may have different meanings in different contexts. It is clear that several layers of art may occur on some stones; older designs were destroyed to make way for new ones. Differences between tombs and between regions may be expressions of different group ident-

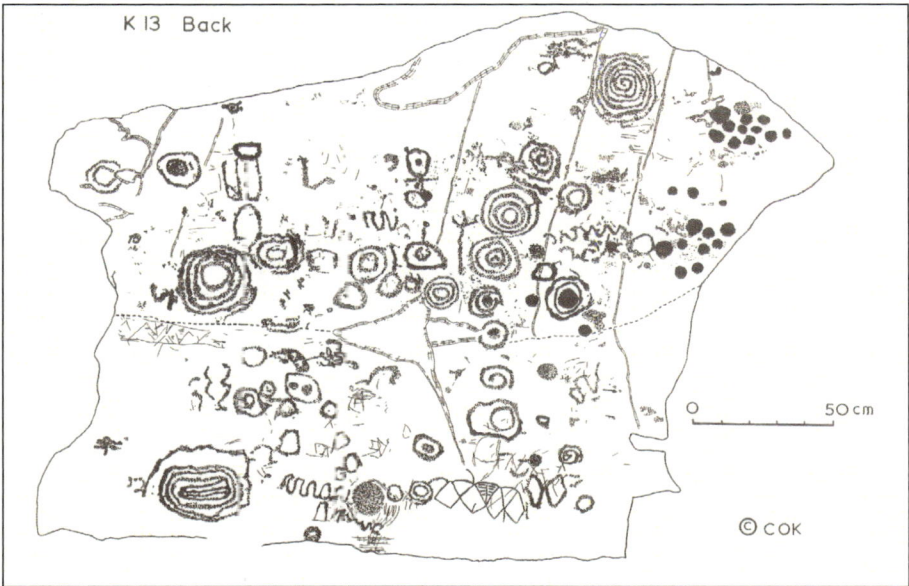

16.5—Over 100 motifs occur in the hidden art on the back of this Newgrange kerbstone.

16.6—Rock art at Kealduff, Co. Kerry.

ities, while shared motifs may have facilitated communication.

The term 'rock art' is applied to the carving of symbols on exposed natural rock surfaces, often on flat or gently sloping faces. Designs may be widely or closely spaced, and motifs may be linked or unconnected to one another. In some cases compositions may be the result of successive carving episodes. Though found in other parts of Atlantic Europe, a quite limited range of basic abstract motifs occurs in Ireland. Particularly common are cup marks, cup marks with a tail or radial groove, cup-and-ring marks and multiple penannular rings.

There has been much theorising on the possible meaning of some motifs: solar and fertility interpretations have been freely offered but no satisfactory explanation has emerged. They may have been a means of imbuing such rock outcrops or certain parts of the landscape with special significance. The designs undoubtedly had some distinctive meaning, perhaps drawing their symbolic power from the earth-fast rock. It is possible that the circle and the cup mark, if related to passage tomb art, were selected because they were especially potent symbols in their own right and lost none of their significance when deployed in a different context. Inscribed on natural rocks, not only did they mark special places but also the size, spacing and intricacy of the design elements may have conveyed complex information.

It is conceivable that some of these rocks marked singular places where solar phenomena might be witnessed—and of course circles might be solar symbols too.

16.7—Above: a time-lapse photograph of the setting sun at various points on the northern slope of Croagh Patrick.

Thus the art on some stones may have been directed at the heavens. This may be the case at a decorated stone outcrop near the sacred mountain of Croagh Patrick in County Mayo. Located south of Westport, in the townland of Boheh, it is an irregularly shaped boulder with several decorated surfaces, and it lies on the western side of a low hill. It is profusely decorated with over 100 motifs, mainly cup marks and circles. A small incised Latin cross on one surface suggests that an attempt was made to Christianise this pagan monument. Indeed, today the stone is known locally as St Patrick's Chair and it lies on Tóchar Phádraig, the pilgrimage route to Croagh Patrick.

The near-pyramidal shape of this famous mountain is clearly visible from Boheh. Observations by Gerry Bracken in the early 1990s confirmed that in late April and late August the setting sun, to the west behind the holy mountain, would appear to roll down its northern slope. This was a slow but dramatic descent only clearly visible from this location. Bracken thought that these two dates, around 21 April and 24 August, might be significant in so far as they could be linked respectively to the planting and harvesting of crops. The stone at Boheh could conceivably have been the focus of ceremonial rites at such important moments in the agricultural year, but the meaning of the symbols is still a mystery.

Almost a century ago R.A.S. Macalister was struck by the resemblance between rock carvings and passage tomb designs and motifs in the art of some Aboriginal Australian peoples. In 1935 in his *Ancient Ireland* he published a photograph of several ground-drawings, as he called them, of the Warramunga people of central Australia. He noted an amazing resemblance between their concentric circle motifs and Irish 'rock-scribings' but dismissed them as having little or no intrinsic significance, they being 'mere mnemonics, aiding the memory of the narrator and of those to whom instruction is being given'. His source was Baldwin Spenser and Frank J. Gillen's *The northern tribes of central Australia* (1904). Their pioneering and painstaking anthropological work and artefact-collecting were hugely significant. They were typical of their time, however, and today, their major contribution to the ethnography of Australian First Nations people notwithstanding, some would see them as condescending agents of paternalistic and racist colonialism.

Robert Hensey, too, has looked to this ethnographic material but in a more measured way. He has concluded that it is plausible that some passage tomb art motifs, though conventionally regarded as non-representational, may have had associations with real aspects of the physical world of the carvers. This is because in the Warlpiri art-making tradition in Australia's Northern Territory, for instance, simple elements that are abstract depictions of real objects, such as burrows, nests or digging sticks, may be combined to form complex non-representational designs.

16.8—R.A.S. Macalister's illustration of a sand drawing or sandgraph of the Warramunga people, taken from Baldwin Spenser and Frank J. Gillen's *The northern tribes of central Australia* (1904).

In other words, though laden with meaning, they are not meant to be an accurate depiction of something.

The anthropologist Howard Morphy has shown that Walpiri graphic art consists of a small number of geometric elements, of which only half a dozen are frequently used. Each is associated with a range of stories of the world of the ancestors. In recounting tales of ancestral events and places, things that are or can be classified as roundish or enclosed—for example, water-holes, fruit or campfires—can be represented by circles. Things that can be classified as elongated, such as rivers, paths, spears and animals lying outstretched, will be represented by a straight line. They create an image of the ancestral world, and a simple circle or an oval may have multiple meanings.

```
  ⬭        Food or water scoop
           Baby carrier
           Shield
           Spear thrower
           Oval "bed" (ngura), hollow in
              ground for sleeping


  ◯        Nest
           Hole
           Waterhole
           Fruits and yams
           Tree
           Hill
           Prepared food
           Fire
           Upright fighting stick
           Painting material
           Billy can
           Egg
           Dog, when curled up in camp
           Circling (as, for example, dancing
              around), or any encircling object
```

16.9—The multiple meanings of a Walpiri design.

Among the Yolngu in northern Australia abstract geometric patterns are often thought to be transformations of ancestral beings—various aspects of ancestral figures being encoded in different elements. Variant lozenge patterns, for example, are associated with different communities connected by the journeys of ancestors. Myths exist which explain the origin of the form of many such designs, and different communities have quite different myths to explain essentially the same form. Secrecy is a feature of much of this art and it should only be understood by people who have been initiated into its significance.

Walpiri art and the geometric component of Yolngu art cannot be described as representational in the sense in which that word is normally applied to art objects in Western Europe. This Australian art is a reminder that what we call abstract designs in passage tomb art may have been redolent with numerous meanings for their carvers. One of the roles of this art may have been to create a sense of participation in the ancestral past and this might explain the reworking or re-carving of some images. These signs and symbols may have had a particularly limited audience, their meaning known only to a committed group. To recover some of the meaning encoded in passage tomb art and in rock art is one of the great challenges in Irish archaeology.

17

A tripartite ideology

17.1—Navan Fort, Co. Armagh.

It has been recognised for many years that the deposition of objects in the earth or in water was a votive action to ensure prosperity or to propitiate an Otherworld below. The land itself was permeated with meaning, and natural features such as hills, rivers and rocks figured in myth and legend. The sky was a focus of particular attention, and the celestial journey of the sun was of major religious significance. This implies a basic division of the cosmic sphere into three zones: a heavenly realm, the earth in a middle region and a nether or underworld. This tripartite cosmology is echoed in elements of the archaeology of Navan Fort, Co. Armagh.

Excavations in the 1960s at the great mound in this enclosure exposed an extraordinary series of circular structures, their construction and use spanning many centuries. This ritual sequence culminated around 95 BC in the erection of the great

'40-metre structure', as it is known—a huge circular building, almost 40m in diameter, formed by five rings of spaced timber posts with a large central post. This oak post was so large that it had to be dragged at an angle into its pit on a sloping ramp, 6m long, cut into subsoil. Its base, about 50cm in diameter, was found in the central pit, which was 2.3m deep. About 1.4m of the post survived because of the damp conditions there and because of a rise in the water-table after this circular temple and its central post were entombed in a great cairn of stones. This in turn was covered by carefully deposited layers of turves and clay, 2.5m deep at the centre.

Chris Lynn has examined the cosmological significance of this composite monument of earth, stone and timber. He has raised the interesting possibility that the mound's threefold hierarchical nature might be a monumental expression of a tripartite belief system. The different materials would represent in turn the three roles or qualities (functions) identified in Indo-European tradition by Georges Dumézil, who in his worldwide studies of comparative mythology identified many traces of a common Indo-European heritage. The timber element would be associated with the sacral first function linked to kingship or a priestly caste, the cairn with the martial second function associated with a warrior class, and the earthen mantle with third-function cultivators.

The idea that the various components of a monument like this might carry different symbolic connotations is entirely plausible. Given the long history of

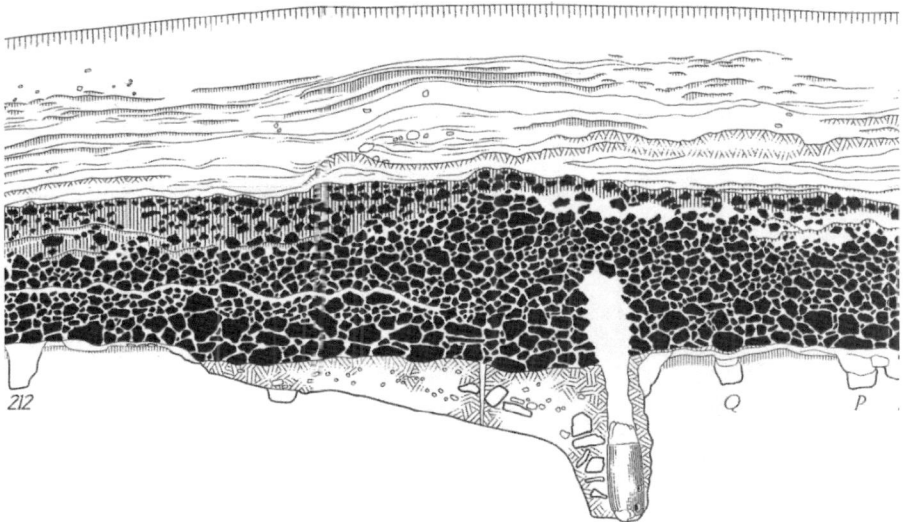

17.2—Part of the cross-section through the great mound in the Navan enclosure, showing the covering layers of turves, the cairn of stones in black, and the socket for the central post dug into the earth below. The mound was 5m high at its centre.

ceremonial wooden structures at Navan, timber might well have been associated with sacral activity. The stones in the cairn appeared to be weathered and not freshly quarried, so they may have come from a significant older monument, even one with warrior connotations. The pollen in the turves indicated that they came from heavily grazed pasture.

The surface of the cairn had been divided into fairly well-defined but somewhat irregular radial segments by the use of different sizes and various arrangements of stones, by slight variations in height and by varying admixtures of soil, clay or turf in the sectors.

These radial divisions, of which there were at least a dozen, did not extend downwards through the mass of stones—they were a surface phenomenon. It is fair to see this wheel-shaped pattern as a solar symbol deliberately created on the summit of the cairn.

The immense central post, perhaps a carved pillar, could have been 13m or more in height and may once have protruded through the top of the cairn. It was the focus of the radial lines in the cairn surface. This configuration presents a crucial

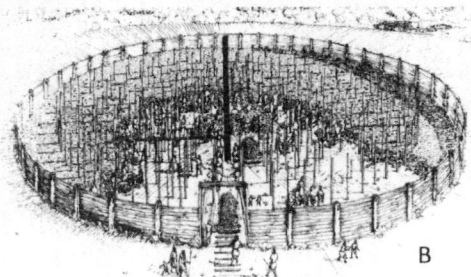

17.3—The *axis mundi* and the solar wheel. (A) The radial divisions in the surface of the cairn at Navan. (B) An artist's reconstruction of the building of the cairn in the 40m structure, with the central pillar emphasised. (C) A *cakrastambha* from Amaravati in the Government Museum Chennai, Madras.

link between solar symbolism and the concept of an *axis mundi*. In many cultures the link between heaven and earth was conceived of as a tree, a mountain or a pillar. In the earliest Indian cosmogony, reflected in the Rig Veda about 1500 BC, the cosmic pillar is the mythical axis of the world, both separating and uniting heaven and earth. Founded in the waters below the earth, this pillar was the channel through which cosmic order was imposed on the world. When the sun unites with its summit, sun and pillar become a metaphysical unity represented by a wheel above the pillar. This is the *cakrastambha* or 'wheel-pillar', a carved pillar surmounted by a solar wheel, a relatively common Buddhist symbol.

This formation of pillar and wheel finds an exceptionally interesting and powerful parallel in the Navan timber post with its superimposed wheel image in the upper cairn. The wet foundations of the pillar may be important too, for the Indian evidence indicates that the presence of water was a necessary element in the foundation of votive pillars, whether of wood or stone.

In addition to the mound's tripartite structure, this is another noteworthy illustration of the survival of an ancient Indo-European tradition. On a level with the sun and at the axis of the world, the flat clay-capped summit of the great mound was an exalted stage for kingly ceremonial, and those who stood here would have been acutely conscious of its cosmic import. The great pillar united heaven, earth and netherworld.

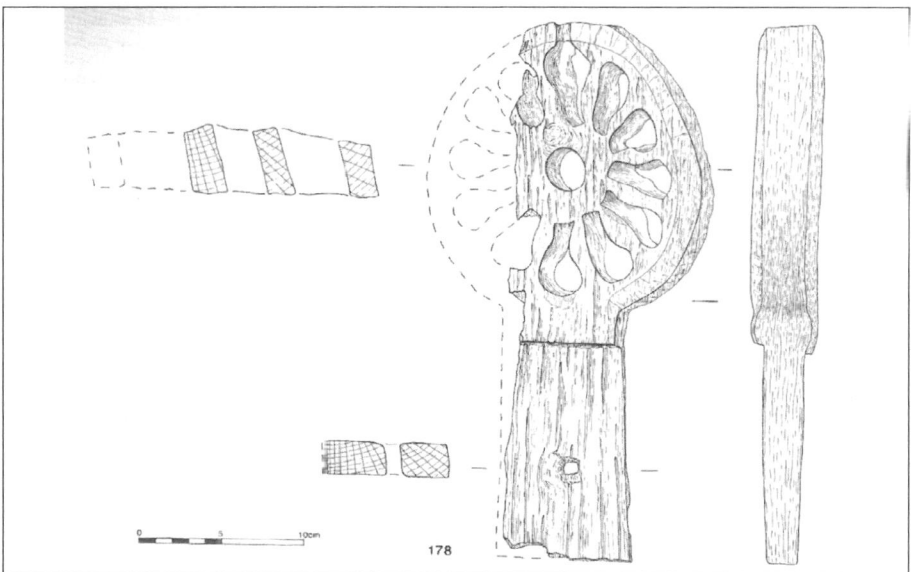

17.4—Small wooden wheel-pillar from Wavendon Gate, Bucks.

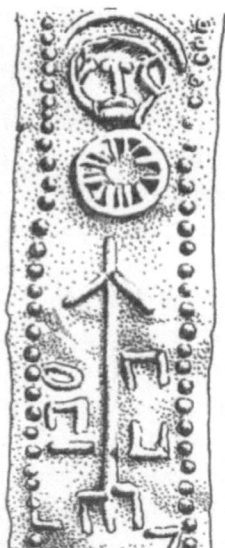

17.5—A portion of the imagery on a bronze sceptre binding from Farley Heath, Surrey, showing a wheel symbol above a stylised pillar or tree (see 24.4).

This belief in the cosmic significance of pillar and wheel found expression in Iron Age England too. Excavation of part of a large Romano-British rectilinear enclosure at Wavendon Gate, Buckinghamshire, dating from the mid-first century to the fourth century AD, revealed extensive settlement evidence. No structures survived, but pottery, animal bones and plant remains were recovered in quantity. Several horse skulls buried on the site may have been ritual deposits. A large pit, 7m in diameter and 3m deep, contained a wealth of material. Its base was below the water-table, but its size and its sloping sides suggested that it was not a water-hole for animals or a well. It may have had a ritual purpose, however, because it was accessed by a series of crude stone steps and, on the opposite side, beside the edge of the pit there was a large hole for a timber post enclosed by a U-shaped ditch. A pottery vessel containing a cockerel had been buried at the base of the post. The pit also contained pottery sherds, an iron spearhead, other iron objects, part of a tree trunk and a wooden wheel-shaped object.

The trunk, that of an ash tree, was a substantial piece; a section 1.35m in length survived. Also found was the greater part of a unique small wheel-like object made of oak. The circular head had twelve spokes and was originally 17cm in diameter. It was mounted on a long, tenon-like piece, presumably for insertion into something, perhaps a wooden post or rod, and probably had a ceremonial purpose. This was a very significant discovery for the small wheel atop a pillar is a miniature version of the Navan combination.

Another possible depiction of this wheel and pillar occurs on a small bronze strip found in the nineteenth century on the site of a Romano-British temple at Farley Heath near Guildford in Surrey. It is believed to be a binding for a staff or sceptre and may bear an image of the god Vulcan, as we shall see. A wheel-shaped motif with a vertical pronged device (a stylised tree?) below is also represented.

In Iron Age Britain and on the Continent, wheel symbolism, in stone or metal, is often associated with a Celtic deity whom the Roman poet Lucan called Taranis. The Wavendon wheel was interpreted as a cult object, perhaps carried in procession or more likely attached to a high post, symbolising the power of such a figure with solar associations. Its carefully cut perforated tenon does suggest that it was probably inserted into a wooden post. Its small size might also imply that it had been placed in a shrine of some description. Despite its modest size, it probably carried the same weighty metaphysical meaning as the monumental wheel and pillar at Navan.

It is obvious that wooden monuments may once have been much more common than stone and, of course, organic artefacts only survive in exceptional circumstances. Therefore it is quite possible that larger wooden versions of the Wavendon wheel were once a feature of the Iron Age landscape in these islands. If this was the

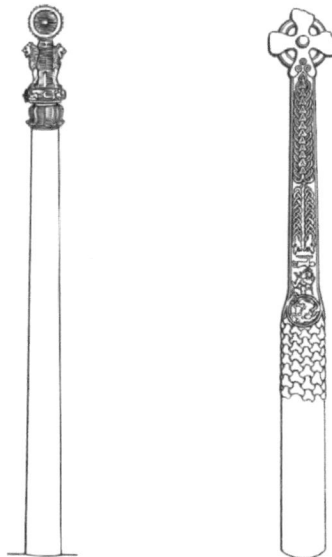

17.6—John Irwin's illustration of a reconstruction of an Asokan Pillar from Sarnath, Utter Pradesh, India (left), and the 'Celtic' high cross at Gosforth, Cumbria (right).

case, one speculative step further raises another interesting question in a Christian context a few centuries later.

There has been much speculation about the origins of the ring-headed 'Celtic' cross but there is general agreement that it was an Irish or north British development. Charles Thomas has shown that the fashion for erecting free-standing stone crosses was preceded by a widespread tradition of wooden crosses at least by the seventh century. Other older cosmic influences may have been in play as well.

In India, the so-called Asokan Pillars are finely carved monuments with wheel-shaped capitals surmounted by carvings of lions or elephants. These are versions of the *cakrastambha* or wheel-pillar. They are believed to have been erected by King Asoka (272–231 BC) and were extensively studied some years ago by John Irwin, distinguished Keeper of the Indian Section of the Victoria and Albert Museum. In one paper he drew attention to the fact that Pope Gregory in the sixth century had directed that pagan shrines in Britain should not be destroyed but adapted for Christian worship. Irwin thought that pillar veneration in pagan times was an expression of the same belief, namely that sun and pillar were a metaphysical unity as in the wheel-pillar. Early Christian crosses are explicitly connected with the sun in Anglo-Saxon poetry, and he noted the solar emphasis on the cross, the instrument of Christ's death, as being described 'in solar terms as "blazing", "the brightest of all beacons", "drenched in gold", "wound round with light", and so on'. Both the

17.7—One face of the fragmentary Mullaghmast pillar, with a solar symbol on its sloping summit.

Christian cross and the *cakrastambha* have been described, in very different contexts, as 'the fulcrum of the universe'. Interestingly, the Gosforth cross, which he illustrated, with its plain, circular lower shaft, has been described as a 'staff rood', an imitation of a slender wooden pole with a small cross attached to its summit (just as the Wavendon wheel may have been mounted).

In Ireland this wheel-pillar is represented in early medieval times by the sixth-century Mullaghmast Stone. This very damaged four-sided stone has a finely carved solar triskele on its sloping summit. The slope was probably an intentional feature to give a clear view of the sun symbol. Once again sun and pillar are combined. Broken in antiquity, this 90cm-long decorated fragment is said to have been incorporated into the masonry of a castle on the hill at Mullaghmast, near the village of Ballitore, Co. Kildare. It may once have stood somewhere on this hill, which is a location rich in archaeological remains. These include a large enclosure (Mullaghmast Rath), several burial mounds and a standing stone. It also has mythological associations, and famous visitors included Óengus, son of the Dagda, Finn Mac Cumaill and St Patrick. Conor Newman (below) has shown how this stone was used in an unusual sword-sharpening warrior ritual, and it was probably the inauguration stone of the local Uí Muiredaig.

With the recognition of the image of a wheel-pillar at Navan and Wavendon, and a version of this concept at Mullaghmast at an even later date, Irwin's thesis deserves to be revisited. Like the adoption of the circular enclosure, the cosmic symbolism of the wheel-pillar image was fully understood and readily absorbed by early Christians in these islands and replicated in the circular head of the high cross. After all, the *axis mundi*, in the form of both the Tree of Life and the Tree of Knowledge, was a central feature of the Garden of Eden (Genesis 2:9).

18

Kingship and sacrifice

18.1—Part of a page from the twelfth-century *Topography of Ireland* by Gerald of Wales, depicting a horse sacrifice in Donegal in former times.

Gerald of Wales or Giraldus Cambrensis first came to Ireland in 1183 and a few years later wrote his *Topography of Ireland*, in part to illustrate the barbarous nature of the Irish and to justify a civilising Anglo-Norman settlement. A number of illustrated copies of this Latin manuscript survive. He deals with the island's topography and natural history, its wonders and its inhabitants. While the Irish are described as handsome and well-built, and are skilled in music, they are a wild and inhospitable people who live on beasts and live like beasts. To emphasise this he quotes a story that he was told about the Cenél Conaill, one of the northern septs of the Uí Néill in Donegal:

'When the whole people of that land has been gathered together in one place, a white mare is brought forward into the middle of the assembly. He who is to be inaugurated, not as a chief, but as a beast, not as a king, but as an outlaw, embraces the animal before all, professing himself to be a beast also. The mare is then killed immediately, cut up in pieces, and boiled in water. A bath is prepared for the man afterwards in the same water. He sits in the bath surrounded by all his people, and all, he and they, eat of the meat of the mare which is brought to them. He quaffs and drinks of the broth in which he is bathed, not in any cup, or using his hand, but just dipping his mouth into it about him. When this unrighteous rite has been carried out, his kingship and dominion has been conferred.'

This is an extraordinary echo of an ancient Indian inauguration rite that was almost certainly a part of Indo-European tradition in some parts of Europe in pre-historic times. The major historical source for this Hindu ritual, the *asva-medha* or horse sacrifice, is the religious narrative the *Satapatha Brahmana*, compiled around 800 BC, but elements are evidently much older, going back to the second millennium BC.

The preparatory Indian ritual began with the selection of a stallion that was purified and allowed to wander for a year, escorted by 100 princes and others. The return of the horse marked the beginning of the elaborate consecration ritual. It was bound to a central stake and various other animals, including goats and cows, were tied to it. When the stallion saw mares penned in the sacrificial area, its neighing was interpreted as the recitation of Vedic chanted verse. It was then attached to a chariot and driven about before being unharnessed and laid on a gold cloth and suffocated, no blood being shed.

The chief wife or queen lay with the dead animal and imitated copulation while priests and other women present engaged in rough and rude dialogue. Finally the horse was dissected; portions were roasted and offered to the god Prajapati, the lord of creation, and then to those present. In India the ritual involved a stallion and a woman while the Irish ceremony concerned a king and a mare, but both in-cluded a symbolic union and the killing and dismemberment of a horse to ensure fertility and prosperity. Both of these rites of kingship culminated in the consump-tion of parts of the animal.

Though the Cenél Conaill story has generally been assumed to be an account of a long-discontinued rite and Gerald did say that he was writing of events and scenes of times past, Tomás Ó Canann has argued that the rite was still practised in the twelfth century. He suggests that the bearded, long-maned figure depicted in the bathing tub was meant to represent Ruaidrí Ua Canannáin, who died in 1188 and whose inauguration took place shortly after the death of Magnus Ua Canannáin, his immediate predecessor in the kingship of Tír Chonaill. Ó Canann also believes that the horse sacrifice probably took place on Carraig an Dúnáin, Doonan Hill, near the modern town of Donegal. This was, in all probability, the inauguration site of the Ua Canannáin kings of Cenél Conaill. The summit of this prominent rock may have been modified and terraced in ancient times, but it was damaged in the late nineteenth century.

Besides the inauguration practices of the Cenél Conaill, there are other clues to indicate that a version of the *asva-medha* was once practised in pagan Ireland. The Gabhra, the 'river of the white mare' that flows by Tara, is probably an allusion to the horse rituals that were part of the ceremonial activities on that hilltop. There may be echoes of this sort of horse sacrifice in the Life of St Molaise of Devenish (*Betha Mholaise Daiminise*), the foundation legend for the monastery on Devenish, Co. Fermanagh, in which there is a contest between the saint and a king for these lands. This is a tale rich in puzzling imagery, including the racing and death of two white horses with red manes, a bull sacrifice, a magical oak tree called the 'Oak of the White Mare' and a feast.

The most striking indication of equine rites at a major cult site is, however, to be found in some of the mythology of Navan Fort. Macha is the female deity associated with this famous place and she has several manifestations in medieval Irish literature. In one tale she is identified as one of the great war goddesses. It is also said that Mag Macha—the plain of Macha around Navan Fort—was named after her and she is thus linked to the land as a sovereignty figure. Sovereignty goddess and war goddess may represent dual aspects of the same character.

The best-known Macha is the one who gave her name to Emain Macha. In one tale her boastful husband claimed that his wife could outrun the horses of the king. Even though she was pregnant, she was forced to race, like a mare, and gave birth to twins. She then cursed the men of Ulster, who for nine generations had to suffer the same debility as she, a weakness that meant that only Cú Chulainn could defend the province when Medb and the men of Connacht attacked, as recounted in the *Táin Bó Cuailnge*.

The unusual equine dimension to this tale is highly significant, for the peculiar contest blurs the distinction between horse and woman. It probably echoes a memory of horse rituals linked to kingship ceremonial at prehistoric Navan. Macha, it seems, was a horse goddess and sovereignty figure, a mare being her earthly surrogate. Land and sovereignty were conceived of as a female entity who was intimately linked to the institution of sacral kingship.

Charles Doherty maintains that Navan was not the inauguration place of a local king but was a location associated with universal kingship, a belief that they ruled the whole world. He agrees that the great central post of the 40m structure was an *axis mundi* because, as in Vedic India, the world king could only reside in the middle, the zone of the sacred. Here the greatest of kings was a wheel-turner, a *cakravartin*, who behaves like the sun, protecting and destroying all creatures with its rays, and who promotes the welfare of his people and governs the world. The final structure at Navan, the clay mound that formed the king's seat or *forad*, was the equivalent of the Indian *prasada*, a seat of divinity and home of gods and kings.

We can be sure that in the act of mimicking copulation with a mare that was the equine avatar of the goddess of sovereignty a king at Emain Macha would present an especially powerful expression of the significance of the sacred marriage. It has been contended, too, that in so publicly professing himself to be a beast, as Gerald reports, the Cenél Conaill candidate for inauguration might have voiced an

18.2—Mistletoe-gathering and bull sacrifice interrupted by the arrival of Christian monks: 'The Druids; or the Conversion of the Britons to Christianity'. Engraving by Simon François Ravenet (1752), after Francis Hayman.

actual ritual utterance such as 'I am *ekwos*, thou art *ekwā*', recalling the Vedic marriage formula 'I am he, thou art she'. This could have been part of the rites at Emain Macha as well.

Bulls were sacrificed too, and this was an element in the inauguration rituals at Tara. Conaire Mór, a king of Tara, had his kingship foretold in a vision. This took place at a bull sacrifice reported in *Togail Bruidne Dá Derga* ('The Destruction of Dá Derga's Hostel'):

> 'Then the king, namely Eterscél, died. A bull-feast (*tairbfheis*) was con-vened by the men of Ireland: that is, a bull used to be killed by them, and one man would eat his fill of it and drink its broth and a spell of truth was chanted over him in his bed. Whoever he would see in his sleep would be king; and the sleeper would perish if he uttered a falsehood.'

There is also an account of a bull-feast held to see who will be king of Tara in *Serglige Con Culainn* ('The Wasting Sickness of Cú Chulainn'). A white bull is specifically mentioned, as are four chanting druids. The reference to a white bull and to druids recalls a description of this ritual in Gaul in Pliny's *Historia Naturalis*, and it would seem to be part of the common inheritance of Gauls and Irish. This account cer-tainly helped to inspire a somewhat idealistic image of the druid in eighteenth- and nineteenth-century Britain and Ireland. Pliny had written:

> 'Having made preparations for a ritual sacrifice and a banquet beneath a tree, they bring there two white bulls, whose horns are bound then for the first time. Clad in a white robe, a priest climbs the tree and cuts the mistle-toe with a golden sickle, and it is caught in a white cloak. Then finally they kill the victims, praying that God will render this gift of his propitious to whom he has granted it.'

Writing in the middle of the first century AD, Pliny was relying on the work of others, so an eccentric detail like the golden sickle can be disregarded. The imple-ment may have been of highly polished bronze.

In the story *Táin Bó Fraích* ('The Cattle Raid of Fraoch') the warrior Fraoch is placed in a bath of 'broth of fresh bacon, and flesh of a heifer chopped under adze and axe'. This took place at Carnfree, some 6km south-south-east of Rathcroghan, a cairn that was one of the medieval inauguration sites of the O'Conor kings of Connacht. This is the earliest example of a common motif of a hero being given a curative bath of broth, but because it is associated with an inauguration place it might represent a confused tradition of a ritual akin to the *tairbfheis* at Tara.

Archaeological evidence for horse or bull sacrifice is hard to come by. It is difficult to distinguish between horse bones that were used for sacrifice and bones discarded after a meal. It may be that animal remains from exceptional places such as Navan Fort or Tara are the product of ritual practices, but this is obviously difficult to prove. At Navan the animal bone assemblage associated with the repetitive construction and use of an extraordinary sequence of Iron Age timber structures was dominated by pig, followed by cattle, all showing a high proportion of butchery marks. Some of the relatively small number of horse bones found (0.8%) were butchered or broken, suggesting the consumption of some horseflesh.

In contrast, cattle were the dominant species at Dún Ailinne, followed by pig. Butchery marks were commonest on cattle foot bones, perhaps for marrow extraction. The modest quantity of horse bones from Dún Ailinne displayed a similar pattern: with the exception of a single cut-mark on part of a pelvic bone, all the cut-marks occurred on lower limb and foot bones. The animal bones from Tara come, for the most part, from two cuttings across the great internal ditch of Ráth na Rí. Cattle were the dominant species recovered, but sheep or goat, dog and horse were also present. Many of the horse bones were broken for the extraction of marrow, and one lower forelimb displayed knife cuts and marks of burning, suggesting that it had been roasted. Given the very special nature of these sacral places, it would be wrong to conclude that all these bones were merely feasting residues. Some may be the product of ritual sacrifice.

Tara and its landscape are closely associated with kingship in myth and history. This is reflected in some of the names given to the visible monuments on the hill about AD 1000: the Forrad (An Forrad) was the King's Seat or inauguration mound, and Teach Cormaic (Cormac's House) was named after Cormac mac Airt, one of the most famous of Tara's kings, often portrayed as the ideal ruler. A pillar stone of Newry granite on the summit of the Forrad is said to have been originally located near the Mound of the Hostages to the north. It is today believed to be the Lia Fáil, the stone of destiny, a stone that uttered a cry at the inauguration of a legitimate king of Tara, but this may have been a recumbent flagstone rather than this standing stone.

Ráth Ghráinne is named after Gráinne, daughter of Cormac mac Airt, and is a large ring-barrow with central circular mound surrounded by a ditch with external bank. Geophysical and aerial survey has demonstrated a remarkable sequence of ring-barrow construction on this part of the hill in what was evidently a major burial-ground. The large ring-barrows called the Claoinfhearta or 'the Sloping Trenches' are situated on the steep western slope of the hill. The northernmost was

18.3—Tara, Co. Meath: the great enclosure of Ráth na Rí is visible in the centre of the photo, with the Mound of the Hostages and the conjoined Forrad and Cormac's House within it. The ring-barrows known as Ráth Ghráinne and the Claoinfhearta (the 'Sloping Trenches') are on the lower right. The parallel banks of the 'Banqueting Hall' are clearly visible in the lower centre.

supposedly the dwelling of the king named Lugaid mac Con that collapsed when he delivered a false judgement.

A large body of ethnographical and historical evidence demonstrates that the institution of sacral kingship was not primarily political—to reign meant to guarantee the order of the world and society. Such a king was accountable for order in the cosmos, and his life and death had cosmic significance. That Tara was once the inauguration place of sacred kings is not in doubt.

Even though no detailed account of these inauguration rites at Tara survives, various tales and mythic themes associated with some of its rulers confirm this. A central concept is that a king was wedded in a symbolic marriage to a sovereignty goddess who personified his kingdom. This supernatural woman appears in *Baile in Scáil* ('The Vision of the Spectre'), where Conn Cétchathach (Conn of the Hundred Battles) is transported to the Otherworld and granted foreknowledge of his future kingship and that of his successors in Tara. The sovereignty goddess appears as a beautiful woman seated beside the god Lugh. She is described as the 'eternal sovereignty of Ireland' and in offering him a drink she confirms his rule.

We know of some of the rites associated with this symbolic marriage. Bull sacrifice, as reported in *Togail Bruidne Dá Derga*, was an element in the inauguration of Conaire Mór. Equine rituals took place on Tara too and are a reminder (like the very name of the Gabhra River) that sovereignty had both feminine and equine connotations. The same Conaire Mór has to pass various tests, described in *De Shíl Chonairi Móir* ('Of the Seed of Conaire Mór'), which included controlling two untamed horses of the same colour that were yoked to his chariot. When the axle of his chariot screeched against the Lia Fáil, it cried out to announce his kingship. Horse sacrifice may well have been a part of these ceremonies.

The sacral king, in an Irish context, was bound by ritual prescriptions and invested with quasi-divine qualities in that sacred marriage. A series of injunctions or taboos were placed on Conaire Mór, for example, whose reign was prosperous as long as this contract with the Otherworld was observed. One by one he broke each *geis* or taboo, all with catastrophic results, for he perished in the destruction of Dá Derga's great house.

The sacral king was also a sacred figure of unblemished physique, the flawless bridegroom of the goddess. Cormac mac Airt, who was renowned for his wisdom and justice, was exiled to Achaill, the hill of Skreen to the east of Tara, because he lost an eye in a confrontation. The mythical Nuadu of the Tuatha Dé Danann lost an arm and was provided with a silver replacement—hence his epithet *Argatlám* 'silver hand'. This blemish had disqualified him from the kingship.

Conaire Mór delivered an unjust judgement which violated *fír flathemon*, the 'prince's truth'. His predecessor as king of Tara was Lugaid mac Con, who is also remembered for a misjudgement, one that is monumentally marked on the Tara landscape. Lugaid delivered a judgement on a relatively minor matter of trespassing sheep that was evidently wrong. This had serious consequences, for his house collapsed; in medieval times, one of the Claoinfhearta on the western slope of the hill was presented as the site of this disastrous event. This was not the only result of Lugaid's action, however, for 'no grass came through the earth, nor leaf on tree, nor grain in corn. So the men of Ireland expelled him from his kingship for he was an unlawful ruler.' In short, the prosperity of the land was dependent on a just ruler who abided by his pact with the Otherworld.

The so-called 'Banqueting Hall' was actually a processional way, and its present name is a medieval invention. Conor Newman has proposed that it was a routeway designed to unite the remains on Tara into a formal, religious arena. The hill and its monuments in effect constituted a sacral theatre. Standing within the routeway's two parallel earthen banks—which were once, of course, even higher—it is impossible to see over them. This is the one monument on the hill where views to the outside world are deliberately denied. Starting at the northern lower end, visitors ascending gently to the hilltop find themselves in an enclosed space and,

18.4—The 'Banqueting Hall' on the Hill of Tara, viewed from the lower northern end. The human figures give an idea of its scale and the present height of its earthen banks. One of the gaps in the banks is visible on the right. The hole on the lower left is due to quarrying.

in an almost literal sense, enter Tara. This sort of procession may have been part of the inauguration rites. A *feis Temro* (the *feis* or feast of Tara) was held once in the reign of each king. A number of Tara's kings are recorded as having held the *feis*, the last being Diarmait mac Cerbaill in AD 560.

As a processional route, however, it has some perplexing features—there are puzzling gaps in the banks on either side that from time to time allow a sight of the world outside. Proceeding along the avenue, glimpses of the burial mounds of the ancestral kings and queens of Tara would have been visible through the gaps on the right-hand side. These would have included Ráth Ghráinne with the Claoinfhearta beyond, so memorably associated with the misfortunate Lugaid mac Con.

Reflecting on the lives of the ancestors, the royal party would have been reminded of the burden of responsibility that comes with world kingship, and of the fact that in re-enacting an inauguration they are about to take their place in history. The hill of Skreen, where Cormac mac Airt was exiled, would have been visible to the left. This is the limbo that awaits those who break the taboos of kingship or fail to live up to the principle of the ideal just ruler. Emerging from the processional way ten centuries ago, a royal party would have entered Ráth na Rí, where the Lia Fáil would announce the rightful reign of the new sacral king.

19

In search of the ritualists

19.1—Image of a shaman. A burial from Bad Dürrenberg, central Germany, of Mesolithic date contained the body of a female shaman covered in red ochre and accompanied by a large array of shells and animal bones. Artist's impression by Karol Schauer.

A young woman from Bad Dürrenberg in Saxony-Anhalt, central Germany, was buried with a strange array of objects, including shells and animal bones. She was placed in a pit and covered with red ochre, and the body of an infant lay between her legs. Unusual items in this Mesolithic grave dating from the seventh millennium BC included a polished stone axe, the long bone of a crane used as a container for 31 microlithic flints, and pendants made from the teeth of cattle, bison, red deer and roe deer. She suffered from a malformation of the upper cervical vertebra that would have interrupted blood flow to the brain, probably causing occasional loss of consciousness and involuntary body movements. It is generally agreed that she was a female shaman or ritualist.

Much has been written on the rituals and beliefs of past societies, who viewed the world in very different ways. Communities sometimes labelled as 'traditional' or 'pre-modern' offer a bewildering variety of evidence. As elsewhere, symbols and rites come and go in prehistoric and early historic Ireland and are testimony to an enduring desire to make sense of the world and to transform human life. Though the evidence for ritual is plentiful, in tomb, grave, settlement and landscape, the creators of these symbols and the practitioners of these rites are quite elusive. The ritualists—whether shaman, druid, wise woman or priest—are difficult to identify.

The term 'shaman' derives from a Siberian word meaning 'one who knows' and refers to a man or woman who engaged with the spirit world in an ecstatic trance-like state, perhaps with the aid of hallucinogenic substances. It has often been used in archaeology in diverse and imprecise ways to denote a ritualist, a seer, a sorcerer, a magician or a religious specialist.

Shamans have generally been associated with small-scale hunter-gatherer societies. They are thought to have disappeared in agricultural communities when sacred rulers or a priestly caste adopted many or all of their functions—even if certain characteristics such as ecstatic practices survived. Identifying ritualists of any complexion in the archaeological record is problematic.

19.2—Yakut shaman costume, seen from behind. Decorated with metal objects and bird bones hanging beneath the sleeves.

In Siberia, in the earlier twentieth century, shaman dress included deer-, bear- and bird-type costumes. These creatures represented assistant spirits, and their hides, feathers or plumes might indicate the shaman's ability to journey to the Otherworld. A shaman costume representing a bird was very common among the Yakut people of eastern Siberia, for instance. Long strips of leather and other attachments hung from under the sleeves as 'wings', lengthening towards the back into a 'tail'. Bird bones hung beneath the sleeves, and small leaf-like or cylindrical pieces of iron were attached all over the garment. Metal objects, along with bones and feathers, were often attached to shaman costumes, each article having its own name, place and meaning.

Recent research has produced the first direct evidence of the use of feathers (rather than just wing bones) in hunter-gatherer burials in north-eastern Europe. Microscopic fragments of feathers have been identified in the soil associated with a skeleton in a number of graves. No species could be identified with certainty but in one the feathers might have been part of a ceremonial mask or headgear. Numerous shaman burials have been identified around the world, sometimes characterised by unusual grave-goods. One problem for archaeological studies, however, is that shamans were not always given their ritual paraphernalia as grave-offerings. This was the case in certain parts of Siberia and Asia, for instance.

Shamans of a traditional sort, prone to impersonating animals to enable them to escape the natural world, were probably a feature of the Irish Mesolithic, but our knowledge of the ritual practices of this period is negligible. Bones of the brown bear have been found on a few Irish sites. This is the grizzly bear well known today in North America, where it has figured prominently in the beliefs and customs of indigenous peoples. Its near-human qualities, occasional upright stance, sitting posture, and omnivorous feeding habits and intelligence all meant that bears were sometimes perceived as kin or ancestors. This was probably the case in Ireland too. Some bones of an eagle found at Mount Sandel, Co. Derry, do at least raise the possibility that eagle plumage may have been a part of Mesolithic dress.

Metal objects with shamanic associations are not easily identified. The occasional odd combination of objects in hoards or graves might conceivably be argued to be the equipment of a ritualist. One peculiar assortment of objects from a Sligo hoard is worth considering with this possibility in mind. Excavation of a crannog at Lough Gara in the townland of Rathtinaun in the 1950s revealed evidence of settlement activity at various times, including the late Bronze Age around 1200– 800 BC. A small hoard of gold, bronze and other objects had been placed in a wooden box at the very edge of the crannog. The box was made of thin pieces of alder and its position had apparently been marked by two wooden pegs.

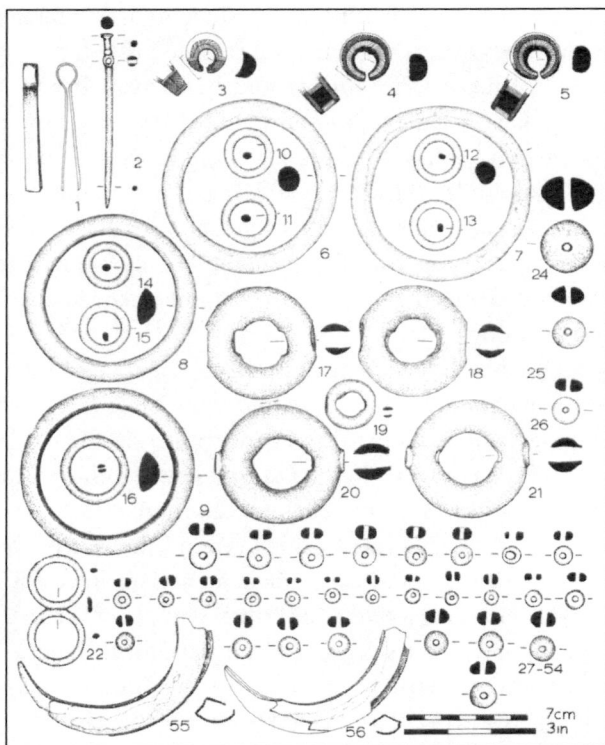

19.3—Part of the hoard of bronze, tin, gold, amber and bone objects from a crannog at Rathtinaun, Co. Sligo: (1) tweezers; (2) pin; (3) penannular gold-covered 'hair ring'; (4–5) pair of gold-covered 'hair rings'; (6–8) tin rings; (9–22) bronze rings, two (20 and 21) with projecting buffers; (24–54) amber beads; (55–56) two of the five boar tusks.

The contents comprised three small gold rings, bronze tweezers, a bronze pin, fourteen bronze rings of different sorts, a tubular piece of bronze, three rings made of tin, 31 amber beads that may have formed a necklace, and five polished boar tusks.

Two of the gold rings form a matching pair, while the third ring is slightly smaller. All were made of decorated gold foil covering a lead core. The three large tin rings are also unusual pieces. Tin, essential for the making of bronze, was a valuable commodity and very rarely used in its own right in metal manufacture. Tin, imported from Cornwall, and amber of Baltic origin had an exotic quality. It has been assumed that the amber necklace belonged to a woman and that the hoard was her personal property. The presence of wooden pegs or markers has also prompted the suggestion that the box of valuables was carefully hidden for safe-keeping, to be retrieved at a later date. Neither of these assumptions is necessarily true, however.

While some of these objects may once have had an ornamental function, there may be magico-religious reasons for their deposition. The range of substances is interesting and surprisingly diverse—wood, gold, bronze, tin, amber and bone are all represented. This and the puzzling variety of objects might imply that this was not someone's personal property but rather a collection of offerings from different sources deliberately combined, with each element carrying some weighty symbolic significance.

The items were deliberately positioned in the wooden container: some of the rings were carefully stacked and flanked by boar tusks. There is a peculiar pattern as well: in addition to the pairs of matching gold rings, two bronze rings had projecting buffers, and two were hollow with transverse perforations; there were two solid tin rings of round cross-section, two solid rings of D-shaped cross-section (one of bronze, one of tin), three pairs of small rings and a double ring. This is a very curious pairing configuration, one that is repeated in a small number of other bronze hoards.

The Rathtinaun objects might have had some divinatory purpose or a role in the oral transmission of ritual knowledge. While some may once have been ornaments or trophies, they may have ended their lives as magical devices. It is even possible that some or all of them might have been part of that sort of ceremonial dress worn by a male or female ritualist on particular occasions. The presence of no less than five boar tusks may be noteworthy because animals, of course, were a persistent feature of shaman identity.

Not all ritual practitioners were shamans. Various uses have been suggested for small bronze blades or razors of Bronze Age date, sometimes found in cremated burials of males. Shaving is an obvious explanation, even perhaps the shaving of the corpse, as was the case amongst the Nuer. They could have been employed by ritual adepts in initiatory rites such as circumcision, or in cosmetic mutilation like tattooing or scarification. The range of possibilities for these small objects neatly illustrates the difficulties involved in any search for ritualists in the archaeological record. In theory, at least, it should be possible to identify their dwellings or other structures associated with them. Unusual or specialised artefacts, animal or bird remains, architectural details or uncommon botanical evidence might be clues worth considering.

Irish druids are equally elusive. They were a feature of pagan Iron Age society and were still an influential priestly caste in the early centuries AD, as the few stories of St Patrick's encounters with them show. In Tírechán's *Collectanea*, a biography of the saint compiled in the seventh century, Loegaire, king of Tara, declines baptism, preferring to be buried in a pagan manner, facing his enemies: 'for the pagans,

19.4—An 'Irish Druid', from Joseph Cooper Walker's *Historical essay on the dress of the ancient and modern Irish* (1818). A learned white-clad druid, with a gold lunula on his head, stands beneath an oak tree laden with mistletoe. A druidic fire burns on an altar behind him.

armed in their tombs, bear weapons at the ready—face to face until the day of *erdathe*—as the druids say'. The meaning of *erdathe* is uncertain but it may mean the end of the world.

While it is possible to glean some information about Continental druidism in the writings of Greek and Roman commentators, early Irish literature offers relatively little detail about their beliefs and practices apart from depicting them as evil people able to foretell the future and ever ready to curse and cast spells. Indeed, in the prayerful incantation known as St Patrick's Breastplate, divine protection is sought 'against the spells of women and smiths and druids'.

Patrick condemned the prophetic skill of *imbas forosnai* and the practice of *teinm laedo* because it and other activities were pagan and involved offerings to demons. The meaning of the latter term is uncertain, but it may mean breaking the marrow and refer to the custom of chewing a bone or a piece of flesh in a divinatory rite. The legendary warrior Finn mac Cumaill famously acquired supernatural knowledge and prophetic power when 'he put his thumb in his mouth and chewed it to the bone, and from there to the marrow and from there to the marrow heart and knowledge was manifested to him'. The peculiar formula of enumerating body parts in this fashion is a very ancient one and has an Indo-European ancestry.

There is one druidic figure named Mug Ruith who does deserve expert study. He appears in a ninth-century poem, *Mug Ruith, rígfhili cen goí* ('Mug Ruith, a royal poet without falsehood'), and in the thirteenth- or fourteenth-century *Forbais Dromma Damgaire* ('The Siege of Druimm Damgaire', also known as 'the Siege of Knocklong'). While much of his story is medieval invention, there are puzzling older elements in it. In the Siege of Druimm Damgaire he defends a Munster king against an unjust attack by Cormac mac Airt, king of Tara. His magical feats include the creation of a well to provide water, the generation of a black mist with his breath and, dressed in a shaman-like druidic costume of bull hide with bird mask, the production of a fire-storm to force the retreat of Cormac's warriors:

'The bull-hide from a horn-less brown bull belonging to Mogh Ruith was now brought to him along with his speckled bird-mask with its billowing wings and the rest of his druidic gear. He proceeded to fly up into the sky and the firmament along with the fire, and he continued to turn and beat the fire towards the north as he chanted a rhetoric: "I fashion druids' arrows ..."'

Unsurprisingly, archaeological evidence for druids is hard to identify in pagan or Christian times. A series of enigmatic bronze spoon-like objects have perplexed British archaeologists for over a century and are thought to be cult objects with some ritual purpose. Usually found in pairs, these spoons are oval-shaped shallow bowls with one end pointed and the other having a short handle. Each would easily sit in an adult's palm. While there is considerable variety, each pair consists of two slightly different spoons; in one the bowl is quartered by an incised cross, in the other there is a small hole on one side. Two of the English finds come from unburnt burials, where they had been placed by the head, and they are dated to the later centuries BC.

Two pairs of these spoons are known in Ireland, but nothing is recorded about their find circumstances. Each pair comprises one shallow spoon with a plain bowl that has a perforation on the left-hand edge, and one with a bowl that is carefully divided into quadrants by an incised line. The handles are simply decorated with La Tène motifs.

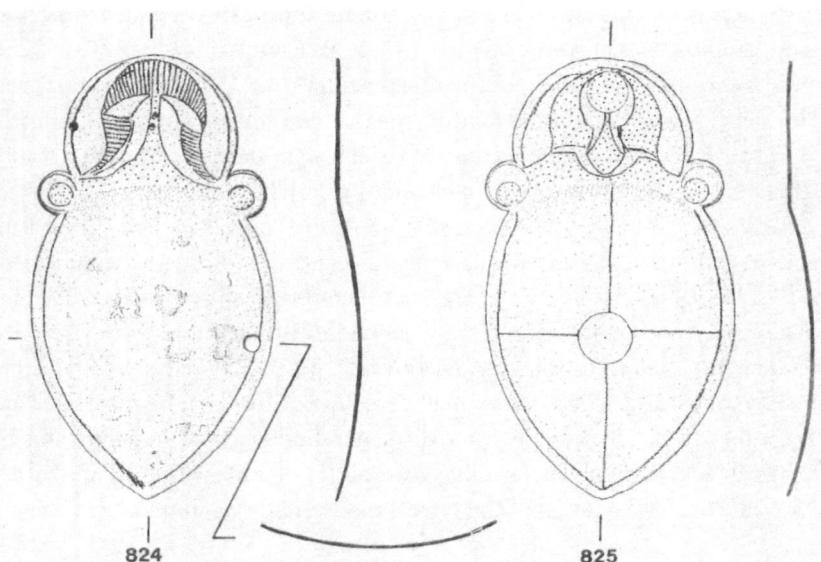

19.5—Pair of bronze spoons from Ireland: no precise provenance recorded. Length: 12.7cm.

It is fair to say that their purpose is a mystery, but they have been the subject of some informed study and interesting speculation. It is possible that a liquid, perhaps blood or an oil-based substance, was dripped from the perforated spoon, held in the auspicious right hand, onto parts of the spoon incised with a cross. The fourfold division on this spoon may have some symbolic significance and could represent the quarters of the lunar month or year. In short, these objects may have been used in divination. The ability to predict future events was powerful knowledge and they may have possessed such potent magic.

It may seem odd to use a pair of bronze spoons to tell the future, but it is surely no more bizarre than predicting events using a sheep's liver. The famous Liver of Piacenza, now in the municipal museum in the Palazzo Farnese in that city, is a bronze model of a sheep's liver dating from around the second century BC. Its surface is divided into sections, each bearing the name of an Etruscan divinity. It had astrological significance too and was used as a teaching aid in the art of predicting the future and determining the will of the gods. Bronze spoons in the hands of an Irish druid may have been just as effective as a sheep's liver in the hands of an Etruscan priest.

Women ritualists may have been common throughout prehistory. They may be represented in a few important prehistoric burials that are unusual in one way or another. These women probably prefigure the 'wise women' or 'women of knowledge', *mná feasa*, of traditional Scottish and Irish folklore. The special gifts of the *bean feasa* included second sight, prophetic capabilities and healing powers.

In Ballymacaward, Co. Donegal, four burials were inserted into an earlier Bronze Age cairn on the northern shore of Ballyshannon harbour. All were slab-lined long cists, and each contained the extended skeleton of a woman, with no grave-goods. Elizabeth O'Brien, in her magisterial study of Iron Age and medieval burials and burial practice, suggests that these women were members of a female cult or community of the fifth to seventh centuries AD, spanning the pre-Christian and Christian eras. They had been buried in an ancestral burial mound and there was no indication that they were associated with a Christian religious community.

One burial, dated to AD 420–540, was particularly interesting. This was of an elderly woman, over 50 years of age, an exceptional age for a woman at that time. She had suffered from post-menopausal osteoporosis of the spine, resulting in severe spinal curvature. Strontium and oxygen isotope analysis indicated that she was of local origin and, as O'Brien observes, she must have been of high standing

19.6—Excavation of the burial of an elderly woman in a long cist at Ballymacaward, Co. Donegal.

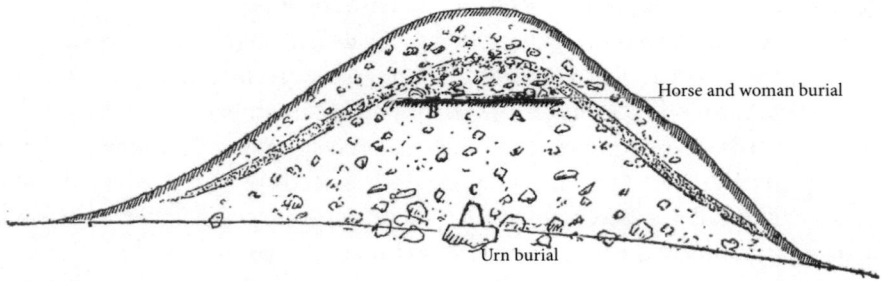

19.7—Cross-section of a burial mound at Farta, Co. Galway, with an urn burial and the remains of a woman and a horse.

in the community, who would have cared for her for some time in her later years. Elevated rank may not, however, have been her only or most important quality. Her disability provides a clue to her special status—she may well have been a ritualist, a *bean feasa*, with special powers.

In 1903 a small burial mound was investigated in the townland of Farta, near Loughrea, Co. Galway (the name being an Anglicisation of the Irish *fert*, 'burial mound'). It had been built to contain a Bronze Age cordoned urn and a cremation inverted on a stone slab and dating from about 1500 BC. Over 1,000 years later, the extended body of a woman aged 20–25 years was inserted into the older monument. She was accompanied by some pieces of deer antler and a seven-year-old stallion, laid on its left side. Strontium and oxygen isotope analysis suggests that the woman was not of local origin but had spent her formative years in eastern Ireland or eastern England. Interestingly, she had an inward twisting of the knee or in-toeing, and this would have given her an abnormal gait.

This woman's remains were radiocarbon-dated to AD 383–536, the horse to AD 388–536, and thus they are contemporary. We do not know how the horse died but, since it and the woman are unlikely to have expired simultaneously, horse sacrifice is a distinct possibility. Horse burial is exceptionally rare and implies that this was a prestigious interment. The deer antler was dated to AD 564–677 and was presumably introduced one if not two centuries later, when the significance of this prestigious burial was evidently still remembered. Again it seems probable that the woman's physical impairment may have afforded her a special status, like the disabled Ballymacaward woman. The deer antler was a significant addition, because antlers are associated with shaman rituals elsewhere and might be an allusion to this woman's special powers. O'Brien notes antler deposits in several other female burials of medieval date and suggests that they may have been symbols of regeneration and fertility.

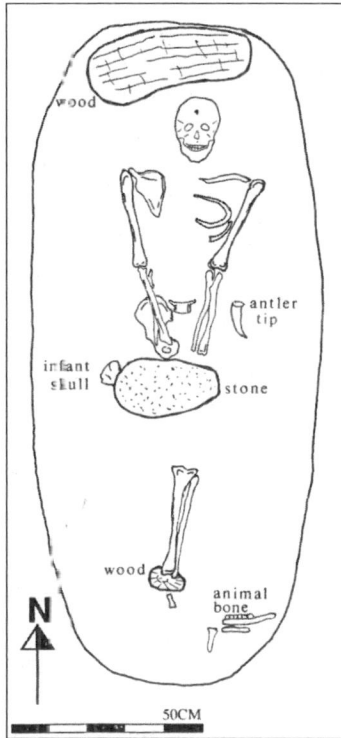

19.8—A sketch-plan of a female burial in a bog at Derrymaquirke, Co. Roscommon.

An antler tine was found in another female burial in a bog at Derrymaquirke, near Boyle, Co. Roscommon. The partial remains of an adult woman were found lying in an extended position with head to the west. There was a large piece of wood behind her head and a large stone lying on top of her lower body. Some bones of a child, a small piece of antler, some animal bone and a small piece of wood were also found in the grave. A sample of animal bone has been dated to 660–240 BC. The atypical rite of unburnt burial at a time when cremation was the norm, the presence of animal bones (sheep or goat and dog) and the piece of deer antler all imply that this woman was of special significance. The burial in a bog and the placing of a stone on top of the corpse were perhaps meant to inhibit her return to the land of the living.

Such unusual female burials are paralleled elsewhere. One remarkable discovery in Iron Age Burgundy is worth mentioning. This is the grave of the celebrated 'princess of Vix', who was buried with all the symbols of superior rank of the fifth century BC. Her timber tomb contained a four-wheeled wagon, rich personal ornaments

157

and a drinking set that included an immense bronze wine vessel capable of holding nearly 1,100 litres and made in a Greek colony in southern Italy. She was not physically distinguished, being of small stature (about 5ft in height), and she was marked by asymmetrical facial features and hip dysplasia that may have impaired her walking. These puzzling details and the quite outstanding nature of the grave-goods have all prompted the proposition that she was a high-status priestess or ritualist with some ceremonial role rather than a mere secular princess.

Another special female burial from Juellinge on the Danish island of Lolland was also accompanied by rich grave-goods that included a bronze cauldron, a ladle, a wine-strainer, two glass beakers and two drinking horns. This woman lived around AD 100 and she too was lame, having a deformity of her right leg caused by an osteochondroma, a large benign tumour on her thigh bone. Both of these women may have had an important role in the sacramental serving of drink, and it may be more than a coincidence that both were physically impaired.

Other special burials of impaired women of early date are known. The skeleton of 'La dame de Bonifacio' was found in a rock shelter at l'Araguina, near Bonifacio in southern Corsica. Her remains were extended and she rested on her back, with her arms alongside her body. Her corpse had been covered with a layer of red ochre as a funerary offering, and the burial has been dated to before 6000 BC. She had many physical problems, including paralysis of the left arm, a malformation of the left foot and arthritis. She died in her thirties and was evidently accorded a special burial. Another burial, dating from the tenth millennium BC, is that of a 45-year-old woman in a cave at Hilazon Tachtit, Israel, who had a deformed hip. Like the shaman from Bad Dürrenberg, she was buried with numerous animal remains; these included tortoise shells, some bones of a golden eagle and a complete human foot.

An important Iron Age burial discovered in the village of Wetwang, east Yorkshire, contained the remains of a woman and a range of grave-goods, including some pig bones, a mirror, parts of a two-wheeled chariot and two bridle bits. The woman was aged 35–45 and tall in stature. Her right shoulder had advanced osteoarthritis, and this and some other injuries might have been due to an accident. It has been suggested that her skull shows considerable asymmetry, and she might have had a marked asymmetry throughout her body. This interpretation is disputed, however, because it has been claimed that these irregularities could also have been due to post-mortem movement in the grave. Her physical status must remain uncertain until full analyses are published.

Widely separated in time and space, and provided with noteworthy funeral rites, many of these women clearly shared the unfortunate distinction of being handicapped in one way or another. It is interesting that the Galway woman, buried with a horse but without any other prestigious goods, may have been just as important in her own community in the west of Ireland as the wealthy 'princess' in eastern France some centuries before.

Early Irish literature offers an interesting perspective on the possibility that some female ritualists may have been distinguished physically by some abnormality. In that story *Togail Bruidne Dá Derga* ('The Destruction of Dá Derga's Hostel') a woman named Calib arrives at night demanding to enter the dwelling. She is of unprepossessing appearance, with long black shins, pubic hair reaching to her knees and her mouth on one side of her head. She declares her many names and is clearly from the Otherworld. She casts an evil eye on the assembled company and, standing on one leg and holding up one hand, she prophesies the destruction to come. This is an instance of the strange theme of irregularity of form. The strange Calib is one of several ritualistic figures in some early tales who display asymmetry of posture— standing on one leg, raising one hand—or physical abnormality, being one-eyed or lame.

20

Wooden idols

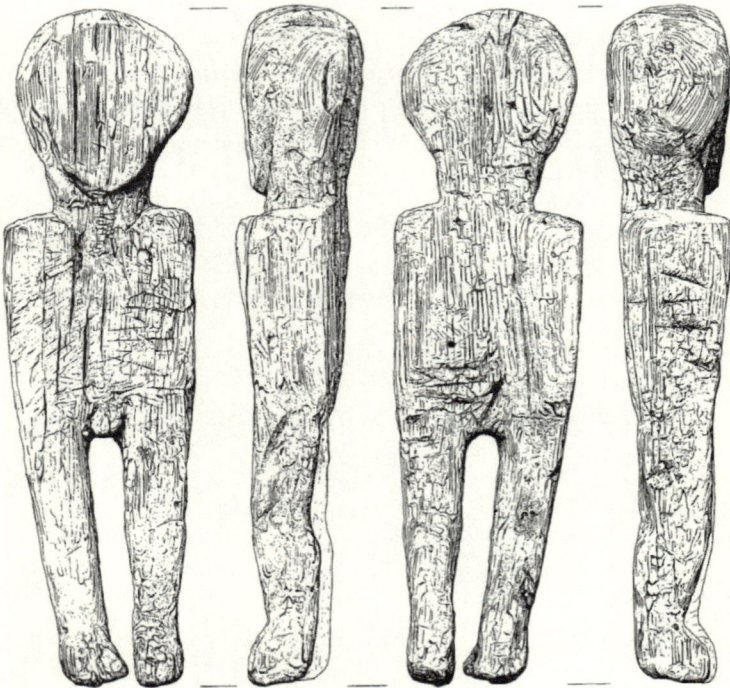

20.1—The four sides of a Bronze Age wooden figure from Lagore, Co. Meath.

A small carving of a human figure was found in excavations at Lagore crannog in the 1930s. It was only briefly noted in the published report. Made of oak and only 47cm high, it was described as a nude male figure of unknown purpose. In an important study of wooden figures from Britain and Ireland in 1990, Bryony Coles noted that the edge of the face and the genital area were polished as if worn by frequent touch. Though it came from a medieval site (with traces of much earlier activity), it was later radiocarbon-dated to 2135–1944 BC. Even if carved from an old

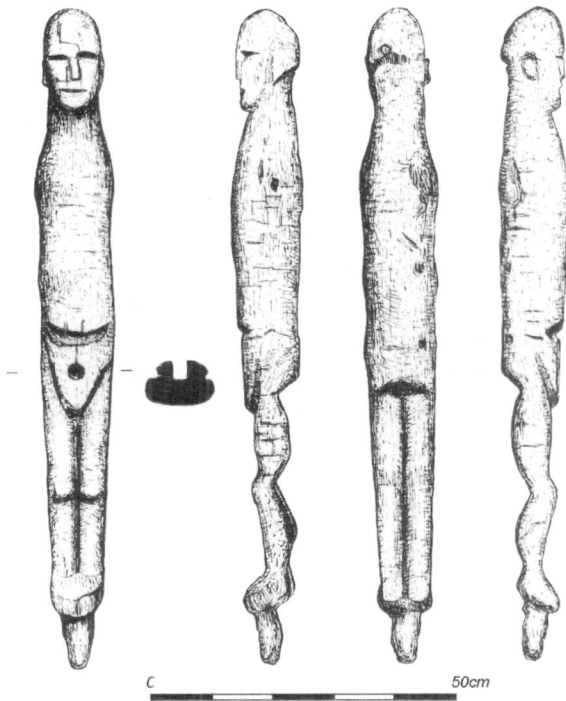

20.2—Wooden idol from Ralaghan, Co. Cavan.

piece of oak, it still probably dates from the earlier Bronze Age. Like some other carvings, it is slightly asymmetrical from head to foot and is assumed to be male—though a deliberate sexual ambiguity may have been intended.

A rather crudely carved wooden idol found in a bog at Ralaghan, near Shercock, Co. Cavan, has been radiocarbon-dated to 1096–906 BC. Carved from yew, this primitive and sexually ambiguous figure stands just over 1m in height. It has uneven eyes, the left eye being higher and less clearly cut than the right one; the nose is off-centre and there is possible damage to the left side of the face. In contrast, its legs are relatively carefully carved, and the knees are clearly shown. Some asymmetry is also evident in the definition of the pubic area, which begins higher on the right than on the left. The puzzling pubic hole may have been intended for a detachable penis. It has a basal tenon that was once inserted into another piece of wood that was not preserved. It is conceivable that it once formed part of some larger wooden structure.

A number of other wooden carvings in Britain have puzzling pubic holes. Five come from Roos Carr, east Yorkshire, and are stylised figures standing in a shallow boat with an animal-headed prow; two appear to be warriors holding round shields. This group is dated to the early Iron Age. One carving from Dagenham, east London, also with a pubic hole, is dated to the early Bronze Age, *c.* 2000 BC. It is particularly interesting because, like the Ralaghan figure, it has relatively simply carved facial features, lacks arms and has one eye very different from the other—the right socket is noticeably deeper than the left. Bryony Coles noted this disparity in both these carvings and tentatively drew attention to the myth of Odin's eye.

The asymmetrical eyes are certainly intriguing. There are various references to one-eyed personages in early Irish literature, where the loss of an eye is associated with the springing forth of the waters of knowledge. The Norse god Odin famously offered one of his eyes at the well of Mimir (at the root of the Tree of Life) to acquire wisdom. It is possible that the Ralaghan figure had mythological associations—as we shall see—and was in some way associated with a source of sacred knowledge. The emphasis on the knees of the figure is peculiar. Oddly enough this takes us back to Scandinavia, where in some Swedish rock art images of warriors some have prominent knees that appear to have phallic-like extensions attached to them. It has been argued that the knee may have been considered as the seat of virile strength.

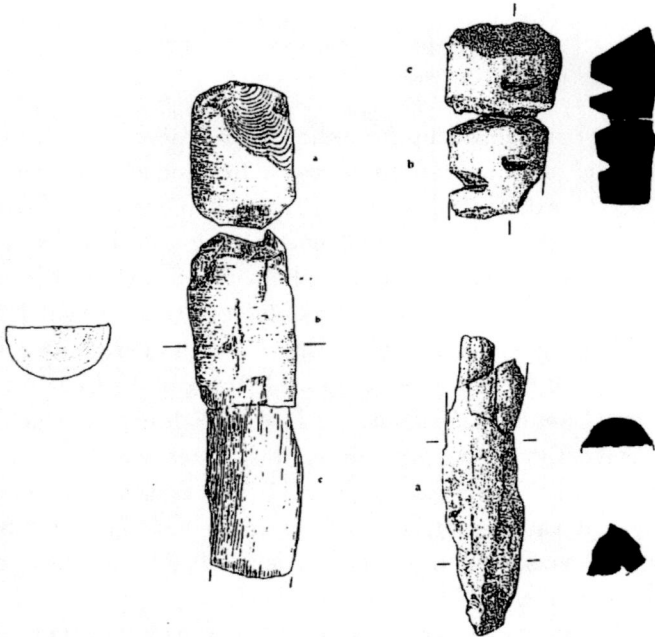

20.3—Fragments of wooden idols from Ballykilleen, Co. Offaly. Both have bulbous heads and that on the right is notched.

Both the Ralaghan idol and the smaller Lagore figure could have been placed in a timber shrine or a domestic dwelling, representing a revered ancestor or a household god. Ralaghan Bog lies at the foot of Taghart Mountain, once a place of Lughnasa assemblies. No connection can be proved between a possible Bronze Age cult site and this hilltop, but it is an interesting coincidence. No less intriguing is the association between the great god Lugh and the 'one eye shut' motif. Before the great slaughter of the second Battle of Moytura, he famously urged the men of Ireland to seek death rather than bondage, chanting a spell while standing on one foot and with one eye closed. The well-known Corleck Head was also found near such a traditional assembly site.

A series of cruder wooden carvings are less obviously representational. These usually consist of a worked timber with a slender pole-shaped body and a roughly delineated head. An example from Cloncreen Bog, Ballykilleen townland, Co. Offaly, was found on the surface of a Bronze Age wooden trackway. Only three fragments survive but it was originally about 1.3m in length. Made of alder, it has

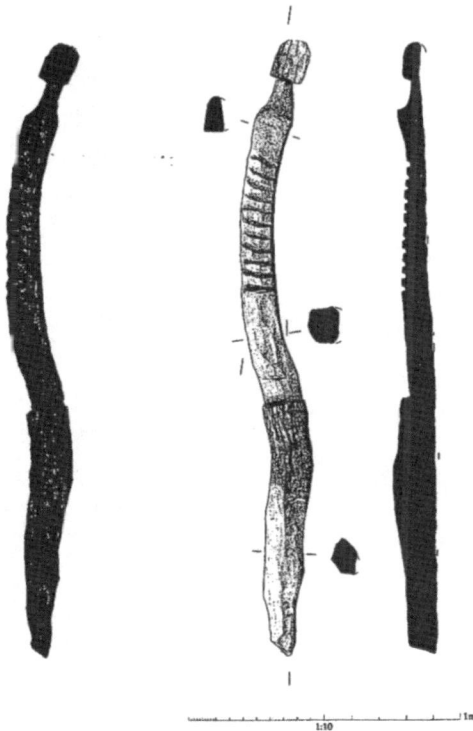

20.4—Notched figure from Kilbeg, Co. Offaly.

a wedge-shaped point, and the other end is notched to create a bulbous head-shaped projection. There is another notch on the body just below this and there may have been similar cuts on the missing parts. A second idol, also found on a trackway, has a surviving length of 43cm. Some other similar pieces of worked timbers of vaguely anthropomorphic shape with multiple notches on their body have been found in the vicinity. They each have ten or eleven incised V-shaped notches and vary in length from just over 1m to just over 2m.

A find from Ballykean Bog in Kilbeg townland, some 7km to the south-west, is made of alder and is 2.31m long. Though heavily damaged, it has a bulbous head, a pointed tip and eleven narrow notches on its body. Like some others, it does not appear to show signs of prolonged exposure.

The largest example found to date comes from a former bog in Gortnacrannagh, Co. Roscommon, a townland a few kilometres north-east of Rathcroghan. Probably once the centrepiece of a ritual site, it is made from a large split oak tree trunk and stands over 2.5m in height. It has a crudely carved head and neck, and nine deep horizontal notches were cut on its upper body. The back of the figure is rough and

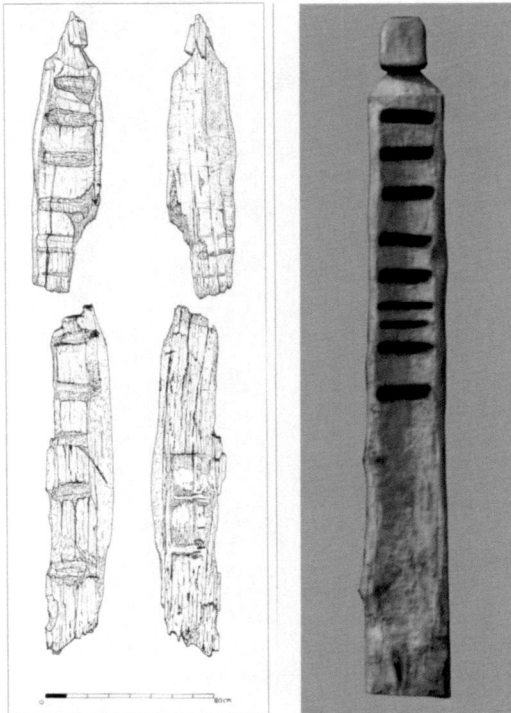

20.5—The fragmentary Gortnacrannagh idol and image of a modern replica.

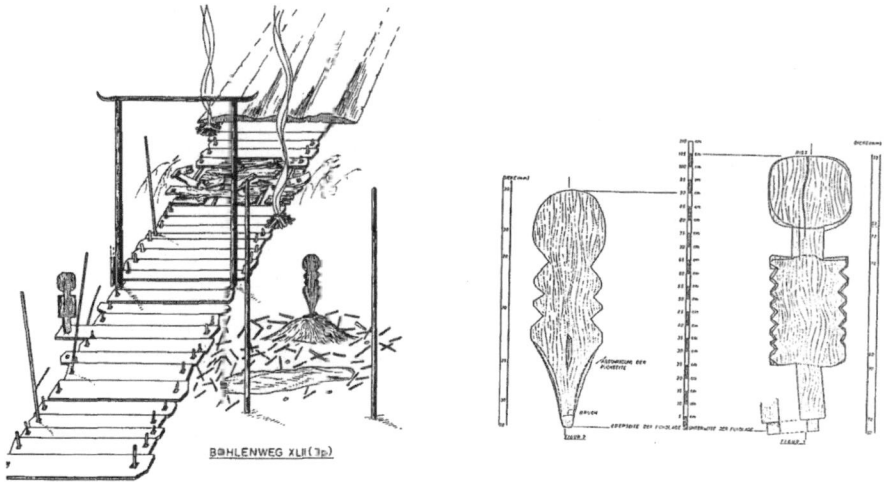

20.6—Reconstruction of a trackway and a pair of wooden idols at Wittemoor, Lower Saxony.

unfinished, and it has been dated to sometime in the later Iron Age (AD 252–413).

A number of similarly schematic wooden figures have been found in bogs in northern Europe, sometimes, as in Ireland, on or near wooden trackways. Two such idols were associated with a timber trackway north-west of Bremen at Wittemoor, Lower Saxony. Carved from flat oak planks with notched sides, they were dated to the Iron Age and were lying flat on the trackway when found. They varied slightly in size and shape and represented a male, 105cm tall, and a female, 95cm tall. The male figure was slotted into a plank, the female placed on a small mound. Three other wooden figures found were more schematic, having slender plank- or pole-shaped bodies with featureless heads. Hearths and vertical posts suggested a cult site, and it is possible that the figures offered some protection against evil forces.

These particular carvings and the Irish examples from Ballykilleen, Kilbeg and Gortnacrannagh are remarkable in their very deliberate avoidance of any semblance of realism. They are not artless creations, however, but display an obvious intent to avoid realistic representation. This suggests a belief that any lifelike reproduction might be injurious in some way. This was once the case among the Pende people of what is today the Democratic Republic of the Congo, and even today their carvings, no matter how naturalistic, must never resemble a named individual, living or dead. Sculpture may serve as a container for a human spirit in the same way that the body does; the border between naturalism and portraiture is always of concern.

A fear associated with the depiction of the human form is found in many traditional societies and may be based on the belief that a copy or portrait drains power from its model. This was the theme of Edgar Allan Poe's horror story 'The Oval Portrait'. An obsessive painter, wishing to create the perfect image of his wife, fails to see her failing health as he progresses. When he finally produces a perfect likeness, his wife is dead. This tale of the ambiguous relationship between life and art inspired Oscar Wilde's 'The Picture of Dorian Gray'.

All of these exceptional prehistoric wooden carvings, whether on the Continent, in Britain or in Ireland, come from wetland contexts where the anaerobic conditions allow the preservation of organic materials. It is certain that wooden figures, whether of Bronze Age or Iron Age date, were once a widespread feature of the landscape in prehistoric times. Many have undoubtedly vanished, but one interesting lost example is recorded in Tipperary.

The Bog of Cullen, north-west of Tipperary town, produced an enormous quantity of gold and bronze objects over a number of years in the eighteenth century. In a report in 1774 to the Society of Antiquaries in London, a Revd Mr Armstrong supplied Thomas Pownall, best known in Ireland for an early description of Newgrange, with the following account of one particular discovery in that Tipperary bog:

'As to the image said to have been found there, I only heard of it in conversation with the late most worthy Mr Damer who told me that his neighbour, Mr William Chadwick, who then rented the lands about Cullen of Lord Thomond, informed him, that a long time before (above sixty years ago) a large wooden image was found in a part of the bog, and that little pins or pegs were stuck in different parts of it; and that Mr Damer imagined that the little gold plates found there, one of which I saw with him, were suspended by these pegs in different parts of that image. Mr Chadwick, who was not curious in such things, told Mr Damer that he made a gate-post of it.'

Sadly, we are not told what the word 'image' means, but the reference to a gatepost indicates that this was probably a carved wooden pillar of some description and brings to mind another gatepost-sized wooden carving found in County Derry. This was a 1.8m-tall wooden carving of a four-faced figure found in a bog at Ballybritain, just north of Aghadowey, in the eighteenth century. It is known only from a crude thumbnail sketch in the Ordnance Survey Memoirs compiled several decades later in 1836. It may be of later medieval date, as we shall see, and one of many indications of the longevity of pagan practices well into Christian times. The veneration of wooden idols may have spanned 3,000 years or more.

21

The sacred tree

21.1—A sacred tree: the 'Big Bell Tree' in Tombrickane, north-west of Borrisokane, Co. Tipperary, in 1834, as illustrated in the *Dublin Penny Journal*.

Sacred trees are an extraordinarily widespread phenomenon, and this belief has a remarkable longevity in Ireland and elsewhere. The Annals of the Four Masters record that Máel Sechnaill, king of Tara, laid waste the territory of the Dál gCais in County Clare in AD 982. He provocatively felled the sacred tree at their royal inauguration site at Magh Adhair near the village of Quin. In this contemptuous insult, the tree 'was cut after being dug from the earth with its roots'. Why such a tree was so important is not clear, but it must have had weighty mythological significance and symbolised age-old wisdom—and the 'rod of kingship', an emblem of legitimate royal authority, may have been cut from it. In any event, it points to some sort of association between tree and kingship ceremonial in medieval times.

Similar trees are recorded at other inauguration sites in Connacht and in Ulster, where the trees (*biledha*) of the Uí Néill at their inauguration place at Tullaghoge, near Dungannon, Co. Tyrone, were uprooted in 1111 according to the same annals. A bardic poem of the early seventeenth century laments the action of a new English landowner who cut down a whitethorn tree on a hill of assembly, the poet declaring: 'My heart in my breast is sad for thy ancient tree, O hill yonder … the ruin of the thorn stirs my sorrow'.

The tradition of the *bile* survived into modern times. In 1834 a large ash, over 7m in circumference at the base, which was called the 'bellow-tree' or the 'Big Bell Tree', was still to be seen in Tombrickane, near Borrisokane, Co. Tipperary. There was a local belief that if any part of it was used for fuel the house in which it was burnt would itself be destroyed by fire. The water that lodged in a hollow between the branches was regarded as holy. Its name is a version of the Irish *bile*.

The Old and Middle Irish word *bile* means a sacred tree, and there are many references to such venerated trees in early Irish literature. In particular, five pri-meval sacred trees are often mentioned: Bile Tortan (the tree of Tortu—an ash tree), Eó Rossa (the yew of Ross), Eó Mugna (the oak of Mugna—the *eó* element in its name here meaning great tree), Craeb Daithi (the bough of Daithi—an ash) and Bile Uisnig (the tree of Uisneach—an ash). The last-mentioned stood somewhere in the great cult centre of Uisneach, Co. Meath, a cosmological central place and the centre-point of the island of Ireland. The Eó Mugna was said to have been hidden since the time of the great deluge, its appearance coinciding with the birth of a legendary king. They reflect the reverence attached to certain trees in early Irish tradition, and the mythical origins of all five imply an older pagan ancestry. Emly, Co. Tipperary, the site of an early foundation by the shadowy St Ailbe, was known as Imblech Iubair, 'Emly of the Yew Tree', and was probably the location of just such a sacred tree.

Trees like these had supernatural qualities and druidic associations, as a tale in the Life of St Berach of Termonbarry, Co. Roscommon, indicates. We are told that the saint built his church on land belonging to a local druid, who brought him to trial before a host of important judges, including Áed Dub, the king of Bréifne. The druid objected to the location of the trial because he wanted it to be held where there was a tall whitethorn tree. A demon lived in this tree and would deliver

21.2—A reconstruction of an inverted tree set within a timber circle found at Holme in Norfolk.

answers to the druid's supporters, and he hoped for demonic support if the trial took place there. The judges refused to move, however, so the saint, after much strenuous prayer, miraculously brought the tree flying through the air to take root beside them. Then the voice of an angel spoke from the clouds above, declaring God's verdict in favour of the saint.

The significance of an individual tree at a very early date has been clearly demonstrated at Holme-next-the-Sea, Norfolk, where a Bronze Age sacred tree has been identified. An oval setting of 55 large contiguous oak timbers with a maximum diameter of 6.78m surrounded a pit containing the lower part of an inverted oak tree, its roots in the air. The end in the ground had been carefully trimmed and side branches and bark removed. Dendrochronological analysis indicated that the Holme tree and its assemblage of timbers were felled in early 2049 BC. Some of the timber posts probably came from the central oak. The monument was constructed on the coast in a salt-marsh adjacent to intertidal mud-flats, and this exceptional waterlogged context ensured the survival of the timber structure.

The large inverted oak was set in a pit 1.5m deep with the remains of its roots deliberately exposed. Since pottery vessels in contemporary burials are often placed mouth downwards, it was suggested that this inversion in a liminal area may have marked the transformation of the tree from the world of the living to the world of the dead. Exposing its roots—and, indeed, the removal of its bark—had some particular symbolic significance.

It was felled early in the year, when the tree itself and everything around it was in full growth. It may have been seen as a symbol of life and its inversion in the ground as returning those life forces to the earth, the source of all life. It may be that the removal of the bark was a purification process that was needed before the tree could release its energies back into the ground.

The Holme tree was a quite exceptional archaeological discovery, and it is no surprise that excavated evidence for special trees is almost non-existent. In Ireland, the burnt roots of a tree were found at the entrance to a small, U-shaped ditched enclosure at Shanaclogh, south Co. Limerick. A number of pits within the penannular enclosure contained cremated bone, and some coarse pottery sherds suggested a date in the middle Bronze Age. The excavator thought that the tree was modern but, situated as it was between the terminals of the ditch, Con Manning's suggestion that it might be the remains of a prehistoric sacred tree should be borne in mind. More of these elusive objects may await identification.

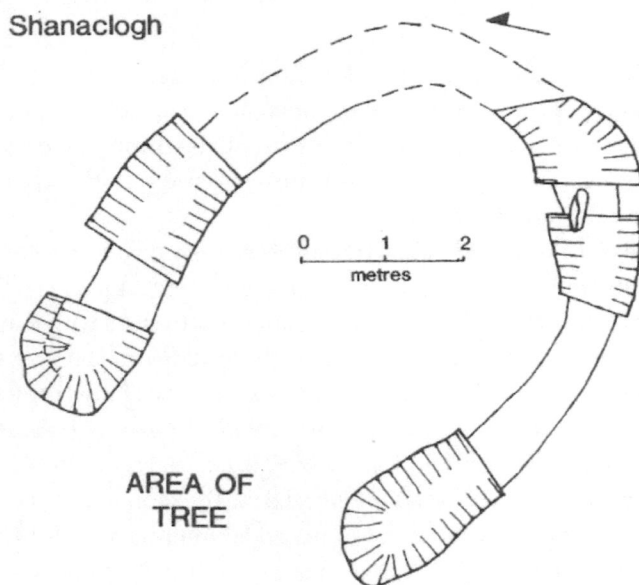

21.3—Simplified plan of a small Bronze Age ditched enclosure at Shanaclogh, Co. Limerick.

21.4—Sketch of an image on a first-century BC sword found at Port, north-west of Bern, in Switzerland. The name 'Korsios' in Greek script is below an impression of the Tree of Life flanked by a pair of animals This is the inspiration of the dragon-pair motif found on other sword scabbards (Fig. 28.4).

21.5—Sketch of a stylised Tree of Life symbol found on a decorated sword scabbard from Bussy-le-Château in the Marne region of north-eastern France.

Such special trees were seen as a source of sacred wisdom, and their presence on inauguration sites imbued a ruler with the necessary knowledge to ensure the fertility of the land and to maintain cosmic order. Like the *axis mundi*, sometimes conceived of as a wooden pillar or even as a pillar stone forming the link between the three levels of the cosmos (heaven, earth and the world below), these trees were a version of the Tree of Life.

The subject of the Tree of Life or World Tree is an exceptionally widespread one and, unsurprisingly, the subject of an enormous body of literature. Images are particularly common in the Mediterranean world and in the Near East as early as the fourth millennium BC. They are to be found in later Jewish, Muslim and Buddhist art and in Christian imagery, where the Tree of Life is often represented by the cross.

A late La Tène iron sword was discovered at Port, Canton Bern, on the Nidau-Büren canal in north-western Switzerland. Dated to the second half of the first century BC, the sword with its scabbard had been ritually decommissioned, being bent almost in two. It may have come from the bed of an old river. It bears the name

'Korisios' in Greek script and above it, just below the hilt, the image of a palm tree is flanked by a pair of rampant horned animals, possibly goat or ibex. They are eating from or protecting the Tree of Life.

More stylised images of this motif occur in the Celtic world on some other decorated sword scabbards and on a series of belt attachments. A noteworthy instance of how stylised this symbol might become is found on a decorated sword scabbard from Bussy-le-Château in the Marne region of north-eastern France. The major decorative elements on the upper part of the piece simply consist of two motifs: one is an inverted palm leaf or palmette motif; the other, placed above it, is a design consisting of a pair of fantastic beasts confronting a leaf-like shape. While the animals, formed by S-shaped scrolls with well-delineated heads, are just about recognisable as such, the tree has been reduced to one large leaf. Here a single leaf represents a tree. This is a remarkable illustration of how a single simple motif in La Tène art may carry a weight of meaning.

In more recent times there is an enormous amount of folklore on remarkable trees, not just in Ireland but also elsewhere. Indeed, one folklore expert has written—almost despairingly—of such solitary trees: 'almost every tree growing in Ireland has a certain amount of traditional information associated with it'. Vestiges of the sacred tree survive in the rag tree superstitiously bedecked with bits of cloth and other items, and its image lives on in the White Tree of Gondor in Tolkien's *The Lord of the Rings*. In 1999 the construction of a section of motorway at Latoon, near Newmarket-on-Fergus, Co. Clare, threatened a 'fairy bush' that was a meeting place of the Munster fairies according to local folklore. Contrary to popular legend, the motorway was not re-routed, but due care was taken and minor works were carried out to protect the tree and to accommodate the fairies. The saving of the tree, a whitethorn, made international headlines. It is now sandwiched between an on-ramp and the highway and stands just north of a flyover, making fairy access difficult to say the least.

22

Agrarian rites and sacrifices

22.1—The boulder circle Carrowmore no. 26, Co. Sligo, that revealed some surprising evidence of Iron Age agricultural ritual.

Even though ritual is one of the many ways in which people attempt to understand and control their world, many such practices have left little or no archaeological trace. Hunting rituals, perhaps performed to mimic the wounding and killing of the animal, probably featured prominently in hunting and foraging societies. The same may be said of ritual practices in the agricultural domain. Farming practices of every sort, crop cultivation, animal husbandry, burning, fencing, weeding and harvesting, all probably involved activities to ward off evil spirits, to appease good spirits, to protect animals and to ensure a good crop. We are remarkably ignorant of this ritual world in prehistory.

Numerous customs related to farming practice in more recent times, as noted by the folklore specialist Seán Ó Súilleabháin, give an idea of the many rituals that may once have been associated with these activities. For instance, salt might be sprinkled on a field before a crop was sown in it. Water in which a plough sock or coulter had been immersed might be sprinkled in a similar fashion—this might be due to a belief that iron had special magical qualities. On May Eve (30 April) or on St John's Eve (23 June) either the farm would be encircled with fire using burning reed-sheaves to ward off evil influences or some burning bushes or sticks from the fires might be thrown into the fields where crops were growing.

Animals needed protection from evil too. It was hoped to protect cows by tying red ribbons to their tails or around their necks. Rings made of rowan might be used as well. Cattle were driven across the dying flames of bonfires on May Eve and St John's Eve, or between two fires. Sometimes the animals were forced to swim in a lake or river to avert illness and bad luck. William Wilde, in an account of the bleeding of living cattle for food at Rathcroghan, records that milch cows, heifers and calves needed particular protection from evil influences at May time. As a magical precautionary custom, some people put a twisted rope of straw around the neck of each cow or made 'each head of cattle to be slightly singed with lighted straw upon May Eve, or to have a lighted coal passed round their bodies, as is customary after calving …'.

Many domestic tasks had their associated rituals. To cite just one example, the churn required protection from those who might want to steal the butter. This was achieved by placing a live cinder underneath it, and many wooden churns had charred bottoms as a result. Horseshoes or iron nails might also be attached for this purpose.

Agricultural rituals of any sort are hard to identify archaeologically but some surprising evidence for a fertility rite was discovered in Göran Burenhult's excavations in Carrowmore, Co. Sligo. This passage tomb cemetery lies below and to the east of Knocknarea. The majority of the surviving monuments are boulder circles, consisting of circles or parts of circles of stones that probably once contained centrally placed stone structures of some description. Megalithic tombs survive within the circles in seventeen cases, and most are monuments with polygonal chambers, some with short passages. They are built of boulders and the capstones are split boulders with a characteristic almost conical shape. Many were in use in the period 3600–3200 BC.

Dated bone or charcoal samples indicate that there was Iron Age depositional activity in several tombs there. Some human cranium fragments and some teeth

22.2—Plan of Carrowmore no. 26: the Iron Age internal ditch and three cultivation furrows are shown in grey. The post-holes of the timber entrance to the secondary circle are on the lower left, and ritual Pit 3 containing grains of barley, rye and oats is on the lower right.

from Carrowmore no. 27 were thought to be possible evidence of the practice of a severed head cult. Quite unusual evidence comes from Carrowmore no. 26. This was a circle of 38 boulders with substantial internal stone packing—a construction technique identified at several other excavated tombs. There was no trace of a central tomb within this circle, however, and the monument had clearly been modified in later prehistoric times.

A penannular ditch 13m in diameter had been dug inside the stone packing, and a formal entrance with four timber posts was constructed on the east where a gap in the boulder circle had been created. A number of pits in the interior contained offerings of charcoal and other burnt material, and one, Pit 3 on the north, also produced a grinding stone and a large quantity of burnt grains of barley, rye and oats. Three shallow cultivation furrows were also dug inside the ditch; they ran roughly north–south, and the southern end of the western example swerved slightly to avoid an earlier pit. Presumably dug with wooden spades, they were about 20cm deep. The low ridges between them were 90cm wide. The pits, the ditch with formal entrance and the ridge-and-furrow cultivation were all dated to the period 580– 490 BC.

The creation of these three furrows was a ritual performance. The ceremonial cultivation of cereals seems to have been practised inside the older monument to produce a sacred crop designed for ceremonial use and, in this instance, for deposition in a nearby pit. The presence of three cereals in the nearby pit is significant because triple sacrifices may once have been a widespread activity in the ancient world. Of course, there is a difference between a bloodless offering and an animal sacrifice, but triple sacrifices were a feature of early Roman religious practice. The Iguvine Tablets, a series of inscribed bronze plaques found at Gubbio (ancient *Iguvium*) in eastern Italy, record the sacrifice of three oxen and three pregnant sows at one of the city gates, triads of other animals being sacrificed at other locations.

This glimpse of a prehistoric agrarian cult at Carrowmore is a telling reminder of how little we know about the magical rites associated with ancient farming activities aimed at ensuring a good farming year. It is easy to forget how all aspects of such work were imbued with ritual significance in the past, and even the north–south axis of the Carrowmore furrows may be significant. Though prehistoric evidence is hard to find, a systematic north-east to south-west alignment has been noted in Bronze Age field systems in Britain and, because it seems to have offered no agricultural advantage and was maintained regardless of topographic variations, this pattern may express a cosmological imperative. In some cases orientation may have been aligned on the winter solstice sunrise.

An Anglo-Saxon rite known as the *Æcerbot*, 'the Land Remedy', is often called a charm but is in fact a lengthy set of liturgical prayers and rituals to heal agricultural land. Though clearly Christian, with references to Christ, Mary and the Apostles and phrases from the Book of Genesis, this day-long series of ritual actions contains traces of pagan practices. Ceremonies included placing a loaf of bread or cake in the first plough furrow; it was made from several kinds of cereal and kneaded with milk and holy water. In addition to many prayers, one invocation may have been inspired by an early Irish source. In this act the supplicant treats his plough with various blessed substances and declaims, 'Erce, erce, erce, mother of earth, may the all-ruler, the Eternal Lord, grant you fields growing and producing …'.

The mysterious *erce, erce, erce* phrase has puzzled scholars but may derive from Old or Middle Irish and mean 'May you increase, may you increase, may you increase'. This is a rare indication that fertility rites like this were probably practised in Ireland too, with offerings being made to the land and agricultural implements magically anointed to improve their efficacy.

For thousands of years cereals and other foodstuffs were ground on saddle querns. This laborious task involved the to-and-fro movement of a rubbing stone on the oval surface of a saddle-shaped stone. The operator had to kneel behind the stone to apply the necessary pressure to grind the material and this was hard physical work. The introduction of the rotary quern was an important technological development. It represented a considerable improvement on the saddle quern particularly because it was more effective. It crushed as well as ground the cereal and, though still a tedious task, was less onerous for the operator.

A rotary quern consists of two circular stones; the upper stone, rotated with a handle, has a central hole which serves as a chute for the corn which is ground between the stones, working its way to the edge as it is ground. The narrowness of the chute or feed-pipe often implies the use of a metal spindle, this pivotal piece sitting in a socket in the centre of the lower stone. There are two basic forms of ancient rotary quern: those with thick grinding stones of relatively small diameter, the heavy upper one being slightly domed—hence the name beehive quern—and

22.3—Beehive quern from Coolcarta, south-east Co. Galway.

the flat disc quern, which in Ireland seems to have replaced the beehive form some-time in the first millennium AD.

It is generally believed that the rotary quern originated in Spain and was intro-duced to Britain in the fifth or fourth century BC. The earliest form is the beehive quern, and the conventional assumption is that this type appeared in Ireland in or about the first century BC, though the evidence for such a late arrival is slim. Their general distribution is mainly confined to the northern half of the island, with only a few examples found south of a Galway to Dublin line. This northern bias is odd and contrasts with the island-wide distribution of saddle querns and the later disc querns. While they may display signs of use, surprisingly few show evidence of damage or excessive wear. All of this might suggest that they were something other than an ordinary piece of domestic equipment.

The fact that a few were decorated may be a further indication of their special character. Occasionally simple motifs occur that are also found on fine metalwork and doubtless had some particular significance. In two instances, on a quern from County Offaly and one from County Galway, the motifs are carefully paired on op-posing sides of the stone. A triple leaf motif occurs on one quern, opposed S-scrolls

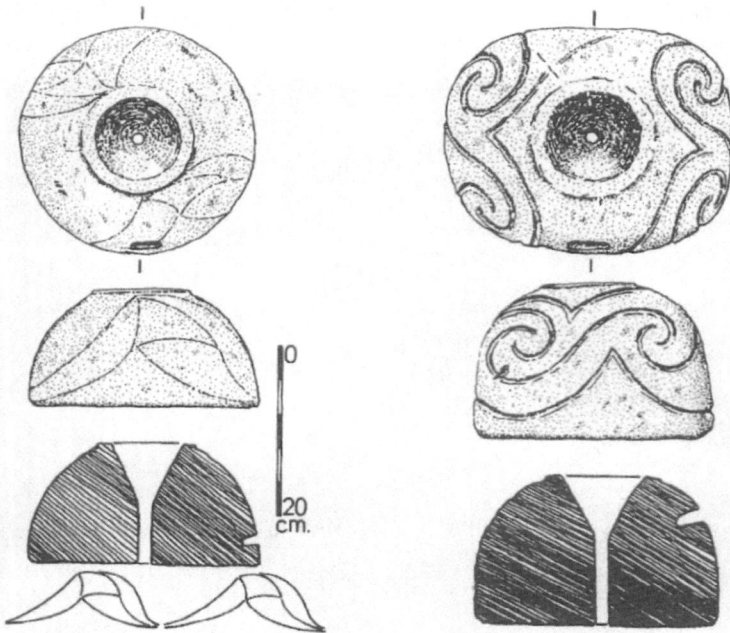

22.4—Decorated beehive querns with opposed motifs: Clonmacnoise, Co. Offaly (left), and Ticooly-O'Kelly, Co. Galway (right).

on the other, and this duplication presumably had some special meaning.

Equally difficult to explain is the fact that none have been found on or near settlement sites but a significant number have been found in bogs. Presumably these querns were sufficiently important to warrant their eventual fate as sacrificial offerings. They would seem to have been more than mere utilitarian tools and had some ideological significance that required their intentional votive deposition.

It is conceivable that initially at least this form of quern was used to prepare cereals for some special purpose—for a fermented drink or certain foodstuffs, for instance. It is interesting that the rotary quern seems to have been a late introduction in Norway and Sweden around AD 200 and is rarely found on settlements. There it may have been used in the preparation of exceptional food—such as bread that was baked and eaten at special places and on special occasions. Bread was part of the ritual meals that the gods expected to receive. When the god Odin hung on the World Tree, he complained that he had been given neither 'horn-drink' nor bread. Bread was sometimes given as a burial gift to the dead, and then mainly to a select category of people. Irish beehive querns may have had a special purpose.

Judging from historical and ethnographic evidence, the grinding task was probably performed by women. This is the case today among the Ouarten, a Berber tribe in Tunisia, and the Lala people in eastern Nigeria, where in recent times lengthy grinding sessions were held as part of the rituals to celebrate female rites of passage such as puberty. The Lala corn-grinding ceremony is an annual event held in the largest village, and people gather from the surrounding hamlets. Corn is ground on saddle querns by a large number of women to the accompaniment of rhythmic drumming. The climax is the incision of the tribal markings on the girls who are then eligible for marriage.

Because both the saddle quern and the rotary quern were associated with the process of turning grain into meal, they were linked to successful harvests and to fertility in many societies. It has been claimed that the operational to-and-fro motion of the saddle quern mimicked the male–female sexual relationship and this can also be seen in the rotary quern, the lower stone (with its vertical spindle) this time taking the male role. Millstones are still described in feminine terms in modern traditional milling terminology.

The circular movement of the rotary quern enabled the development of new mythologies and meanings based on a rotary motion. The turning of the upper stone came to symbolise the turning of the earth, or of the heavens with its revolving constellations, or the passage of time itself. In Nordic mythology there are brief allusions to a cosmic mill. The giant Bergilmir was ground in a mill to produce the soil and sand of the beaches. He is a being who furthers the fecundity of the earth through being ground up. The image of a cosmic mill may lie behind a reference to a certain Mundilfari who is cryptically called 'the father of Moon and also of Sun, they are to turn heaven every day for the reckoning of years for men'. According to Clive Tolley, the name Mundilfari has been designed to signify the mill-like device that turns the heavens by means of a 'handle'. Sun and Moon are, according to this genealogical fiction, his children who operate the device for him or by means of him. This turning of the cosmos, pictured as a mill, is the daily and yearly movement of the heavens.

We know very little about the ancient beliefs connected with the rotary quern in Ireland, though some associations with fertility are almost certain. In early times the laborious task of grinding (like milking and churning) was part of the work of a female slave. Seán Ó Súilleabháin, writing in the early 1960s, records that on St Martin's Day (11 November) no action should be performed that involved twisting or turning: no spinning, no use of wheels, no fishing (which involved the turning of boats) and, above all, no grinding of corn in mills or by quern-stones. In Ireland many mills remained idle on that day. The legend to explain this taboo tells that St Martin was ground to death in a mill—hence the prohibition against milling on his feast-day.

As no such death appears historically to have been the fate of any Christian saint of that name, Ó Súilleabháin thought it possible that we have here an echo of a much earlier belief. It may be that, as people in the Middle East once believed that the god Tammuz (or Dumuzid), who had given them the harvest, was being ground to death along with the corn between the quern-stones, so too in Ireland Martin, the Christian saint, replaced some pagan deity who was associated with the grinding of the harvest. The tradition connecting St Martin with milling can be traced back to medieval Germany, however, and this is where this element of the Irish tale may have its roots.

That said, the folklore scholar Billy Mag Fhloinn, who has comprehensively studied the customs associated with St Martin, also documents the more widespread custom of killing animals or fowl especially on the eve of the saint's feast-day. The cult of St Martin originated in fourth-century Gaul and spread to many parts of Europe, where it became associated with revelry, wine-drinking, feasting and excess at the end of harvest. Meat was widely consumed and animals that would not survive the winter were slaughtered. In Ireland Martin was considered an important saint, along with Patrick and Columba. By late medieval times he was certainly associated with the killing of animals, notably pigs. Abundant later folklore links his feast-day with shedding of the blood of a fowl or a farm animal on behalf of the saint, cockerels, chickens and geese being favoured in more recent times.

Their blood was often spread around doorways or in the four corners of the house, demarcating it with a protective substance.

The great pagan festival of Samhain was in time eclipsed by the Christian All Saints' Day on the same date (1 November) and All Souls' Day (2 November). Aside from its well-known supernatural aspects when the barriers between this world and the Otherworld were removed, Samhain was a moment that marked the end of harvest, and medieval sources record it as a time of feasting of some seven days' duration. This centred on the consumption of pork and on a pig specially raised for the occasion, the *banb samna*, the Samhain piglet. The eating of meat was forbidden on All Saints' Day and Mag Fhloinn suggests that this was probably one reason why rituals associated with the slaughter of animals and such an integral part of pagan customs at Samhain were displaced to St Martin's feast-day a little later in November.

23

Offerings in a midden

23.1—A section of a shell midden at Culleenamore, Co. Sligo.

Shell middens of various dates are a widespread phenomenon in Atlantic Europe and are known around much of the Irish coast. Some of these deposits of molluscs and other material are of late Mesolithic date and were evidently created over 6,000 years ago by hunters and foragers. These shell mounds were also fashioned by coastal visitors throughout much of prehistory, in the Neolithic, in the Bronze Age, in the Iron Age and well into the medieval era.

One Mesolithic midden at Sutton, Co. Dublin, measured some 100m in length but had a general depth of only 30cm. It had been formed at a time when Howth was an island, and the shell layer proper was composed of over twenty varieties of shellfish, including limpets, whelks, cockles, scallops, periwinkles, oysters and mussels. It also produced flint implements and bones of wild pig, hare, dog or wolf, and fish were identified. Its use spanned many centuries around 5000 and 4000 BC. It is a reasonable assumption that this and other middens like it were places where coastal resources were exploited on a seasonal basis by inland communities. It is also fair to say that excavation of these sites has been very limited indeed and their formation is poorly understood.

Some were seemingly used in a sporadic manner for 1,000 years or more. For example, two middens at the north-western end of Dalkey Island, Co. Dublin, seem to have accumulated over just such a long timespan in the Mesolithic and Neolithic periods. The deposition of stone and other material in pits and the presence of a disarticulated human burial beneath the shell deposit (with its cranium filled with periwinkle shells) suggest a ritual dimension to the activities here. This is the one site where there is evidence that seals were hunted, and one seal bone has been radiocarbon-dated to 5970–5560 BC. The seal was certainly exploited in prehistory. Its meat and the oil extracted from its blubber are nutritious foodstuffs, and its skin is a valuable material for clothing and other uses. Some bones of mature seals were found in later Bronze Age contexts in Dún Aonghasa on Aran, and they were an important resource in the early medieval period—some coastal ecclesiastical communities had fishery rights over seal colonies.

At Culleenamore, Co. Sligo, an extensive complex of shell middens on the shore of Ballysadare Bay was also used over a prolonged period of time, and one contained a hearth that produced a Neolithic radiocarbon date. These middens extend for about 100m, are 30m wide in places and have a depth of up to 3m. They are

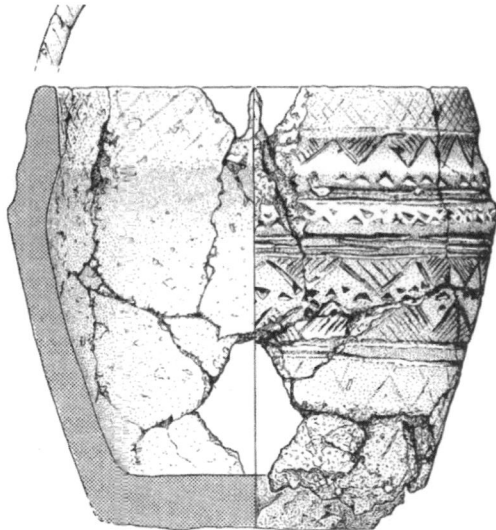

23.2—Bronze Age pottery vessel from a pit in the Doonloughan midden.

comprised mainly of oyster shells, but other species such as cockles, mussels, periwinkles, scallops and limpets are also present. It has been suggested that they were one of a series of food sources seasonally exploited by the builders of the nearby passage tombs on Knocknarea and at Carrowmore. Such a straightforward functional explanation for midden formation may well be the case in many instances. Small collections of shellfish, hearths and other remains probably represent seasonal visits to the seashore by local communities to augment their normal diet or in times of scarcity.

This sort of exploitation occurred in Truska townland, Co. Galway, where the remains of an early Bronze Age midden at Doonloughan Bay, near Ballyconneely, were excavated. Many middens have been damaged by erosion by wind and sea, by animal action and by farming activities, and this was the case here. This one survived as a thin triangular spread, about 30m across, of oyster shells and burnt stone. Limpets, winkles and the occasional cockle shell were also noted. Finds included a few chert scrapers, pottery sherds, some burnt grains of barley and a cattle bone. A

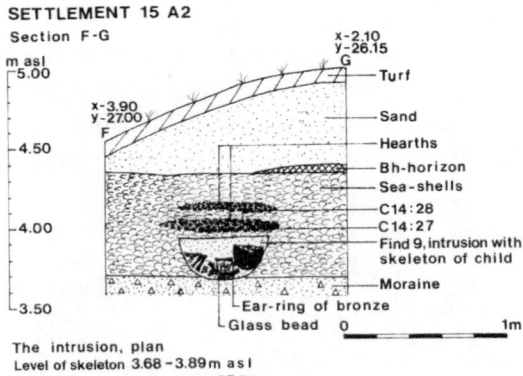

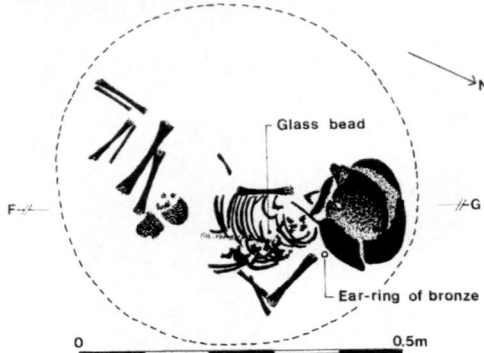

23.3—Plan and section of a circular pit inserted into a shell midden at Culleenamore, Co. Sligo, and containing the skeleton of an infant.

sample of charcoal produced a radiocarbon date of 2094–1880 BC.

There was one puzzling feature: a small pit, about 30cm in diameter and 50cm deep, had been dug into the midden and it contained lenses of sterile sand, shells, burnt stone and some large pottery sherds representing the greater part of one Bronze Age vase. This would appear to have been a carefully structured deposit of different materials inserted into the midden in a ritual act.

Another unusual pit was found in the midden complex at Culleenamore. While cremation was the common Iron Age burial rite, an exceptional unburnt burial was thought to be of Iron Age date. Excavation directed by Göran Burenhult in 1981 revealed a circular pit about 50cm in diameter. It had been dug into the midden near its base, and later deposits of sea shells and burnt material representing two hearths were placed above it. In the prosaic language of the excavation report the pit is described as 'the intrusion'. It contained the crouched burial of a child about eighteen months old who had been carefully interred in the mass of shells along with a small blue glass bead and a miniature earring of bronze.

We can only guess as to why this tiny child was buried in this place and what the meaning of the bead and the ring may have been. The bead may have been a protective charm, for it was once widely believed that children needed special protection against malign forces such as the evil eye and beads like this were perceived as surrogate eyes.

A number of other infant burials accompanied by glass beads are recorded and are of late Iron Age and early medieval date. Five infant burials were found in a relatively confined area on the lower slopes of Mullaghmast Hill, Co. Kildare, close to a townland boundary. They were dated to between the second century BC and the first century AD. Aged from a few months to less than a year, they had been buried with care in small circular pits, and two were accompanied by bronze or iron rings. As Elizabeth O'Brien remarks, the Mullaghmast graves present a conundrum. Finds in the general area suggest that it was a place that was visited from time to time for various activities. Occasional post-holes and roasting pits were excavated but no traces of permanent habitation were uncovered. Did the infant burials represent some sort of ritual on an ancient territorial boundary or even the sacrifice of first-born children?

The Culleenamore infant had also been buried in a liminal place, on a boundary between land and sea, and in a context where people gathered from time to time to consume food. This is one case where the dictionary definition of a midden as a 'prehistoric refuse heap' may be quite misleading. It is possible that some of the shellfish-gathering and food-processing at large middens like Culleenamore were ritualised activities. Some small deposits might represent intentional and repeated activities by small groups of people, and larger accumulations could be the result of major communal feasting occasions. The shell mounds might then be visible markers of these important social events, their symbolic value enhanced by the inclusion of other material such as animal and human remains. These places may have acquired a symbolic power and the repeated events created a story-line about a mythical and a real past that was recalled again and again over time.

The Torres Strait islanders of north-eastern Australia occupy a series of islands between Australia and Papua New Guinea. This region has a rich tropical marine life, including fish, shellfish, turtles and dugongs (a large marine mammal like the seal or the manatee), that formed an important part of the subsistence economy. Traditionally, procurement of turtles and dugongs was a male activity, shellfish were procured by women and children, and fish by both men and women. Public or communal feasts resulted in large quantities of food being shared, and the capacity of males to contribute generously to these occasions was a key part of their status and leadership. Hunting dugong was particularly important and the making of mounds of their bones was a structured and formal process, bones being carefully selected and arranged.

Large midden deposits have developed over many centuries, and they contain varying quantities of shells and bones of fish, turtles and dugongs. Middens continue to be created today. On one island, Goemu, extensive middens, graves and shell arrangements stretch for 300m along the coast and 150m inland. A sampling excavation in one 1,000-year-old deposit produced a quantity of teeth of dogs and children, all possibly extracted post-mortem. These remains of children were considered a way of deliberately linking midden deposits with particular families or communities.

Linear and circular shell mounds were made in and around the settlement at Goemu village and were intended to be highly visible and conspicuous markers. They reflected a desire to record the fact that they were the product of shared social actions. Over a number of centuries these people did not simply use one place for depositing food remains but made over 100 discrete midden mounds across a 2ha area in purposeful acts of public remembrance and display that became a part of everyday village life. Ian McNiven described this as 'living architecture for pedestrian engagement'.

Some of the finds on Dalkey Island, the pit containing an offering of pottery and other material at Dooloughan and the infant burial at Culleenamore do suggest that there may have been more to midden-building activity in Ireland too. Dietary needs and subsistence requirements were perhaps just a part of the story. Some were probably more than a mere 'wholeborrow of rubbages on to soil', as James

Joyce called them in *Finnegans Wake*. It is widely recognised that feasting is regularly associated with ceremonial activity, so there may have been a ritual element in their formation. This could have involved different communities, but even extended family events, with shared participation in diverse activities such as seal-hunting, shellfish-gathering, processing and consumption, would serve to strengthen social bonds and affirm identities. Special events may have been commemorated by special offerings.

24

The magic of ironworking

24.1—A divine blacksmith: Vulcan with his hammer and iron tongs as depicted on the *Pilier des Nautes* in the Musée de Cluny, Paris.

In the reign of Tiberius, around AD 40, an influential company of Parisian boatmen, who managed the transport of goods on the River Seine, erected a monumental pillar in Lutetia, the future Paris, in honour of the emperor. Known as the *Pilier des Nautes*, it is the oldest piece of Gallo-Roman sculpture in that city and is on prominent display in the Musée de Cluny. It bears Latin and Gaulish inscriptions and images of the Roman gods Jupiter and Vulcan. Also represented are named Celtic deities: Tarvos Trigaranus (meaning 'the bull with three cranes'), a horned figure called Cernunnos and a god named Esus, who is portrayed cutting branches from a tree with a billhook.

Vulcan was a relatively popular cult figure in Gallo-Roman iconography, particularly when compared with the rest of the Roman Empire, and this is presumably because he assimilated an important indigenous Gaulish deity with metalworking associations. This was Gobannus, whose name is cognate with the Welsh Govannon and the Irish Goibniu, who was one of the Tuatha Dé Danann. These several manifestations of a divine smith exemplify the exceptional importance attributed to this craft in these early societies.

The historical and ethnographic record around the world contains an enormous number and variety of myths and rituals associated with metalworking but a constant feature is the sacredness of metallurgical work. It was a transformative process inextricably linked with status and gender, and with the mastery of fire. It was often considered a dangerous activity and the social position of its practitioners varied through time and from place to place. In early medieval Ireland the literary evidence indicates that skilled blacksmiths were of high social status but were feared for their magical abilities. As already mentioned, prayers might be offered 'against the spells of women and smiths and druids'.

The same was true of their Iron Age predecessors. Some limited evidence hints at an early date for the introduction of iron, probably in the eighth century BC. A large number of sites have produced evidence for later ironworking, however, and it was widely established after 500 BC. It is not known whether there was a distinction between those who smelted iron and those who worked it at this time. Iron was probably a prestigious material when it was introduced and both tasks may have had religious significance, perhaps being preceded by rites of purification and then surrounded by ritual and taboo.

The extraction of iron ore, whether from a bog or rock source, was just the first step in a sacramental process. In some traditional African societies offerings and sacrifices were made to mollify the earth, to release the ore and to propitiate the ancestors whose land it was. Even the collection of suitable timber for the production of charcoal may have been circumscribed by customary regulation. This was an area where women may have had a role.

The production of iron required relatively simple equipment. Iron was extracted through heating the ore by burning charcoal in a small furnace with a shallow bowl-shaped base and a low cylindrical clay shaft about 70cm high. Charcoal was made by carbonising wood under oxygen-limited conditions so that the wood was roasted but

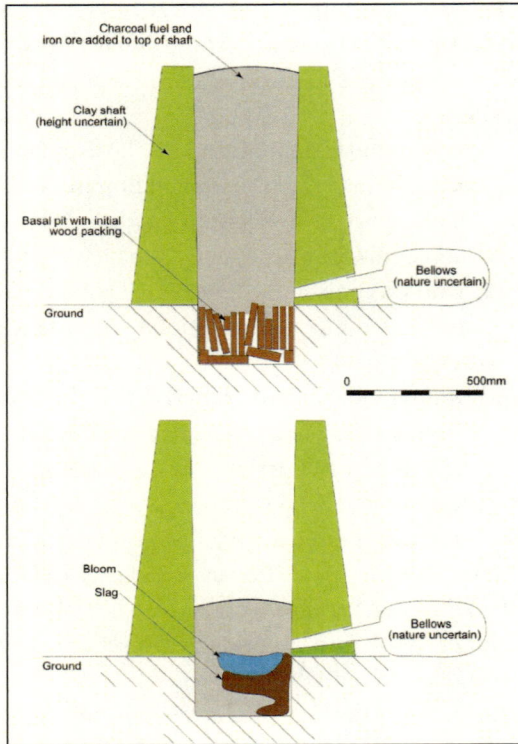

24.2—Schematic reconstruction of a clay shaft furnace.

not burnt. The required furnace temperatures of 1,100–1,250° would be achieved comparatively easily with bellows. This smelting process would produce a deposit of slag, which would accumulate at the base of the furnace below a bloom. The bloom, a spongy mass of metallic iron, had to be reheated and carefully hammered to weld the iron particles together and to remove extraneous matter such as slag. When this was done, a smith had a piece of iron from which artefacts could be made.

We can only guess at the rituals that may have accompanied this process. In many traditional African societies, the smelting of metal was metaphorically equivalent to copulation, gestation and birth. The work of the smith was a creative act like the act of procreation. Smelting was analogous to intercourse, the bellows and its nozzle were the equivalent of testicle and penis, while the furnace was perceived as a woman. The metal bloom growing in the furnace was akin to a foetus, and the male smelters were simultaneously husbands and midwives. In some cases this symbolism was displayed on the furnaces themselves in the form of female breasts,

24.3—Clay shaft furnace from Nyanga, eastern Zimbabwe, with breasts, navel and waist belt that enhanced fertility depicted.

genitalia, navels and the waist belts that women wore to enhance fertility.

While smelting and smithing may have been practised in different places in the Irish landscape, and the production of finished iron objects such as axes, swords and spears was a diverse and more complicated undertaking, both tasks may have had their own exclusive rituals, and both were transformative and regenerative activities with symbolically charged products. Writing of Iron Age metalworking on the Hill of Tara, Roseanne Schot quotes some telling lines from a ninth-century Irish text, 'The Triads of Ireland', where the three renovators of the world are named as 'the womb of a woman, the udder of a cow, the *ness gobann* of a blacksmith'. The latter puzzling object was one of the smith's tools and one translation renders it as 'moulding-block'. In some African societies too the smith's stone anvil was a weighty symbol of his fertile power. As Schot points out, working among the burial mounds of ancestors on Tara would have surrounded the smith's creative ironworking there with a particular aura of sanctity.

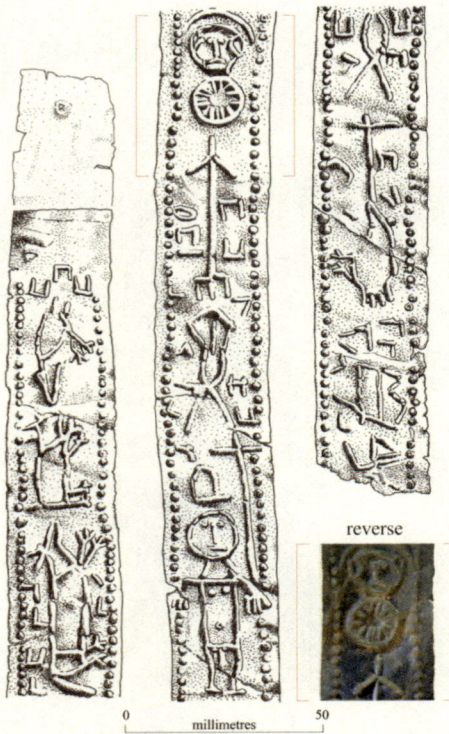

24.4—The Farley Heath bronze binding strip: identifiable motifs in descending order. Left: bird and two animals. Centre: helmeted head, wheel, tree(?), tongs and anvil or altar, human figure. Right: tongs, hammer, bird, animals(?).

The association of smiths with powerful esoteric knowledge and with magic and sorcery is also reported among many African societies. They had occult as well as technical abilities and thus their help might be sought on fertility matters, or they might be asked to mediate between communities and families to resolve disagreements. Their skills might also include performing circumcision, and some engaged in diverse types of healing and oracular activities. Some of these additional pursuits may have been performed by smiths in Iron Age Ireland too. John Carey shows how the smith Goibniu sometimes appears as the possessor of harmful knowledge and magic: he is called a prophet of knowledge, and in one cryptic phrase 'very harsh is the knowledge of Goibniu'.

While a few small images of Vulcan with his characteristic hammer and tongs are known in Roman Britain, the native god of the forge is quite elusive. One possible depiction of this divine smith occurs on a small bronze strip found in the nineteenth century on the site of a Romano-British temple at Farley Heath, near

Guildford in Surrey. When found, it was a twisted spiral with a length of 43cm and a width of 2.5cm. It is believed to be a binding for a staff or sceptre, and it has the remains of a spirally twisted iron handle. A very similar binding was found in the famous Celtic Iron Age hoard in Llyn Cerrig Bach, Anglesey. This collection included decorated metalwork, weapons, chariot fitments, part of a bronze trumpet and several iron tongs. The presence of tongs in such a great votive deposit is probably an indication of their symbolic importance. The ribbon of bronze had an incised central line along its length and had been wrapped around a piece of ash, the remains of a wooden staff.

The Farley Heath object bears simple embossed decoration, and the recognisable motifs include two birds, several four-legged animals and some enigmatic symbols. One human head appears to bear a helmet and lies above a wheel-shaped motif with a vertical pronged device (possibly a stylised tree) below. A nude human figure below this is clearly phallic; it has a pair of tongs above it and another pair of tongs and a hammer(?) are represented below.

The human head and wheel have prompted the suggestion that this might be a representation of the Gaulish deity Taranis with his characteristic wheel, but the combination of this device and what may be a stylised tree recalls the Wavendon Gate wooden wheel-shaped object. Since Vulcan is rarely depicted naked, the nude figure with associated smith's implements and obvious fertility connotations is likely to be a depiction of a native godlike smith.

25

The bodies in the bog

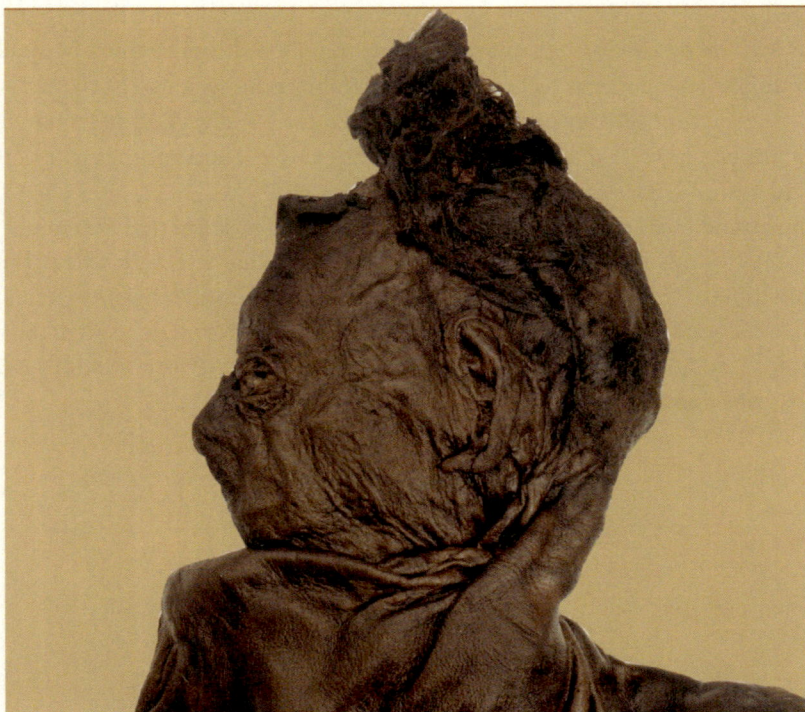

25.1—Part of a bog body labelled 'Clonycavan Man' in the National Museum of Ireland.

Several bog bodies form part of a public exhibition in the National Museum of Ireland, Dublin. It is a well-designed if rather ghoulish presentation entitled 'Kingship and Sacrifice', and its central premise is that a number of these remains are those of kings sacrificed in the Iron Age. The principal bodies have been labelled Gallagh Man, Clonycavan Man and Oldcroghan Man. They do share some features in common, especially the fact that they were found in bogs and are greatly damaged, but they are different in many other ways.

At least 100 bog bodies have been found in Ireland, and many more have been discovered in Britain and northern Europe. The famous Tollund Man was found in Denmark in 1950 and achieved international renown when Peter V. Glob's book *The bog people* was published in English translation in 1969. The soft tissues of this corpse were well preserved, and he was apparently hanged before being placed in Tollund Moss. The evocative images of his 'peat-brown head', his violent end and the flat bogland where he was found inspired several poems by Seamus Heaney.

Having received little attention for many years, bog bodies eventually became the subject of serious multidisciplinary research. When another well-preserved body was found in Lindow Moss, near Wilmslow in Cheshire, north-west England, it was considered sufficiently important to be acquired by the British Museum. This man too met a violent end: according to reports, he suffered some blows to the head, was possibly strangled and then his throat was cut, all in quick succession. He was placed face down in a bog pool, and it has been suggested that this was a ritual sacrifice, even a ritual druidic killing. This triple assault invited comparisons with the threefold death, a motif found in early Irish literature, where it usually consists of a combination of wounding, drowning and burning. A number of kings are said to have died in this fashion, including Muirchertach mac Erca and Diarmaid mac Cerbaill, both kings of Tara and of the northern and southern Uí Néill respectively. Assuming that this was not just a literary motif, it seems that this dubious honour was not confined to kings; a herdsman and murderer named Grác was also done to death in this fashion in the seventh century. In one account he was wounded by a spear when climbing a tree, fell down into a fire and then drowned.

Determining the cause of death of a body retrieved from a bog presents many challenges. Preservation mainly depends on the conditions in the bog in question. Tannic acids contribute to good preservation of soft tissue but cause demineralisation of all skeletal elements. Partial exposure, watery conditions or the pressure of the peat in an unstable bog may damage the corpse, and post-mortem damage by human agency, especially by mechanical turf-cutting, may be even more extensive. Only the upper half of this Lindow body was recovered, for instance.

The evidence of forensic pathologists is of course critical, and it is interesting to note that in the case of the Lindow corpse there was some disagreement. Two medical experts did agree that the man's skull had been fractured twice by blows, but one believed that a third blow had broken the neck while the other thought that he was garrotted by a thin cord that was found around the neck. One believed that the man's throat had been cut; the other considered this gash to have been caused by later damage to the body in the bog. In short, one believed in a ritualised

25.2—The Gallagh, Co. Galway, bog body in the National Museum of Ireland.

threefold execution, the other in a violent attack. Other injuries to the body, such as a broken rib and a possible stab wound in the chest, would be consistent with the latter interpretation. Obviously, these are significantly different interpretations. Though they may have met violent ends, not all bog bodies were ritual sacrifices.

In at least one Irish case a bog find may have been a deliberate interment in the peat, though not a sacrificial one. This is that female burial found in a bog at Derrymaquirke, Co. Roscommon. The unusual contents of this Iron Age grave—the piece of wood behind the head, the stone lying on top of her, the bones of a child, a small piece of antler and some animal bone—all suggest, as we noted, that she may have been a ritualist.

The Gallagh body in the National Museum raises other questions. Also of Iron Age date, it was found in 1821 in a bog in the townland of that name near Castleblakeney, Co. Galway. As William Wilde reported in 1861, it was reburied and exhumed more than once as a curiosity before being deposited in the museum of the Royal Dublin Society in 1829.

Little survives of this man's clothing, but he was not half-naked, as has been claimed. Neither was he wearing a cloak but rather had a close-fitting deerskin garment that extended to elbows and knees, rather like some of the clothing depicted on the Gundestrup cauldron. There was a 'band of sally rods' around his neck, and a pointed wooden stake had been placed on each side of the body. There is no evidence that the willow band was a spancel or a garrotte of withies. It may have been a symbolic torc. He may or may not have been murdered but his unburnt burial in a bog, like that of the Derrymaquirke woman, was a deviant one for some reason. Again, such a departure from the norm may have been prompted by a fear that the spirit of the dead might have some malevolent capability, or it may have been a punitive act. In the circumstances, human sacrifice is the least likely explanation.

Two other Iron Age bog burials may, however, have been ritual murders. Both were found in 2003 in the course of mechanical turf-cutting and both were grossly damaged in the process. Full reports have yet to be published and the precise find-spot of one is not known. This was just the torso of a young man that survived the action of a peat-harvesting machine in Clonycavan, near Ballivor, Co. Meath. He was killed by a series of axe blows to the head, and there was a 40cm-long cut to the abdomen. He was apparently of slight build and small stature (perhaps just over 5ft tall), but his head was intact, with a clearly distinguishable face and a very distinctive hairstyle. His hair in front was shaved from ear to ear and was gathered into a topknot. It was infested with lice and held in place by the application of a sort of gel made from vegetable oil and pine resin from *Pinus pinaster*, a tree that grows in the French or Spanish Pyrenees. This material may have been imported from France or Spain—possibly a mark of his high rank or just applied as part of some elaborate preparatory ritual prior to sacrifice.

The second body was found during the mechanical digging of a bog drain at Oldcroghan, near the village of Croghan, Co. Offaly. Only a severed torso was recovered, but a few fingernails found undisturbed in the drain face marked the original location of the body. Pollen and plant fossil analysis indicated that the body had probably been completely submerged in a bog pool. The remains were those of a tall, powerfully built man who was killed by a stab wound to the chest, but a defence wound on his upper left arm indicated that he tried to fend off the fatal assault. He was then decapitated and his thorax severed from his abdomen.

The surviving part of the body was in good condition and both hands were well preserved. He had carefully manicured fingernails: this and an absence of wear to his hands suggested that he was a person who did not engage in heavy manual work. There was a plaited leather armband with decorated metal mounts on his left arm, and withies had been inserted through cuts in his upper arms as if to spancel or hobble him.

Both men had a plant-based last meal and, in a peculiar ritual, both bodies had their nipples partially cut, but whether this was done before or after death is not known. There seems to have been a pagan Irish custom whereby a man indicated his fealty to another by sucking the latter's nipples. It is recorded by St Patrick in his *Confessio*, for instance, that when he was escaping from slavery the men with whom he was sailing expected him to suck their breasts, and when he refused to do so they relented and allowed him to 'make friendship with us in whatever way you wish'. It also figures in the Old Irish story *Echtra Fergusa meic Léti* ('The Adventure of Fergus mac Léti'), where the warrior king receives submission in this form from a water-spirit. It is an important detail, but this custom was evidently a form of male bonding with a leader and not confined to kingly individuals and their subordinates.

The National Museum exhibition presents the Clonycavan and Oldcroghan men as deposed sacral kings who were sacrificed in a quite forceful and ritualistic manner. Their deposition in what are often thought to be liminal boundary locations is seen as an important supportive detail, for these are places where rites of one sort or another were often performed. Even though their status may have been special, and their deaths and mutilation were ritually complicated, it does not follow that they were kings or even surrogates for kings.

Prehistoric boundaries may not have been neatly defined in geographical terms and some were probably fluid concepts personified by powerful leaders. Nonetheless, the ritual of human sacrifice in wetlands, as a public display of extreme cruelty, was doubtless a dramatic expression of the power and authority of such individuals. These murderous rites transformed a living being into an inanimate object and invested the violence with sacral significance. It is of course probable that, like so many offerings of metalwork in watery places (like the Gundestrup cauldron itself), these bodies were also sacrifices in haunted bogland to appease some supernatural power.

26

Lost mythologies

26.1—The 'Cork Horns'.

The object known as the 'Cork Horns' was found in 1909 in river mud on the shores of the River Lee. When recovered, a strip of metal connected two of the three horns together, and it is generally thought that they once decorated a helmet or headdress of some perishable material. All three horns are elegantly decorated with curving trumpet motifs in low relief. The design on the middle horn is a clever and more elaborate variation on the elongated patterns on the side ones. The central element in the design on the side horns is an inverted version of that on the middle one.

Given its complexity, it is probable that the middle horn and its decorative design had some special significance. The Cork object could well have been a helmet embellishment offering its wearer the prowess of such a well-endowed horned animal. It could also have decorated a bovine headdress and mask, perhaps worn with a bull-like costume in a ritual performance as part of a bull cult. It may even have decorated a model bull made of some organic material. Of course, animals with two horns, notably bulls, are common enough, but three-horned creatures are

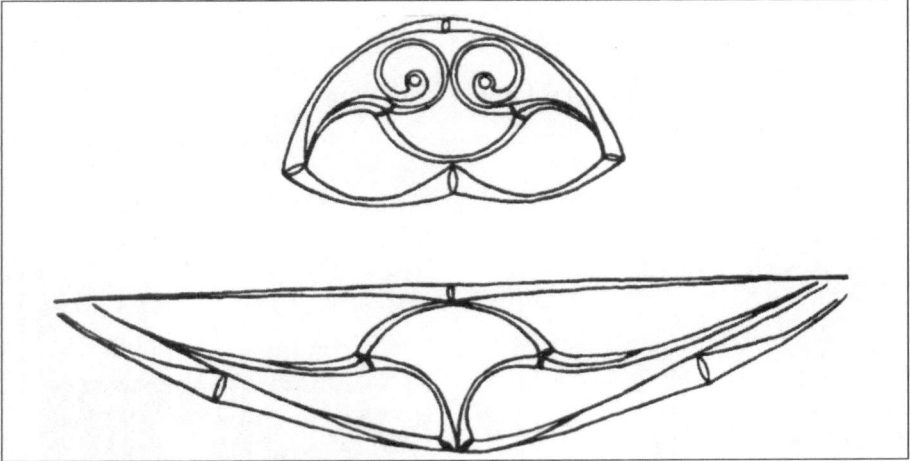

26.2—Decorative design on the central horn (above) and an inverted version of this on the side horns (below).

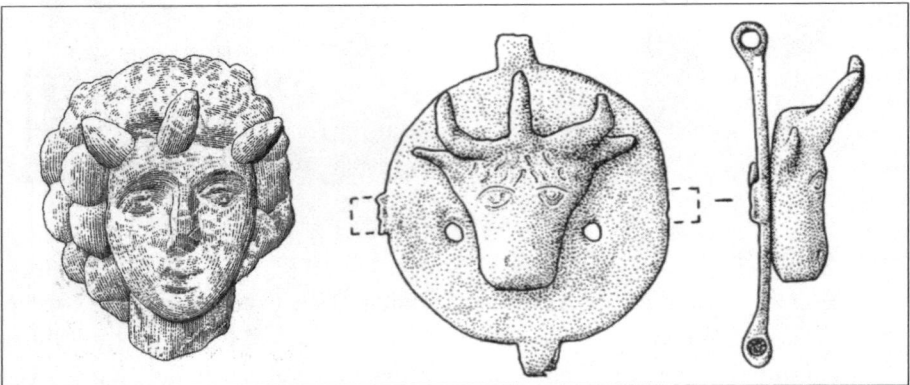

26.3—Triple-horned human figure from Beire-le-Châtel and the Cookham bull.

harder to find. Triple horns are sometimes represented in a variety of ways, and Miranda Green instances some images of horses and humans depicted in this fashion.

A small human head, only 13cm high, from a Gallo-Roman sanctuary at Beire-le-Châtel, north-east of Dijon in eastern France, is a rare example and presumably had some cultic significance. Maybe the horns were an expression of some exceptional supernatural energy. A hollow-cast bronze head from a Romano-British sanctuary at Great Walsingham in Norfolk is only 4.9cm high. It is a bearded male head with a torc round its neck and has three knobbed horns projecting from what appears to be a helmet or cap Whatever its meaning in a particular context, the depiction of three horns is sometimes considered an instance of a Celtic appetite for triplism in which a set of three motifs such as spirals, triskeles or faces are expressions of the greater power of three.

As far as animals are concerned, however, three-horned bulls are commoner. According to Miranda Green, nearly 40 examples in stone, bronze and clay are known in Gaul. A small bronze mount from Cookham, near Maidenhead, Berkshire, consists of a circular plaque 4.5cm in diameter that has the head of a three-horned bull riveted to it. The animal is simply portrayed with oval eyes, a forelock and two ears plus the triple horns. Somewhat larger, the great bronze statue of a three-horned bull known as the *Taureau d'Avrigney* is probably the most impressive surviving example. Now in the Musée des Beaux-arts et d'Archéologie in Besançon, and over 70cm high, it must have been a prominent cult object in a Gallo-Roman sanctuary. It was found in the eighteenth century in the commune of Avrigney, north-west of Besançon in eastern France.

According to writers like Anne Ross, these representations are images of divine bulls, a thesis supported by the bull depicted on one side of the column of the *Pilier des Nautes* in Paris. As already mentioned, three named Celtic deities are represented on this famous monument, including Tarvos Trigaranus ('the bull with three cranes'). This divine bull, with two horns, stands behind a tree; two cranes are perched on his back while a third stands on his head.

26.4—P.-M. Duval's drawings of the divine bull with three cranes on the *Pilier des Nautes* (left), and a bull's head and three cranes in a tree on a fragment of a pillar in Trier (right).

A pillar bearing an inscription to the deity Esus is preserved in Trier. It depicts a man cutting down a tree whose branches contain the head of a bull and three crane-like birds. Here a small square temple was dedicated to the bull-like divinity in the early centuries AD. The meaning of these striking images of a divine bull accompanied by three water-birds is a mystery. Mythical bulls, like the great Findbennach and the Donn Cuailnge of the *Táin Bó Cuailnge*, are well known in Irish tradition. Bull sacrifice does figure in early Irish literature, as we have seen, and various individuals have bull epithets, like Eochaid Marc-cend, a 'bull-king' of Tara, but no bull-like deity can be identified with any certainty.

A Gallo-Roman stone sculpture of the head of a bull was found in the city of Dijon in 1840. It was possibly part of a door pillar but is of particular interest because this bull's head had two holes for detachable horns. The horns may have been of metal, though why they should have been removable is hard to fathom—maybe they themselves were particularly significant. It raises the interesting and real possibility that there were other bulls with detachable horns and that the Cork horns might have been attached to a carved wooden bull rather than to a helmet or a headdress. These triple horns from Cork may be the material echo of a lost and forgotten cult of a divine bull.

That a powerful bull mythology and its associated rites should leave little or no trace is unsurprising. As one writer has said, 'in the course of human events

26.5—'The time of the wolves': P.-M. Duval's rendering of the wolfish image on a Gaulish gold coin.

societies pass and religious systems change; the historical landscape is littered with the husks of desiccated myths'. Such fragments of ancient beliefs and cult practices survive in some of the more bizarre images on Gaulish coins.

For example, one gold coin from the Cotentin peninsula, the region of Cherbourg and home of a Celtic tribe, the Unelli, has been examined in detail by Paul-Marie Duval. It is just under 2cm in diameter with a human head on one face, but on the other there is some remarkably complex imagery. Some minute details are obscure, but the main elements are clear enough: there is a winged creature, perhaps an eagle, and a possible palmette motif placed respectively below and above a large animal. This is a monstrous wolf-like beast with prominent claws that has its head, with open jaws, turned backwards. It appears to be about to devour a solar wheel and a lunar crescent.

Duval suggested that this was a representation of the cataclysmic end of the world, 'the time of the wolves'. In Norse mythology the apocalypse begins when the giant wolf Fenrir and his wolfish offspring devour the sun and moon and plunge the world into darkness. Duval thought that its representation on a Gaulish coin could indicate that this sort of account of the end of the world was once a feature of Celtic mythology.

In Ireland there must have been many myths and pagan practices that early Christian writers chose to ignore or suppress when recording early traditional lore. This is surely the reason for the absence of any extensive trace in early Irish literature of solar mythology, of the cremation of heroic warriors, or of those great myths about the creation and end of the world that are such a feature of other Indo-European mythologies. We find a mere hint of the latter event at the end of *Cath Maige Tuired* ('The Second Battle of Moytura'), for instance, when the last words are chanted by the war-goddess the Morrígan, who prophesies the end of the world, foretelling the evils that will occur then: 'I shall not see a world that will be dear to me, Summer without blossoms, Cattle will be without milk, Women without modesty, Men without valour, Conquests without a king …'. This is an echo of the Norse Poetic Edda in which 'Brothers will fight and kill each other, sisters' children will defile kinship. It is harsh in the world, whoredom rife—an axe age, a sword age— shields are riven …'.

The Ralaghan idol raises some other questions about another lost myth. Two gods in Nordic mythology, Odin and Tyr, are respectively one-eyed and one-armed and are an example of an interesting divine pairing. Odin exchanged his eye for knowledge at Mimir's well and was essentially a divine sage and magician. According to the Icelandic poet Snorri Sturluson (1179–1241):

'Odin was called "Allfather". From his seat, Hlidskjalf, set at the edge of heaven, he watched over the entire world. He had one eye, having traded one for wisdom. And he had a hall, Valhalla, that was thatched with shields. In that hall he sat, flanked by two wolves, while two ravens whispered all the world's news to him, and there he hosted an army made up of the greatest kings and warriors who have ever lived. In the world's final battle, he will ride ahead of that army in a golden helm and shining armour, wielding a mighty spear.'

Various images in Scandinavia with one eye or with an altered or damaged eye have been identified with Odin. Of course, there is a huge chronological gap between Bronze Age Ireland and medieval Scandinavia, but if this concept of a one-eyed deity is an Indo-European one, as some have argued, then Ralaghan just might be a representation of this. It is debatable whether a removable penis was intended to mimic castration in some fashion, but a number of Indo-European deities were also said to have undergone this mutilation that paradoxically increased their powers.

The one-armed Tyr was closely associated with oaths and contractual relationships. He pledged his hand as a guarantee to the monstrous wolf Fenrir and lost. This pairing of a one-eyed and one-armed figure is found in other Indo-European mythologies. The Roman tale of Mucius Scaevola in the Etruscan wars who heroically burns his right arm to prove his honesty and the equally brave warrior Horatius Cocles who lost an eye in battle is thought to reflect a similar mythic duo. There are Irish echoes of this theme too. In the medieval tale *Aided chlainne Tuirenn* ('The Fate of the Children of Tuireann'), the one-armed Nuadu, famous for his silver arm, appears with his one-eyed doorkeeper. The brothers Miach and Oirmiach replace the missing eye of the doorkeeper with the eye of a cat and provide a replacement arm for Nuadu.

In a complicated story, *Talland Étair* ('The Siege of Howth'), an Ulster poet named Athirne extorts various favours around Ireland on pain of satire. These include demanding a single eye from Eochaid mac Luchta, king of south Connacht, and sexual favours from the wife of Mess Gegra, king of Leinster. This starts a battle between Ulster and Leinster in the region of Howth. After this, when the Leinstermen depart, Mess Gegra and his charioteer stay behind, camping at Clane on the Liffey. While the charioteer sleeps, Mess Gegra sees a nut as big as a man's head floating on the river and divides it between them; when the charioteer awakes, however, the king claims to have reduced the charioteer's share. The charioteer attacks Mess Gegra, shearing off his arm, but kills himself when he finds his share intact. In this strange tale of two kings' misfortunes, Eochaid, like Odin, gives an eye to a

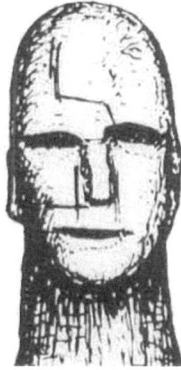

26.6—The head of the Ralaghan figure with a disfigured right eye.

26.7—Three coins of the Bituriges Cubi, showing cranes perched on a horse's back.

poet (associated with hidden knowledge), though here only for a negative reward. Mess Gegra, like Tyr and Mucius, loses his arm because he was untruthful.

There are other instances of missing eyes or arms in early Irish literature, but the pairing of a ruler who gives an eye for magical foresight and one who loses a hand because of his deceitfulness suggests that behind these tales lies an older myth akin to that of Odin and Tyr. There may once have been Irish twin deities, one associated with cosmic knowledge, the other with the maintenance of social order. If the Ralaghan figure, with its puzzling facial asymmetry—which might indicate a blind or altered right eye—is a Bronze Age representation of a one-eyed deity, a precursor of Odin, it is an intriguing possibility that there was once another ancient version of a one-armed divine figure too.

Some years ago the bird specialist Lorcán O'Toole published a study of the Eurasian crane (*Grus grus*) in the *Irish Naturalists' Journal*. These tall, wading birds are famous for their elegant beauty, their elaborate courtship dances and their booming

26.8—A reconstruction of a model crane from Castiglione delle Stiviere.

cry. It is a species that was once very common in Ireland but became extinct in the sixteenth century. O'Toole was struck by the numerous place-names containing the element *corr*, many referring to the crane, indicating its importance in the country in former times. The picture is complicated, however, because *corr* may also mean a rounded hill. Another difficulty is that unambiguous references to cranes in early Irish literature are relatively rare. The allusion to Manannán's mythical crane-bag, the *corrbolg,* is a notable exception. O'Toole confesses that 'it must be stressed that there is currently little in the way of expert acceptance or support for the concept of a Crane Cult in Ireland from any of the leading Irish glossators, historians, linguists, Celtic scholars or archaeologists', but it is worth looking further afield.

The scattered but significant evidence for images of mythological cranes in parts of the Continental Celtic world has now been documented by Venceslas Kruta. As we have seen, these birds are a significant element in the imagery on the *Pilier des Nautes,* for instance, where the divine bull Tarvos Trigaranus is represented with three cranes. These birds also appear on various pottery vessels in Spain, France and the Czech Republic. Cranes and horses figure prominently on some Gaulish coins, notably on some attributed to the Bituriges Cubi, a tribe in central France. Clearly some mythological scene is represented in this puzzling combination of crane, horse and other symbols.

Kruta has also published a most unusual find from Castiglione delle Stiviere, north-west of Mantua in northern Italy. A rich burial was discovered here some time before 1914. The contents were dispersed but some survive. The grave-offerings included five bronze vessels, a pottery cup, two iron knives, and several pieces of decorated sheet bronze that were old when buried and perhaps dated from the third century BC. These pieces bear repoussé ornament and include fragments decorated with La Tène art and a pair of model bird's wings. Kruta tentatively and ingeniously suggests that these disparate elements were once attachments on a model crane that may have stood about 60cm high. Much of the body of this cult object was, he thinks, made of some organic substance such as wood or leather.

Because the crane is represented in so many different ways in very distant parts of the Celtic world, it does seem likely to have played an important role in the mythological bestiary of the Celts in general. Cranes may once have played an important role in Irish myth as well, but were eradicated, like much solar mythology, by scrupulous Christian scribes. Images of this exceptional bird may have been common too, just like effigies of three-horned bulls.

27

Graven images

27.1—The Corleck head.

A ruined 'Giant's Grave' stands on a low hill in Drumeague townland in the parish of Knockbride, south-west of Shercock, Co. Cavan. It is a megalithic tomb of the wedge tomb class and was probably built around 2500 BC. Some stones to the north of the tomb were probably the remains of another monument about which nothing is known. Here in or about 1855 a local farmer, in search of building material for a house in Drumeague, discovered several carved stones. One of these is the famous

Corleck head, named after a nearby hill.

It seems that a passage tomb may once have crowned Corleck Hill. One John O'Reilly told local historian Thomas J. Barron in 1936:

'In around 1836 there existed in the townland of Corleck a stone circle, which was surrounded by a rampart of earth. This all surrounded a great mound of earth in which there was a stone entrance to a collapsed tunnel. As the stones were drawn away the tunnel was discovered to lead into a cruciform shaped chamber. the stones from the mound were used to build a dwelling house nearby, which was named locally as Corleck Ghost house.'

Some of the circle of flagstones had already fallen by 1836, and there was an outlying standing stone some distance away with a hole through it. The earthen part of the mound was levelled in 1900. Apparently, some stones from this monument were also used by that farmer, James Longmore, to build the Drumeague house in the middle of the nineteenth century.

The Corleck–Drumeague area was clearly significant in prehistoric times, and the stone carvings found in the nineteenth century are certainly testimony to its special status as a cult centre in the Iron Age. This may have been the reason for its later importance as a Lughnasa assembly place. Gatherings there on the first Sunday in August in former times involved bilberry-picking, dancing, courtship, games and athletic sports. The coincidence of prehistoric cult site and later Lughnasa assemblies recalls the situation at Taghart Mountain, several kilometres to the east, where the Bronze Age Ralaghan wooden figure was found in an adjacent bog.

The Corleck head is the finest of its kind. Carved from sandstone, it is just 33cm high and has three faces, each consisting of round eyes, a simple mouth and a wedge-shaped nose. One mouth has a small circular hole in its centre—a puzzling feature found in a few other stone heads as far apart geographically as Anglesey and Bohemia. A hole in the base would have held a tenon to secure it to a wooden or stone base. Presumably it was a prominent feature along with other carvings in a shrine of some description.

Though single-faced heads are numerous, a number of other three-faced heads are known in Britain and continental Europe, and most of the insular examples are crudely carved specimens. This form of triplication is also seen as an expression of mystical intensification.

Other carvings found at Drumeague included a two-faced sculpture with a human head on one side and a ram's head on the other. According to Thomas

27.2—The Corraghy head shown attached to a ram's head.

Barron's informant, the ram's head was accidently destroyed around 1865 and the human head was lost until it was rediscovered built into a barn at Corraghy, near Shercock, in 1969. This carving of a man's head is in a fairly naturalistic style very different to the Corleck piece. Based on the hearsay description provided about this find, Barron published a reconstruction of the combined heads as a single carving, showing the human head, that of a bearded male with clearly delineated hair and a long neck, attached to the ram's head by a long stone cross-piece. While depictions of ram's heads, even with human heads, are not uncommon, if accurate this combination in this form is unique. It is probably further testimony to the exceptional importance of the Iron Age cult centre at Drumeague.

There must have been innumerable small ritual sites like this in pre-Christian times, perhaps marked by some wooden or stone carvings. Some of these sacred places may have become the focus for later traditional Lughnasa assemblies; others may have been destroyed by Christian iconoclasts and then forgotten.

This may have been the case at Killycluggin, near Ballyconnell, Co. Cavan. A pillar stone decorated with La Tène ornament once stood on a low hillock some-where in the vicinity of a small stone circle about 20m in diameter. Three pieces of the decorated stone survive; two bear engraved designs and one is an undecorated fragment. The cylindrical body bore several rectangular panels containing curving tendrils and spiral motifs; the domed top was partly ornamented with a segment

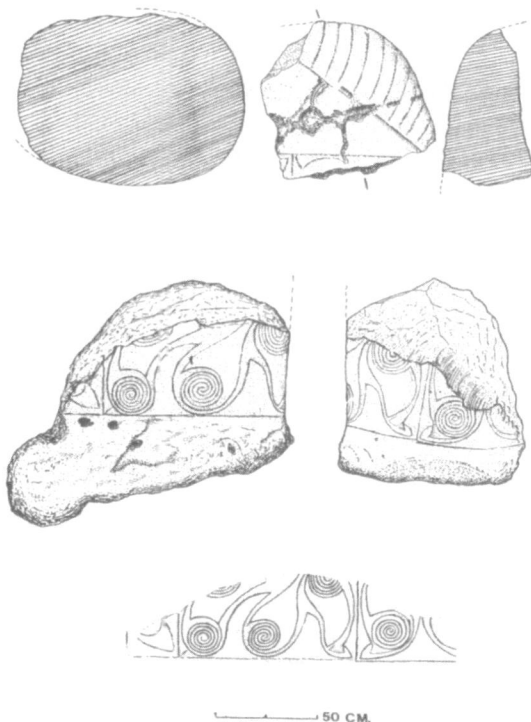

27.3—The Killycluggin stone.

containing parallel lines. The stone had clearly been deliberately broken, the larger piece partly buried and the smaller fragment rolled some distance down the low hill. Some very limited excavation revealed an area of intense burning to the north-west of the pit containing the larger stone and produced no evidence to date the stone circle. Unfortunately, no attempt was made to see whether any other stone fragments had been buried nearby.

A text of the eighth or ninth century records St Patrick's visit to this area of ancient Mag Slécht in County Cavan, where he encountered pagan happenings at a stone circle. Some have thought that this may have been the Killycluggin monument, a thesis difficult—if not impossible—to prove:

'There was a certain idol in the plain of Slecht decorated with gold and silver, and twelve bronze gods were placed here and there around the idol. And the king and all the people worshipped the idol, in which lay hidden the most evil demon who used to give answers to people, on account of

211

which they revered him as a god. But Saint Patrick came as he preached all around to the plain in which the idol was placed, and raising his right hand with the Staff of Jesus which he held in his hand threatened to kill the idol. And the demon who was in the idol, fearing Saint Patrick, turned the stone away to the south and the mark of the staff remains on the north side, and yet the staff did not leave the hand of the saint. Moreover the earth swallowed the twelve other images up to their heads, which alone can be seen as a reminder of the miracle ...'

Elsewhere this idol is described as Crom or Cenn Cróich, who at least from the eighth century onwards was known in the literature as the 'chief-idol' of Ireland. His destruction is portrayed as one of the saint's great achievements in his missionary work. The description of the idols adorned with precious metals is an echo of Old Testament depictions of false gods. Patrick's staff, like the rod of Moses, is both a symbol of authority and an instrument of destruction. Later medieval texts embroider even further the legend of the 'mystic ring' of 'Crom Cruach and his sub-gods twelve', as the poet Samuel Ferguson called them. Though greatly embellished with imaginative details borrowed from biblical sources, the reference to a stone circle is clear and the allusion to the earth swallowing the twelve stones of the circle 'up to their heads' does suggest a prehistoric circle of low boulders. Evidently a monument somewhere in Cavan was still a location of pagan ritual activity in early Christian times.

The fate of Killycluggin has interesting parallels with the story of the Turoe stone. It too had once stood on a low hill beside a circular monument now interpreted as a penannular ring-ditch. This enclosure contained the centrally placed burial of a woman dated to the fifth–sixth century AD and produced traces of ironworking. There were a number of other stones in the vicinity, but the celebrated decorated stone had apparently been dislodged at some time and rolled down to the bottom of the hill. Fortunately it was undamaged, and it was moved from here, as a garden ornament, to the grounds of Turoe House in the middle of the nineteenth century.

Nothing is known about the original location of the Castlestrange stone in County Roscommon, but it may once have been deliberately buried. Some of its upper surface shows signs of weathering, as if this part was once exposed to the elements and the rest shielded in some fashion, perhaps in a pit.

We have no idea when and why these three cult stones were displaced. Even though the Christian writers of the period were well able to accommodate many traditional pagan themes in their writings, some idolatrous expressions of ancient beliefs and practices may have been unwelcome. St Patrick in his *Confessio* alludes to the pagan worship of 'idols and unclean things'. Certain heathen stones may have been deemed more powerful than others and may have attracted destructive attention for this reason. This iconoclastic behaviour could well have happened in medieval times.

Those saints who are said to have overthrown demons may have been engaged in this sort of activity. Tales of the defeat of monstrous creatures may be imaginative and inflated medieval accounts of the eviction of pagan idols. One example is the expulsion of a murderous monster from Scattery Island (Inis Cathaigh) by St Seanán. The terrifying amphibious beast was named Cathach, 'the attacker', and gave its name to the island. It had 'two very hideous, very thick feet' and 'a whale's tail'. The saint banished it to a lake called Dubhloch (Doolough) near Slieve Callan in west Clare.

Another example is to be found in a fourteenth- or fifteenth-century poem that is probably a versified version of a lost life of St Brecán. He is associated with Teampall Bhreacáin, also known as the Seven Churches, on Inis Mór, Aran. He declared that he was originally named Bresal and was the son of Eochaidh, king of the Dál gCais, whose father had been baptised by St Patrick. When he went to Aran he destroyed an idol named Brecán at a place called Iubhar. He took the idol's name and turned a pagan sanctuary into a Christian hermitage. As he declaimed:

'I came to Iubhar and established my settlement, everyone was pleased in turn when I expelled the devils.
Fierce Brecán Cláiringnech was in Iubhar before me, I undertook to expel him and I sanctified his place.
I acted in the matter of Iubhar, a little story that is no harm to read, through the will of God without harshness I expelled the fierce one …'

The exorcism of evil spirits was a widespread practice in the early Church and several saints were noted exorcists, including Lomán of Lough Gill and Usaille of Killashee. The devil is famously depicted as a sinister winged black figure on one of the illuminated pages of the Book of Kells. The image has been stabbed repeatedly with a sharp instrument, and Roger Stalley has suggested that the mutilation of just this figure was a deliberate act that took place during rites of exorcism.

We may never be able to recover the rituals associated with monoliths like Killycluggin and Turoe, but the fact that some of their ornamentation is arranged in discrete panels does suggest that each panel and the designs within them may have offered a sequence of meanings to the participants. Some motifs are difficult to interpret. The meaning of a tightly coiled spiral, as on the Killycluggin stone, is far from clear, for instance, but this motif was important enough to be engraved on a number of bronze sword scabbards in Ulster. Triskeles and birds' heads are perhaps more easily explained: one a rotating solar symbol, the other having otherworldly associations.

The Turoe stone is a challenging monument to try to decipher. Several writers have considered it a phallic symbol, but glacially deposited granite stones of this elongated rounded sort occur naturally in the area. One commentator, in a Joycean turn combining the two possibilities, did describe it as a 'glacial erotic' and the stone may well have been chosen for its suggestive shape. That fertility symbolism is encapsulated in both shape and design is very possible.

This pillar is profusely decorated with superbly executed La Tène designs delimited below by an irregular step pattern. Set in the ground, it stands about 1.2m high, and it may well have been painted originally. At first glance, the curvilinear pattern appears to cover the stone in a seamless fashion, but a detailed analysis has revealed that the decorative scheme constituted four separate and distinct compositions in two broad D-shaped and two narrower triangular panels.

If the participants in the rituals at Turoe performed a circuit of the stone, they would in all likelihood have moved sunwise or *deiseal* around it. Each panel may have had a story to tell, the various motifs or combinations thereof being memory aids in the narrative that had to be told. The continuous step pattern probably had a role in such a sequence because it seems to emphasise two panels in particular. At two points the single step becomes a double step: there is one double step beneath the triangular panel containing a triskele and a bird's head, and three are placed below an adjacent D-shaped panel. It is unlikely that an incompetent carver would have been allowed to mutilate a sacred stone, so it is safe to assume that this variation in the step pattern was intentional.

27.4—The Turoe stone: four panels of curvilinear ornament with a continuous step pattern below.

This D-shaped panel contains an array of three-limbed whirling motifs, curving-sided background voids, leaf motifs and a single roundel. To modern eyes the overall pattern seems incoherent. The opposite panel, in contrast, seems more balanced—at least to us—with a central three-limbed motif, curving tendrils, elegant background voids and a profusion of leaf motifs.

The two triangular panels contain some more recognisable motifs, including roundels, a symmetrical triskele and a bird's head. A swirling mass of tendrils, the triskele and the bird's head dominate one panel that is connected to its opposite number by a sinuous line across the top of the stone. This is the only instance when two panels are visibly coupled, and this link probably represents a chain. The otherworldly associations of aquatic birds are a noteworthy feature of early Irish mythology, and in various tales supernatural birds are linked together by chains of precious metal. To cite just one example: in the story *Compert Conculainn* ('The Birth-tale of Cú Chulainn'), the lands of Emain Macha have been laid waste by a flock of birds, and King Conchobar follows the birds southwards in his chariot, accompanied by the warriors of Ulster. Nine score beautiful birds, each pair linked by a silver chain, lead the hunting party far from the wasteland until they arrive at the place where Cú Chulainn will be born.

The connecting tendril on the summit of the Turoe stone represents a chain linking one world with another. The solar symbol in a roundel on one face and the noticeably empty and sunless roundels on the other may be an allusion to the contrasting daytime and night-time voyages of the sun. Certainly an empty roundel—conspicuously lacking any content—may have had some potent significance, perhaps an illusion to a sunless world.

The larger D-shaped panels are decorated with an extraordinary proliferation of leaf motifs and tendrils. These florid compositions in particular are dominated by one or more asymmetrical swirling three-limbed motifs whose very asymmetry accentuates an appearance of luxurious growth with a clever interplay between background and foreground designs. It is an interesting possibility that this vegetal imagery contains multiple references to the Tree of Life. In La Tène art on the Continent the Tree of Life protected by a pair of creatures might be quite schematically represented. It may even appear as stylised dragon shapes or opposed S-forms on either side of a leaf-like motif, as we saw on that decorated sword scabbard from Bussy-le-Château, where a pair of stylised beasts stand opposed on either side of a single leaf-shaped motif. This one leaf represents the tree as a whole.

We can imagine that a clockwise circumambulation of the Turoe stone might evoke a narrative that included multiple references to the cosmic importance of the Tree of Life as a link between heaven and earth and to the mythical story of the sun's descent into and emergence from the Otherworld. The stone itself may have been imbued with the mystical significance of this sacred tree.

The bird's head is the only motif that approaches a degree of naturalism and must have had a special otherworldly significance. This may be true as well of a stylised bird on a fragment of an Irish bronze horse bit with no recorded provenance. The surviving portion of the bit, which is made of cast bronze, comprises one broken side-link joined by a central link to another complete side-link. The rings for the bridle are missing. A skilful combination of four curving lines cast on the complete end form a stylised human face or mask with pointed oval eyes but no mouth. The other, inner end of each of these links is decorated with a bird's head. The birds too have oval eyes but also have crested heads and recognisable duck-like bills.

Writing of the human mask on this piece, Barry Raftery was of the opinion that

'the Celtic craftsman was less concerned with realism than with subtle suggestion. Thus, a face with no mouth is not in any way unusual. At times the craftsman seems to take deliberate delight in mystifying the beholder, to such an extent, in some cases, that it is uncertain whether a particular combination of curves is really intended to convey the idea of a human face or not. The face becomes a creature of Celtic fantasy and in its treatment we get a hint of the essence of the Celtic spirit: ambiguity, deviousness, subtlety and a predilection for mystery and half-suggestion.'

Such a belief in a unique or exceptional 'Celtic art' has a long and interesting history. In part it harks back to the daft racial theories of the nineteenth century, when the sensitive, imaginative and tremulous Celt was compared to the sturdy

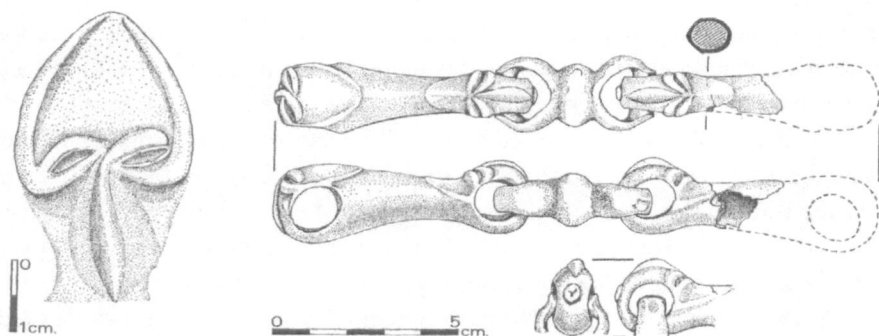

27.5—Part of a bronze horse bit decorated with a human head and birds' heads.

and disciplined Saxon, whose Teutonic respect for rank and blood derived from his noble forefathers in the forests of Germany. Unsurprisingly, in England the popularity of the Germanic myth did not survive the First World War, but Celtophilia and Celtic exceptionalism had a longer life in Ireland. Even if La Tène art does not reflect a particular ethnic essence or some odd playful quality, it is an art style redolent with symbolic significance. To see it merely as inventive decoration would be a great underestimation. It is not at all unreasonable to seek to see meaning in almost every motif. Even a grossly transformed human head spoke to its designer in some way.

Raftery compared the head on the horse bit to some representations on the Continent where a series of leaf-like motifs were combined to produce a 'foliate' image. On a gold disc from Schwarzenbach (Saarland) a nose is represented by a single leaf, with a pair of narrow tendrils forming the head. On a wine flagon from Basse-Yutz in eastern France a series of leaves are combined in an elegant floral composition. Combining elements of plants with human features was a deliberate strategy. It was not without meaning and may have been intended to symbolise fertility and seasonal renewal.

An image of a bird had similar expressive possibilities, though the example on the horse bit is especially puzzling. When the bit was in use it would be quite invisible. Why put a bird in a horse's mouth? As already noted, birds have otherworldly connotations, and perhaps its presence provided the animal with some magical support. On this horse bit it probably had a talismanic quality bringing speed and good luck.

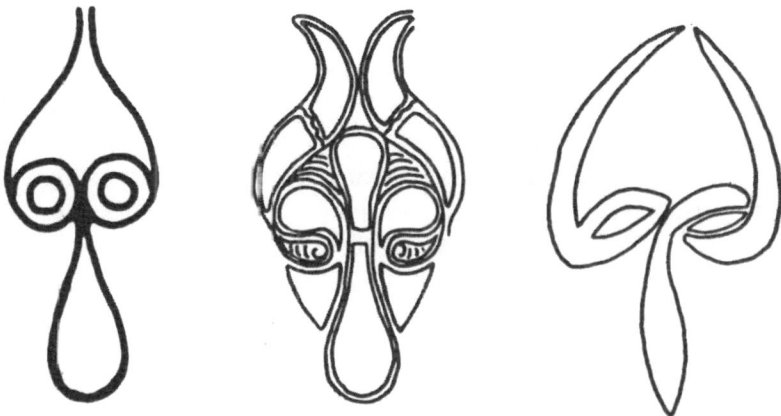

27.6—Stylised human masks: (1) Schwarzenbach gold disc; (2) Basse-Yutz flagon; (3) Irish horse bit.

28

Warriors, wolves and swords

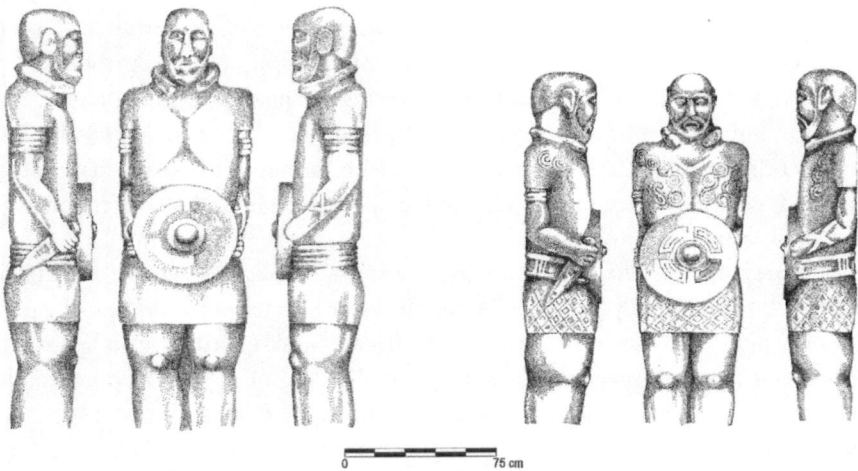

28.1—Two Iron Age warrior statues from Castro de Lezenho, Vila Real, Portugal.

There is a remarkable amount of warrior imagery in Spain and Portugal dating from the Bronze Age and the Iron Age. Stylised depictions of warriors engraved on stone stelae include helmeted figures along with swords, shields, chariots, mirrors, combs, tweezers and razors, brooches, lyres and harps. It is an iconic language that has much to tell us about the equipment and regalia of this élite caste. Some of the earliest depictions of shields are very similar to Irish examples. Later statuary, exemplified by a pair from an Iron Age hillfort at Lezenho, near Vila Real in northern Portugal, are monumental stone figures wearing decorated tunics with belts, and carrying torcs, bracelets and short swords or daggers. They carry round shields and, interestingly enough, some emphasis is given to their knees. They and other statues seem to have once guarded the entrances to hillforts, and the warriors they represented probably used the stone-built saunas in these places for ritual purification or initiation rites.

The emergence of warrior societies is a widespread European phenomenon in later prehistory, and the numerous swords, spears and shields that survive in Ireland give a very warlike appearance to society here from at least the thirteenth century BC. While some exceptionally fine weapons may have been primarily for display, the signs of damage on many swords and shields indicate their use in combat. A mix of prestige weaponry and more ordinary pieces, like leather shields, suggests a warrior society with a hierarchical structure.

Indeed, not everyone would have been entitled to possess a sword; this may have been the privilege of leaders of kin groups or heads of families. Exceptional weapons along with horses and wheeled vehicles may well have been part of the flamboyant equipment of an élite. Beyond that we have very little evidence about their customs and activities. It is probably safe to assume that an exclusive warrior caste had exacting initiation rites to prove personal courage. They may have had various means, in dress or personal ornament, of indicating their special status. Warrior ideology may have included an ethos of bodily perfection and a strong fraternal and martial identity. Their weapons may have been imbued with magical properties and mythical associations. Disputes were perhaps settled by single combat, and war was probably an important social phenomenon. Raiding by war bands may have had a seasonal pattern of spring and autumn campaigns. Much of what has been written about the Fianna is a romanticised version of one sort of pagan institution of this warrior kind.

Geoffrey Keating wrote his *History of Ireland* or *Foras feasa ar Éirinn* around 1630. In this monumental narrative of the deeds of kings and warriors and of clerics and saints, he documented and popularised the great antiquity and the heroic qualities of the Irish story. For him the existence of Finn mac Cumhaill and his warrior band, the Fianna, was a historical fact, and their noble duty was 'to uphold justice, and to prevent injustice, for the kings and lords of Ireland'. He provided a lengthy description of a *fulacht fiadh* or burnt mound. These, he asserted, were the cooking places of the Fianna, who hunted between Bealtaine and Samhain and roasted and boiled their meat at these sites. They also used boiling water for washing and bathing.

This idealistic view of the chivalrous Fianna would persist well into the twentieth century. Lady Augusta Gregory in her popular book *Gods and fighting men* would write of the time of Finn mac Cumhaill: 'the number of the Fianna of Ireland at that time was seven score and ten chief men, every one of them having three times nine fighting men under him. And every man of them was bound to three things, to take no cattle by oppression, not to refuse any man, as to cattle or riches; no one of them to fall back before nine fighting men.' In a preface, William Butler Yeats remarked on the heroism of the Fianna, their pride and joy in one another, and their good fellowship. He saw comparisons with the noble knights of the Arthurian Round Table. In contrast, Flann O'Brien would mock this adulation. He wrote of the initiation rite of an imaginary Fenian youth in *At-Swim-Two-Birds*: 'For five days he must sit on the brow of a cold hill with twelve-pointed stag-antlers hidden in his seat, without food or music or chessmen. If he cry out or eat grass-stalks or desist from the constant recital of sweet poetry and melodious Irish, he is not taken but is wounded …'.

The romantic picture of the Fianna comes from texts of the twelfth century or later, in the literary Fenian Cycle, that tell of their heroic feats, hunting expeditions and great feasts. Many exploits of Finn, his son Oisín and other members of the Fianna are recounted in the lengthy twelfth- or early thirteenth-century tale *Acallam na Senórach* ('Tales of the Elders of Ireland'), for instance, where the few surviving and very old members of the *fían* describe events of the past in a sequence of dialogues with St Patrick. When the saint asked what kept these warriors alive for so many years, he was told that it was 'the truth of our hearts, the strength of our arms, and the constancy of our tongues'.

Romantic as the medieval and later tales may have been, the original *fían* was a very different pagan institution. One of the earliest allusions to this phenomenon occurs in Tírechán's seventh-century life of St Patrick, which refers to the killing of a swineherd by members of a *fían*. There is a ninth-century entry in the Annals of Ulster to 'a large *fían*-band of the sons of death of the Luigni and Gailenga who had been ravaging the *tuatha* in the manner of pagans'. This plundering and marauding activity was known as *díberg* and it is clear that the members of the *fían* and the *díbergaig* were synonymous. In *Togail Bruidne Dá Derga* ('The Destruction of Dá Derga's Hostel'), the story that recounts the life of the ill-fated king of Tara Conaire Mór, the sons of Donn Désa engage in *díberg* and are said to be behaving like wolves in the territory of Connacht. In the eighth-century *Táin Bó Fraích* ('The Cattle Raid of Fraoch'), that great warrior had a company of 50 young men the same age as he and like him in form and appearance. The quintessential warrior Cú Chulainn once had a following of 150 youths.

The size of a *fían* might vary greatly. Another king of Tara, Cormac mac Airt, says of his days as a *fían*-warrior: 'I would slay a boar, I would follow a track when I was alone; I would march against a band of five when I was one of five; I was prone to ravage when I was one of ten; I was prone to raid when I was one of twenty; I was ready for battle when I was one of a hundred. Those were my deeds.' The reference in the Annals of Ulster shows that such activity was still a social reality as late as the mid-ninth century and, unsurprisingly, these bands of roving warriors, 'sons of death and perdition', were frequently condemned by the Church. They are said to have had *signa diabolica* or devilish marks on their heads—perhaps a particular hairstyle or form of headgear.

It is not surprising either that they are often associated with hounds and wolves. One Laignech Fáelad is described as a man who used to go wolfing, and he and his offspring used to kill the herds after the fashion of wolves. Another individual, the warrior son of Dub Dá Roth, is called 'a wolf of vagrancy'. Names with the *Cú* element, 'hound', are common too, but *Cú*, of course, might be a metaphor for 'wolf'.

These references indicate that a *fían* in early medieval Ireland was mainly composed of young, unmarried, landless men cut off from their kin, who practised a roving lifestyle devoted to hunting, raiding, plunder, sexual licence and occasionally murder. This negative picture may have been coloured to some extent by clerical distaste for a pagan institution. For some young men this was a passing phase that lasted until they acquired the necessary property to become a member of their *tuath* with legal rights; for others integration into settled society may not have been possible.

This was an ancient social institution in the Indo-European world, where wild wolfish youths formed vagabond societies in various parts of Europe and elsewhere. This form of all-male society or *Männerbund* was a widespread phenomenon manifesting itself in diverse ways in various times and places, from war bands like the *comitatus* of the ancient Germans to the *Galates*, who were wild young Gaulish warriors sometimes sent away from home. Animal imagery, initiation rites, special insignia and beliefs, exclusivity and misogyny were probably among the characteristic features of such groups.

The wolfish connotations of the *fían* may be reflected in names like Cunomaglos, and this is one interpretation of a name in a Roman inscription from Nettleton Shrub in Wiltshire. The dedication, to one Apollo Cunomaglos, is considered to be to a Celtic deity identified with Apollo and is often read as 'hound prince'. 'Wolf lord', however, is a possibility and, just as the Greek Apollo was also known as a wolfish Apollo Lykaios, the existence of an insular deity with wolfish attributes is conceivable.

The early existence of such groups was not a figment of the imagination of students of Indo-European mythology. In fact, it would now seem to be confirmed by archaeological evidence and studies of ancient DNA. Major migrations took place from the steppes of southern Russia, between the northern shores of the Black Sea and the Caspian Sea, into central and northern Europe between 3000 and 2500 BC. The resulting population, a mix of steppe immigrants and local late Neolithic farmers, was directly ancestral to most modern Europeans and, it is believed, to their languages. This migratory process was led by a dominant élite and probably included male war bands.

Evidence for animal rites associated with just that sort of social group comes from a small settlement at Krasnosamarskoe, on the Samara River in southern Russia, dated to 1900–1700 BC. Excavation there produced a large quantity of dog and wolf bones cut in unusual ways that did not resemble ordinary butchering practices. Skulls, for instance, were broken into small, geometrically shaped fragments. The animals were ritually killed and their age at death suggests a seasonal ritual. Charring on the bones indicates that they were filleted and cooked. This has been interpreted as a repeated rite of passage for males in which they became dogs and wolves through the consumption of dog and wolf flesh.

Such a warrior initiation rite is probably depicted on one of the panels of the Gundestrup cauldron. This was found in a Jutland bog in 1891 and is dated to around 100 BC. It is of Celtic and Thracian inspiration and its fourteen plates are decorated with a range of mythological images that have been the subject of extensive commentary. The scene in question represents a procession of armed warriors approaching a giant figure on the left of the panel who is suspending a smaller figure over a vat or tub. While the large standing figure is assumed to be a deity, the panel as a whole has been interpreted in various ways: as a sacrificial ceremony involving the immersion of an individual in a vessel in an act of ritual drowning or, if the individual is being raised, a representation of the resurrection of a warrior from the dead. The scene has also been described as depicting an army on the march or a warrior initiation rite in which the lower group of individuals is transformed after immersion into mounted warriors, a leafy tree being a symbol of regeneration.

28.2—The warrior initiation scene on the Gundestrup cauldron.

A complex narrative is presented here, and an initiation scene is a very likely explanation. In the lower register, a line of six warriors with spear and shield process to the left towards the giant officiating figure who is immersing one of their group in a vat. They are followed by a sword- or wand-bearing figure and three trumpet-players. They also confront a rampant wolf-like creature and appear to support the horizontal tree on their spearheads. Above the tree, four mounted figures with different helmets ride to the right and are preceded by a serpent. The lower warriors are on foot, and this may be an allusion to their landless class and the fact that they cannot keep horses. In contrast, the mounted warriors, after initiation, are now adult members of the tribe.

The wolf is a significant motif and links these warriors to such youthful war bands as the Irish *fían*. On the cauldron they are about to be transformed into members of normal society, the tree marking the transition from the wild to the domesticated. The giant figure might well be a 'Lord of the Wolves'.

Traces of warrior initiation rites are to be found in early Irish literature. The legendary associations of Oweynagat in Rathcroghan are a remarkable testimony to its ancient importance. It is an interesting possibility that some of these legends may provide a clue to some of the uses to which the cave was once put. Various legendary heroic warriors such as Fraoch, Cú Chulainn, Conall and Lóegaire are linked to the site. The tale of the monstrous triple-headed Ellen killed in single combat by Amairgene may imply that the cave was once the location of initiation rituals. A hero's combat with a triple-headed monster was probably a transformation into myth of an ancient warrior initiation rite that involved a mock combat with a three-headed wooden image. It is probably relevant that the cave has wolfish associations too: a certain Olc Aí is an Otherworld figure whose name, Olc, has dog or wolf connotations, and three hounds or werewolves are among the malevolent creatures that emerge from this cave to molest wethers and sheep in the surrounding countryside. Rites of terror and the subterranean testing of young warriors may lie behind some of these stories.

It seems likely that roving groups of juvenile males, living on the margins of settled society, were a feature of prehistoric times in Ireland. These young warriors could have identified themselves with hounds or wolves, worshipped a wolf-like deity, practised initiation ceremonies and other rituals, engaged in hunting and cattle-raiding, had dietary taboos and sported special insignia and clothing. To become animal-like they may have had to undergo psychological trials of isolation, torment and privation.

The advent of radiocarbon dating demonstrated once and for all that the burnt mounds or *fulachta fiadh* were prehistoric monuments with no connection with the early medieval Fianna, as Keating once imagined. Nevertheless, given the Indo-European dimension of this male brotherhood, it is very possible that they were a social institution in Bronze Age Ireland. It is worth considering the possibility, too, that some burnt mounds may indeed have been cult places where bands of youthful warriors ceremonially bathed themselves as part of their initiation rituals.

While spear and axe were important weapons at various times in the past, the sword in particular became the authoritative weapon in the European Bronze Age, and its importance persisted for millennia thereafter. In medieval times it was the weapon of choice and, aside from its important role in combat, it was also the symbol of the free-born man and the knight, and an emblem of chivalry. Its use in many military and civic ceremonies today is a reminder of its former importance. Some swords were symbols of royalty. The Irish annals record that in AD 995 'the sword of Carlus' was forcibly taken by Máel Sechnaill, king of Tara, from the Viking settlement of Dublin, and 30 years later this prestigious object was part of a king's ransom for Sitric Silkenbeard, king of Dublin, who had been captured by Mathgamain ua Riacáin of the southern Uí Néill. This enormous pay-off included the royal sword, 1,200 cows, six score Welsh horses and 60 ounces of gold. The last we hear of this symbol of the kingship of Dublin is in 1058, when it was seized by Diarmait mac Máel na mBó, king of Leinster.

There are, of course, many legendary swords with kingly and warrior associations, of which Arthur's Excalibur is certainly the most famous. The best-known special sword in early Irish tradition is the Caladbolg—the hard sword—wielded by the Ulster king Fergus mac Léti, who employed it in a victorious fight with a sea monster in Dundrum Bay. After his death, Fergus mac Róich became the owner of the sword and in a moment of frenzied landscape redevelopment used this powerful weapon to cut off the tops of three hills in the county of Meath.

In both prehistoric and historic times most swords were undoubtedly valuable items and may have been especially prized gifts. In all probability they were the possessions of persons of elevated status, were closely linked with masculine values and were symbols of male authority. Some special swords may have been considered almost as living objects with their own names and life histories. Over 170 named swords are mentioned in Old Norse literature alone. Such swords may have been handed down from generation to generation, acquiring significance as markers of kinship bonds and rights of inheritance.

Identifying exceptional swords is obviously not an easy task. A singular quality might be a quite intangible trait, though context, such as a richly furnished burial, or biographical details such as frequent and expert repairs may provide some clues from time to time. Finely decorated scabbards may be another indication of a

28.3—Aubrey Beardsley's depiction of Bedivere's return of Excalibur to the lake from which it came, in a nineteenth-century edition of Thomas Malory's *Morte d'Arthur*.

sword's special status. Several such scabbards are known in Ireland and four in particular are amongst the finest examples of Irish La Tène art. These decorated scabbards contained swords that were exceptional weapons, reflecting the role and status of their owners. The art of these scabbards has inspired considerable comment and discussion, much of it concerned with stylistic affinities, origins and chronology. Though each one is different, they have some features in common, including overall ornament and designs that are based on sequences of S-scrolls and spirals.

Various writers have emphasised the aesthetic qualities of this scabbard art, and the minute detail of some of this decoration may mean that the designs had a very personal significance, perhaps to be seen by a select few. As on other metalwork, some motifs had a symbolic significance. The loosely delineated S-shaped scrolls with their bifurcating finials on one from Lisnacrogher, Co. Antrim, have been compared to the so-called dragon-pair motif (two opposed stylised creatures). This

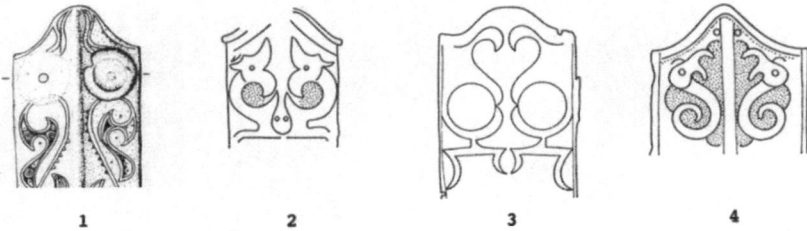

28.4—Part of a decorated scabbard from Lisnacrogher, Co. Antrim, with opposed S-shaped scrolls (1). Dragon pairs—as illustrated in Fig. 21.5—on sword scabbards from Münsingen (2) and La Tène, Switzerland (3), and Taliándörögd, Hungary (4).

is a variation on the design of paired beasts associated with the Tree of Life and is a warrior emblem known on a sword scabbard in Britain and found on scabbards across the Continent from France to Romania.

It was a mark of distinction and may have been a symbol of rank and achievement in battle. According to Ruth and Vincent Megaw, it most probably had the intention of warding off harm, and the protection of fierce and exotic beasts might well have had a particular value. There may have been great Celtic hero-tales associated with the dragon pair which have been lost to us. They may have been similar to the tale of that warrior combat with a triple-headed monster associated with Oweynagat. The tiny opposed pair of sinuous S-shaped motifs at the top of the Lisnacrogher scabbard may also be an attenuated echo of this dragon pair, and the suite of motifs on the rest of this piece may be an extended variation on the same theme, repetition giving added emphasis to its symbolic charge.

The other Irish scabbards are decorated with designs essentially composed of a descending running wave of S-scrolls with a clear tendril or vegetal element that is probably related to Tree of Life imagery. The idea that swords might speak of their famous deeds is a widespread one and figures in early Irish literature. Some scabbard decoration might conceivably have been a mnemonic scheme for those who prized them and wished to remember and recount their prowess. Maybe these swords were named and belonged to exceptional individuals, even adherents of a heroic cult.

There are a number of references to oracular swords in early Irish literature. In *Serglige Con Culainn* ('The Wasting Sickness of Cú Chulainn') we are told that '... they had their swords upon their thighs when they were boasting; for their swords would turn against them when they made a false boast. That is plausible; for demons used to speak to them from their weapons ...'. In *Cath Maige Tuired* ('The Second

Battle of Mag Tuired'), 'Ogma drew the sword and cleaned it. Then the sword related everything which had been done with it, for it was usual for swords in those days, when they were drawn, to reveal the deeds which were done with them.'

One unusual medieval custom can probably be seen as an indication of the quasi-magical properties of certain weapons at this time. Conor Newman has studied sword marks on a diverse group of special stone monuments. A cross-inscribed pillar stone at Kilnasaggart, Co. Armagh, has some 55 narrow grooves incised near the base on its northern side. These were apparently executed by the repeated to-and-fro movement of a sword blade.

The Mullaghmast stone is a fragmentary decorated pillar now in the National Museum of Ireland. Its finely carved curvilinear motifs, including that solar triskele already mentioned, are found on sixth-century AD metalwork. Deep grooves, clearly later than some of the ornament, occur on several faces and again appear to be marks created by repeatedly moving part of an iron blade to and fro in these narrow V-sectioned channels. There are also some areas of burnishing or polishing

28.5—The Kilnasaggart stone, dating from the eighth century AD: the blade marks (inset) are on the lower left.

on the stone resulting from more orthodox blade-sharpening, with a blade being honed with a lateral motion. Mullaghmast was the royal seat of the Uí Muiredaig and, as Newman suggests, this stone and the sword rituals associated with it may have been part of inauguration ceremonies there. Such sword marks also occur on a stone at Finlaggan on Islay in the Southern Hebrides, the centre of the MacDonald lordship of the Isles.

Along with Finlaggan, Newman has identified a whole series of other special or unusual stones in Ireland and Britain that have also received this puzzling treatment. For example, a memorial slab with an early Latin inscription from Penmachno, Gwynedd, north Wales, has several deep grooves near its base. A reused memorial slab from Roman Wroxeter in Shropshire with a fifth-century inscription in Latinised primitive Irish, which includes the name Cunorix ('Hound King'), has one deep blade groove. Other significant stones bearing blade grooves include several ogham stones and high crosses. Over 30 blade marks are to be seen on the base of the ninth-century high cross known as the Market Cross at Kells, Co. Meath.

These and other iconic stones were deliberately selected for this treatment. While the polished areas, where they occur, are probably due to a normal lateral sharpening action, the grooves, used in a to-and-fro fashion, might sharpen the tip of a blade but would tend to blunt its edge. As Newman states, 'the ostensibly contradictory actions that produced respectively the blade grooves and the burnished surfaces are reconcilable when visualised through the prism of ritual and ceremony'. This was a symbolically and ideologically charged rite in which the polished stone bestowed sharpness and potency on a sword while the grooves that blunted its edge symbolised the return of its potency to the stone.

This symbiotic relationship between a sacral stone and a warrior's weapon, and the ritual act of drawing a blade across a stone, are probably two of a number of influences behind the celebrated Arthurian motif of the 'sword in the stone'. This is the story of the youthful Arthur who was able to extract the sword Excalibur that had been embedded in a stone to demonstrate that he was the legitimate king. Though not found in the early Welsh literature on Arthur, it does appear in Arthurian tales of the thirteenth century and later and has been called one of the most famous episodes in medieval European romance.

Of course, there is an obvious difference between drawing a sword across a stone and pulling one out of a stone, but the latter action has been traced back to the steppes of southern Russia, where the Alans, a Sarmatian people, had a custom of plunging a naked sword, a symbol of sovereignty, into the earth—and then extracting it. Some of these folk found themselves in Roman legions and some settled in various places in the west, their name surviving in place-names such as Alençon in France and Alano in Spain. Their sword cult may have contributed an element to the Arthur story. There may be no single explanation for the tale of the 'sword in the stone' but Newman has identified one piece of archaeological evidence that very probably contributed to its genesis. In any event, it was a ritual action that imbued a sword with some distinctive meaning.

In any consideration of warriors and weaponry it is easy to overlook the probability that 'war magic' was an important aspect of prehistoric combat. The role of ritual practitioners in warfare is documented in various ethnographic sources. Bronislaw Malinowski recorded it in the Trobriand Islands, where it was considered an indispensable part of battle. Each community had a family of experts in war magic whose members handed down the sacred formulae from generation to generation. These included chants to be made over the shields to give them the power of warding off all spears. Other chanting over the fighting men aimed to make them strong, enduring and fierce.

The ancient Chamorro people on the Pacific Mariana Islands took ancestral skulls into warfare against the Spanish in the period of the Spanish conquest in the seventeenth century. In 1671, 2,000 Chamorros armed with slings attacked 31 Spanish soldiers stationed in a church and dug earthworks to defend themselves against the assaults of the better-armed Spaniards. They sought the protection of their ancestors and deployed their skulls in their trenches, but the trenches were overrun by the Spaniards and the skulls taken and destroyed. The Chamorros then accepted that defeat was inevitable, since the protective power and assistance of their ancestors was no more. Needless to say, this sort of activity would leave no archaeological trace.

Presumably ritualists were a feature of prehistoric warfare in Ireland. Certainly the custom of carrying relics into battle was a standard practice in medieval times. The best-known battle talisman is the Cathach of St Columba, held by the O'Donnells of Donegal. 'Cathach' means 'Battler' and it was said to have been carried right-handwise or *deiseal* three times around the armies of the Cenél Conaill to bring them victory. This is a book of psalms, now in the Royal Irish Academy, which may date from the sixth century and which was enshrined in a later reliquary around the year 1000.

There are a few references to druids and warfare in early Irish literature. The druid Mug Ruith's exploits in the 'Siege of Druimm Damgaire' in defending a Munster king against an unjust attack by Cormac mac Airt, king of Tara, is one example. His magic included the creation of a well to provide water, the generation of a black mist with his breath and, dressed in his shaman-like druidic costume of bull hide with bird mask, the production of a fire-storm to force the retreat of Cormac's warriors. The Annals of Ulster record the creation of a druidic fence (*erbe ndruad*) that killed anyone who jumped over it during the Battle of Cúil Dremne (AD 561).

Trophy-taking was probably just as common but is equally hard to identify. Sword, spear or shield are mute witnesses to this sort of practice, and even skulls and bones might only rarely survive. Indeed, the Bible reminds us just how elusive the evidence for trophy-taking might be. It is claimed that David brought 200 fore-skins as trophies to King Saul after he slew 200 Philistine soldiers (1 Samuel 18:27). What happened to these prizes is not recorded.

29

The old gods

29.1—The Tandragee idol, now in St Patrick's Cathedral, Armagh.

The Tandragee idol is one of a group of stone carvings found in the Armagh region. It is a ferocious-looking figure with cap or helmet, with vestigial horns, and with arms in a ritual pose. It has generally been considered a representation of a pagan god. The posture of the arms can be paralleled on Continental images of Iron Age date. Anne Ross saw this figure as a proof of the cult of a horned god in Ireland, an insular version of the deity called Cernunnos depicted on the *Pilier des Nautes*. The open mouth and heavy lips are replicated on a crudely carved stone head with ram's horns around its ears from Netherby, north of Carlisle, perhaps of Roman date. Helen Lanigan Wood thought that it might be a representation of Nuadu, that king of the Tuatha Dé Danann who had his arm severed and who was given a silver arm, enabling him to return to power. She suggests that the sculpture depicts the mythical king wearing his horned helmet and triumphantly displaying his new arm for all to see.

When he left Ireland around 590, Columbanus is said to have claimed that the island was a Christian country. This was probably wishful thinking and quite far from the truth. In the early ninth century the author of the Martyrology of Óengus rejoiced in the triumph of Christianity and contrasted the flourishing Christian sites with the pagan centres, which he claims were deserted:

'The great settlement of Tara has died with the loss of its princes;
great Armagh lives on with its choirs of scholars ...

29.2—Stone carving of a solar deity from the Armagh area.

The fort of Emain Macha has melted away, all but its stones;
thronged Glendalough is the sanctuary of the western world …'

This was pious propaganda. In fact, there was a long and complex overlap between the old religions and the new Christian faith in medieval Ireland, one that extended well beyond the ninth century. The old gods had not gone away, and some may still have been worshipped in the Armagh region, where various carvings of uncertain date suggest a former cult centre.

One carving in particular from the Armagh area is identifiable as a solar deity. It is a fairly crude representation of a standing figure, about 65cm high, with out-turned feet. The head, with simple circular eyes, wedge-shaped nose and simple mouth, is surrounded by radiating lines. This motif was probably inspired by late provincial Roman representations of a solar deity in Britain. Given the evidence on Iron Age metalwork for an indigenous and ancient preoccupation with solar matters, as on the Petrie Crown, to find an image of a sun god inspired by Roman iconography somewhere around Armagh is unsurprising.

British examples include a small bronze figure of the sun god Sol found near a temple or shrine at Osbournby, Lincolnshire. Another version of this radiant figure is depicted on a small bronze roundel found near a Roman temple at Lydney Park, Gloucestershire. An intriguing image comes from a shrine near the Roman fort at

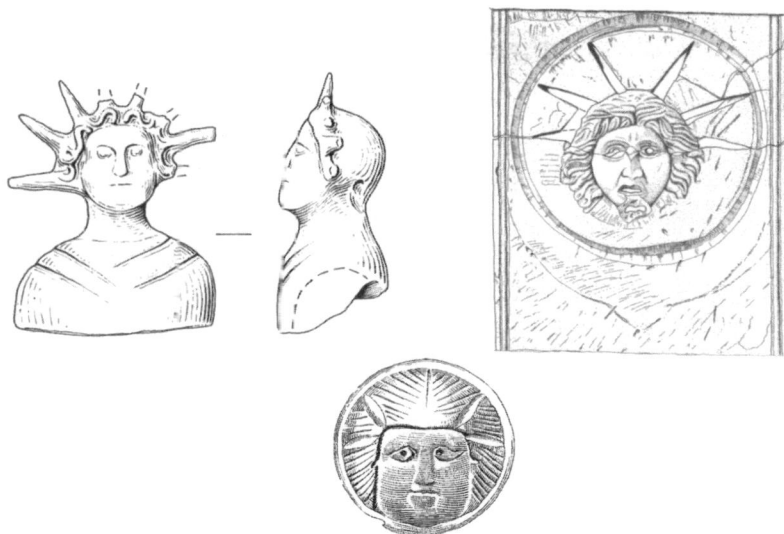

29.3—Above left: small bronze figure of Sol from Osbournby, Lincolnshire. Above right: image of Sol on an altar at Inveresk, Scotland. Below: bronze roundel from Lydney Park, Gloucestershire, bearing the image of the solar deity. Various scales.

Inveresk, just east of Edinburgh. It contained two stone altars, one dedicated to Mithras, the other to Sol. The latter is decorated with a large image of the solar deity almost 40cm across. The six rays springing from his head are openwork and, along with perforated eyes and mouth, would have allowed light from the flames of a lamp set in the back of the pillar to shine through the carving. This would have been a dramatic depiction of the sun god in Scotland in the mid-second century AD, and sound as well as light may have been part of the rituals there.

The absence of unambiguous traces of a sun god in early Irish literature is not surprising. Such a major figure would certainly have attracted the attention of scrupulous Christian censors. The Celtic scholar Proinsias Mac Cana admitted that this was very likely to have been the case:

'Anthropologists have shown that Christian missionaries elsewhere have tended to concentrate their fire on ritual and certain other areas of belief which conflicted with central tenets of Christianity while at the same time tolerating the continuance of less crucial areas of popular indigenous religion … It is hardly surprising therefore that Irish monastic redactors, for all their inherited empathy with native tradition in general, did not choose to record substantive accounts of native cosmology and eschatology, though it should be said that there are indeed many scattered fragments that point to the existence of such mythologies in pre-Christian oral literature.'

Nonetheless, it is still possible to outline some of the more important figures in the pagan pantheon. A host of supernatural personages are to be found in early myth and legend, and many—if not most—of these are refracted pagan figures of some importance. It is very likely that the myths recorded in these medieval texts were not just stories confined to vellum but were still part of a lived religion.

Some were clearly major figures, like the divinities of the Tuatha Dé, the people of the gods. Some were minor gods or goddesses; others were Otherworldly beings of different sorts. The Dagda was one of the principal deities. He was known as Eochaid Ollathair or 'great father', like the Norse god Odin, who also bore this appellation. He and his son Óengus were associated with Brugh na Bóinne (Newgrange). The great god Lugh was linked to Tailtiu (Teltown, Co. Meath) and is prominent in various tales concerning the kingship of Tara. He is depicted as an able warrior 'of the long arm' and as a person of many accomplishments. He was worshipped in various parts of the Celtic world, his name surviving in place-names such as Lugdunum (modern Lyon) and Luguvalium (Carlisle).

Ogma, said to have invented ogham writing, has been equated with the Gaulish Ogmios, and both are associated with eloquence and the magical power of words. Nuadu is the equivalent of the Celtic god Nodons, who was venerated at various temple sites in England, including Lydney Park. There he seems to have been associated with fishing, hunting and healing around the third century AD. Goibniu, a god of smithing, had a counterpart in Gofannon in Wales and Gobannos in Gaul. Manannán was a god of the sea, and he too had a close, though not exact, counterpart across the Irish Sea in the Welsh Manawydan.

Donn, 'the dark one', a god of the dead, is associated with Tech Duinn. This, 'the house of Donn', is said to be the Bull Rock, near Dursey Island, Co. Cork. Little survives of his mythology. He was one of the sons of Míl and upon his death his brother, the poet Amairgen, declared that his people would forever travel to this his last resting-place. A ninth-century poet, Máel Muire of Othan, wrote how Donn himself established the realm of the dead for all his children: 'A stone cairn was raised across the broad sea for his people. A long-standing ancient house which is named the House of Donn after him. And this was his mighty testament for his hundredfold offspring: "You shall all come to me, to my house, after your death".' Here he appears as a divine ancestor who bids his descendants, the people of Ireland, to all come to his home. He was the Irish equivalent of figures such as the Gaulish god who was called Dis Pater by Julius Caesar and whose Celtic name is

29.4—The 'house of Donn', Bull Rock, near Dursey Island, Co. Cork.

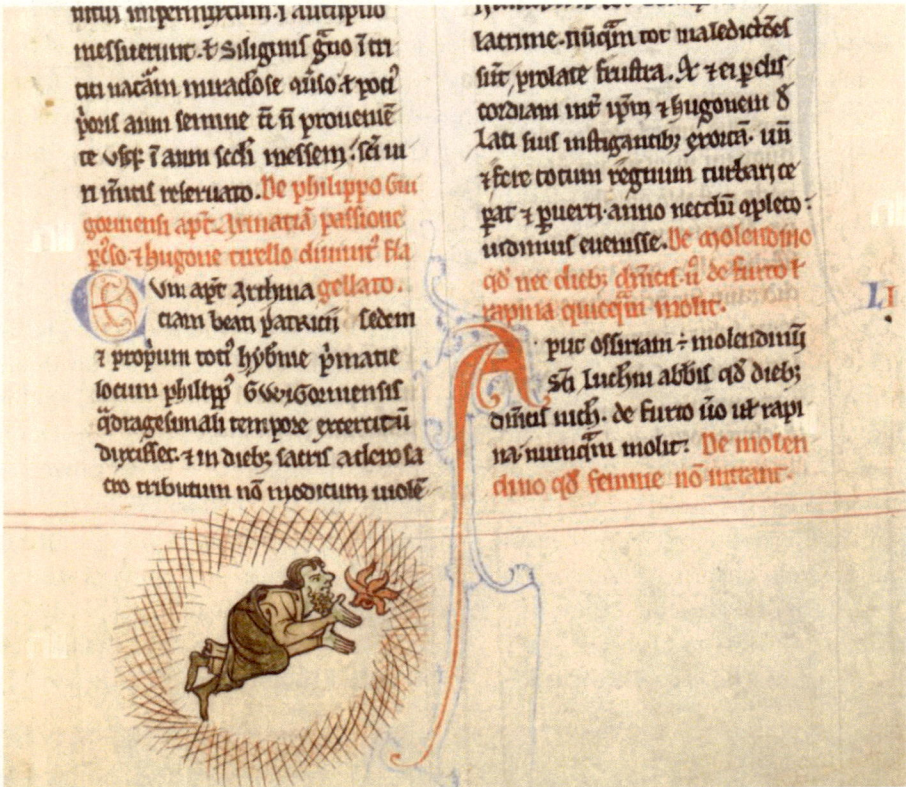

29.5—A marginal illustration on a page from the twelfth-century *Topography of Ireland* by Gerald of Wales, depicting an imprudent Anglo-Norman blowing on St Brigid's sacred fire. He went mad, running through the houses in the town, blowing on any fire he saw. When caught by his companions, he drank so much water that 'he burst in the middle and died'.

unknown. He has even more distant parallels in the Indo-European world in the god Yama in ancient India.

There were a number of major female deities too. Bríg or Brigid was a divinity who inspired the cult of the saint of that name in Kildare. In contrast to the Christian figure, little is known about the pagan goddess. Writing in the twelfth century, Gerald of Wales recounted a tale of a perpetual fire maintained at St Brigid's sanctuary in Kildare, and many writers have assumed this to be a survival from pagan times. This miraculous fire was said to have been kept alive by nineteen servants of the Lord in a circular enclosure surrounded by a fence of withies. Even though it was carefully fuelled over the years, the ash it produced never increased. No man might enter its precincts, and Gerald tells the story of an Anglo-Norman archer who entered the enclosure and blew on the sacred fire and immediately went mad.

Another put one leg in and the limb perished; while he lived, he was lame and became an imbecile.

In all probability Gerald was recording a memory of an ancient rite in which a sacred fire was maintained by a group of women who were originally devotees of the pagan deity. She and the later saint share an association with fire in various guises. The goddess is said to have been a daughter of the Dagda. Her name is found in Britain as the tribal divinity of the Brigantes—'the exalted one'. Her association with a perpetual fire in Kildare is one attribute that has prompted comparisons with the Gaulish goddess Minerva, who had a famous sanctuary in Britain at Bath. The Roman writer Caius Julius Solinus remarked that her temple fire produced no ash but turned into 'rocky lumps', a reference to the coal that was burnt there. This paucity of ash is a significant correspondence, recalling the puzzling ash at Kildare. It is also noteworthy that St Brigit's feast-day, 1 February, coincides with the pagan feast of Imbolc.

At some time the site of the fire in Kildare was enclosed in a stone structure. One visitor around 1580, following in the footsteps of Gerald, reported: 'I travelled of set purpose to the town of Kildare to see this place, where I did see such a monument like a vault, which to this day they call the Firehouse'. This vault-like monument has not survived.

The Morrígan is one manifestation of a war goddess who had other names as well. A harbinger of death, she also influenced the course of battle and sometimes appeared in the guise of a crow. In Britain a deity named Andraste may have been one of her Celtic counterparts. According to the Roman historian Dio Cassius, she was a war goddess of the Iceni who was invoked by Boudica in her battle against the Romans. The name Morrígan may mean 'great queen' and it has been suggested that she was a multi-aspect deity and that war was not her only concern. She is occasionally associated with cattle and with some places in the landscape that are designated as her property or as locations she frequented. These associations with the earth and with animals may indicate that she had some of the qualities of a goddess who offered protection to the land.

There are allusions in early literature to mythical female figures who are the personification of the land and who have a role in the affirmation of sacral kings. The most prominent of these sovereignty goddesses were associated with the major cult sites of Tara, Navan and Rathcroghan: Medb Lethderg, Macha and Medb of Crúachain respectively. At these great ceremonial centres the goddess, intimately linked to the institution of sacral kingship, would preside over various rituals of kingly inauguration.

There are quite a few lesser-known supernatural female figures who may, in some instances, have been territorial goddesses too—for instance, Mór Muman of

Munster, who was 'sought after by the kings of Ireland', and Áine of Knockainy, Co. Limerick, who is associated with a hill bearing significant burial mounds and other monuments.

It has been argued that much of Ireland's medieval literature, a rich heritage of saga, legal and genealogical writing, was the product of a monastic milieu that presented a version of a past which was profoundly transformed—if not actually created—by Christian writers. Today no one would deny that many early tales were sophisticated literary compositions frequently influenced by biblical or classical models, but there is also no doubt that they display a deliberate engagement with pagan personages, beliefs and customs.

Figures like Medb, associated with Rathcroghan, and Macha, associated with Emain Macha, who have long been held to be pagan sovereignty goddesses in origin, have been re-evaluated. In the case of Medb, the limited nature of her mythical

29.6—Medb of Crúachain: an imaginative depiction of Maeve, the warrior queen, by the American illustrator J.C. Leyendecker. It was commissioned for a 1907 article on the ancient Irish sagas in *The Century Magazine* written by Theodore Roosevelt, president of the United States. He, like many others at the time, believed that Maeve was a historical figure.

qualities, found mainly in later texts, has been emphasised and her role as an ancient goddess questioned. As for Macha, her several manifestations have been deemed to be either late scholastic inventions or simply representations of an ancient war goddess. Notwithstanding these objections, often born of a narrow disciplinary focus, for an archaeologist faced with the exceptional evidence for protracted pagan ritual activity at Emain Macha and Rathcroghan over many centuries, if not thousands of years, an obvious question to ask is what was the purpose of all of this and to what supernatural entity was this activity addressed?

The fact that these female figures with their specific supernatural qualities were intimately linked to great ceremonial centres is a telling one and cannot be ignored. Their diminished status in medieval literature has certainly something to tell us about the objectives of Christian writers who, however, had no qualms about including tantalising scraps of pagan material when it suited their purpose. There is an interesting parallel here with the actions of the forerunners of these Irish scribes who wrote the Christian gospels and who also were content to include fragments of older eastern mythic themes such as virgin birth, divine child and slain god in the creation of a new and powerful story.

Following (after a fashion) the sort of literary excavation employed by Jim Mallory in his important book *In search of the Irish dreamtime*, it is possible to identify various strata in the depiction of the character of Medb of Crúachain. Embedded in medieval texts, their careful excavation and possible time-depth have something to tell us about both the medieval mind and the more distant past. One example of a late medieval element in Medb's story is the famous pillow-talk in Rathcroghan with her husband Ailill that begins the epic in the second recension of the *Táin Bó Cuailnge*. Here the author demonstrates a knowledge of early law regarding women and early twelfth-century concerns about female succession.

A description of Medb's grandiose palace at Rathcroghan in another tale takes us to another and somewhat older level. This and a similar description of the royal house at Emain Macha probably drew on many sources, including Classical accounts of great buildings and contemporary descriptions of Carolingian royal apartments. Christian writers had their own agendas in this creation of a heroic past for their medieval audience, a past peopled by intrepid warriors and illustrious kings who lived in splendidly decorated dwellings. At the same time as inventing epic stories, they were anxious to obscure the potent symbolism at these places linked to pagan rites of kingship.

Motifs in older strata probably stem from pagan Iron Age times and allude to aspects of these kingship ceremonies. Medb's name, generally thought to be related to the word 'mead', is an indication that she was originally a goddess with an Indo-

European dimension who—representing the sovereignty of the land—bestowed a drink on the man who would be king in an acknowledgement of his right to rule. Her name may have had the added attraction of ambiguity because, while the association with drink and mead (*medhw-o-) is generally acknowledged, there may also be an allusion to one who rules or commands (*med-wo-). Her multiplicity of husbands is believed to be an echo of the numerous sacred kings who symbolically wed the sovereignty goddess. Her aggressive sexuality is also a characteristic of other female goddesses, including Aphrodite, Venus and the Nordic Freyja. Clerical writers would be happy to emphasise Medb's apparent promiscuity, of course, because it offered a good illustration of pagan bad behaviour.

Those historians who boldly assert that figures like Medb were literary inventions in early medieval times forget that many literary figures have a basis in fact. Presumably, if the writings of Plutarch, Cicero and numerous early commentators, along with portraits and statues of the last queen of the Ptolemies, had not survived, these same writers would claim that Shakespeare's Cleopatra was no more than a literary fiction. The Medb of ancient myth was not a scholarly fabrication. In pagan minds she had a real presence.

We know next to nothing of the rituals associated with the pagan Irish pantheon. Some of these supernatural figures were probably invoked on great ceremonial occasions at major cult sites: Lugh at Teltown and the Dagda and his son Óengus at Newgrange, for instance. It is probably fair to say that the worship of others, like Donn, Nuadu or Goibniu with their respective links with death, healing and smithing, may have been part of domestic everyday cult practices. There must have been innumerable other supernatural figures connected to aspects of the landscape such as hills, wells, rivers and prehistoric monuments. They were still venerated well into Christian times. There is a reference, in a text seemingly of early eleventh-century date (*Aided Crimthann*, 'The Death of Crimthann'), to the worship of a supernatural woman, the 'síd-woman Mongfind', by 'women and the rabble' on the night of Samhain.

Countless pagan practices, over thousands of years, are testimony to the abiding power of the Otherworld and its supernatural inhabitants. The numerous ritual practices reflected as patterned activities in the archaeological record in all periods are evidence of diverse traditional beliefs and, presumably, the worship of a multitude of major and minor deities and spirits. While some historians still question archaeology's capacity to understand or reconstruct such mental constructs in the absence of persuasive historical evidence, it is now accepted that ritual does leave material signatures. This is evident in the burial, religious and domestic spheres. It is true that we cannot know with certainty the deeper meaning of these activities, but the use of ethnographic analogy, the study of comparative mythology and the ever-expanding role of the biological sciences in archaeology all allow us to offer plausible explanations for many of these actions.

The population of Ireland was estimated to be around 1,500,000 in the seventeenth century and, at a guess, it may have been well under 1,000,000, perhaps as low as 500,000, in the medieval period. Whatever the number, the great majority were non-literate, literacy in Irish and Latin being confined to a religious caste and a secular élite. This majority, including the multitude who worshipped Mongfind and other supernatural beings, certainly retained many pre-Christian practices and beliefs. The notion that much medieval piety was in essence amended pagan magic is quite plausible.

It seems that Christian writers in Ireland accommodated the old gods in a uniquely sophisticated way. In medieval Europe these deities were considered to have been either supernatural demons or pagan humans who lived long ago, whereas in Ireland, according to John Carey, they were ingeniously interpreted as immortal beings who were descended from Adam but escaped the Fall. In other words, in this 'baptism of the gods', as he described it, they were given a Christian identity as a branch of the human race who had escaped the contagion wrought on humanity by the sin of Adam and Eve. These were the *aes síde*, the people of the hollow hills, whose Otherworld was an Irish version of the Garden of Eden. They survived in modern folklore as the fairies or 'good people'.

30

The pagan continuum

30.1—Ask, Co. Wexford: a small gilded cross found with cremated bones and dated to the seventh century AD.

The Christian belief in the resurrection of the body was a major factor in the spread of the custom of unburnt burial in medieval times. Burial practice preserved rather than cremated the corpse, with the motive of keeping it for reunion with the soul at the end of days. The dead person was normally buried in an extended position with head to the east, but the traditional pagan rite of cremation continued for many centuries. It was the principal burial rite in Iron Age Ireland before the advent of the new religion. Thanks to extensive radiocarbon dating, it is now evident that the practice continued until the twelfth century AD. This is a clear indication that religious change did not constitute a straightforward and comprehensive replacement of pre-existing beliefs and ritual practices.

A small medieval cemetery excavated on the western slopes of Ask Hill, near Gorey, Co. Wexford, consisted of seven cremations in small pits placed within a circular palisaded enclosure. Only very small amounts of bone were present, and they were highly fragmented and unidentifiable. Such token deposits of burnt bone are very much a late prehistoric custom, so in all probability these were pagan burials. Two produced seventh–eighth-century AD radiocarbon dates, and a tiny cross is of a similar date. This is a gilded object measuring just 28mm across and was probably originally mounted on leather or wood. It may have been deposited as a powerful talisman representing the new religious magic. Of course, it is possible, too, that the people of Ask were Christians who still preferred some of their pagan customs.

A striking example of the long survival of such customs is to be found in the Annals of Tigernach. A great plague is recorded in the year 1084 and its cause is explained by Óengus, the son of the Dagda, to one Gilla Lugan when he visited the *síd* mound of Óengus, namely Newgrange:

'A great pestilence in this year, which killed a fourth of the men of Ireland. It began in the south, and spread throughout the four quarters of Ireland. This is the *causa causans* of that pestilence, to wit, demons that came out of the northern isles of the world, to wit, three battalions, and in each battalion there were thirty and ten hundred and two thousand, as Óengus Óc,

30.2—Newgrange at sunset.

the son of the Dagda, related to Gilla Lugan, who used to haunt the fairy-mound every year on Halloween. And he himself beheld at Maistiu one battalion of them which was destroying Leinster. Even so they were seen by Gilla Lugan's son; and wherever their heat and fury reached, there their venom was taken. For there was a sword of fire out of the gullet of each of them, and every one of them was as high as the clouds of heaven. So that is the cause of this pestilence.'

It is particularly interesting that half a millennium after the introduction of Christianity some of the old gods were evidently alive and well. It is significant that in the eleventh century this Gilla Lugan should commune with Óengus and be a persistent annual visitor to the otherworldly mound at the great feast of Samhain on 1 November.

In 1224 Cathal Croibhdhearg, king of Connacht, died and the succession of his son Aodh Ua Conchobair was celebrated in a bardic poem, *Congaibh róm t'aghaidh, a Aodh* ('Keep your face before me, O Aodh'), that prophesies that he will have many victories and inflict slaughter on the foreign Anglo-Normans. Katherine Simms points out that the poem carefully distinguishes between prophecies attributed to saints and those more sinister prognostications ascribed to fortune-tellers and soothsaying women. Clearly pagan prophets were active and pagan prophecies were in circulation in the early thirteenth century.

When Gerald of Wales visited Ireland in or around 1183, he was able to record the famous horse sacrifice that was part of the inauguration rites of the kings of the Cenél Conaill in Donegal. Even if discontinued, it was evidently still in living memory in the twelfth century. Certainly, idol worship is attested in Donegal at an even later date. In 1256, in response to a report that some 'sons of perdition' in Donegal were worshipping idols, Pope Alexander IV authorised Maol Pádraig Ó Scannail, bishop of Raphoe, to excommunicate them. We have no idea what these idols were, but it is a distinct possibility that wooden idols were a feature of some parts of the medieval landscape. Whether the eleventh-century veneration of Mongfind took the form of idol worship is an intriguing if unanswerable question.

A wooden carving 1.8m tall was found in a bog at Ballybritain, just north of Aghadowey and south of Coleraine, Co. Derry, in the eighteenth century and is known only from a crude thumbnail sketch in the Ordnance Survey Memoirs, compiled in 1836. The brief accompanying account, however, is quite informative:

'In a bog in the townland of Ballybritain or, as it was formerly called, Mut-tonhole, a man and boy were cutting turf about the year 1793 when there

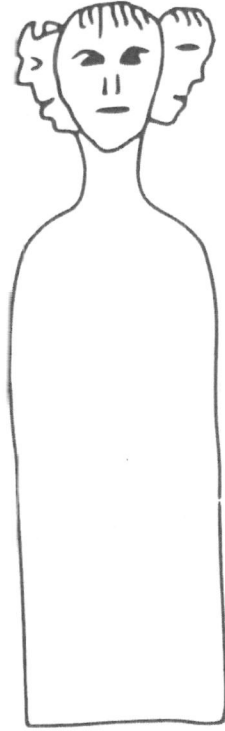

30.3—The Ballybritain wooden idol.

was suddenly turned out from beneath the spade a heathen image or god so hideous that the boy, a weak sickly lad, fainted with horror. It was a long circular block of wood like the trunk of a tree and about 6 feet long. At the top there were 4 heads each looking different ways with 4 faces and carved hair. The elder of the labourers immediately set it up on his garden wall where multitudes of country people flocked to see it. After a few months by the action of the weather it decayed and fell to pieces. Many of the parishioners recollect seeing it and can still accurately describe it.'

Four-headed images are uncommon: the few recorded are widely scattered geographically and differ greatly in date. The Pfalzfeld pillar, found in the Rhineland, is probably the best known; this tapering stone sculpture is of rectangular cross-section, with a stylised human head and La Tène art on each face. It dates from the later fifth century BC. The Sutton Hoo sceptre or whetstone, from the famous Anglo-Saxon burial in east Anglia, is some 58cm in length, has four human heads at either end of its four-sided stone bar and is dated to the early seventh century AD.

A tall, four-sided stone pillar found in the River Zbruch near Horodnytsia in western Ukraine has four heads sporting a single hat or crown. The large, stylised figures below, on each of the four faces, have a long garment and share a common belt. One has a carving of a sword and a horse below this belt. Two have breasts and are presumably female (one holding a horn of plenty, the other a ring), and all four have their arms in a ritual pose—one hand on the chest, the other on the stomach. Below these are four small standing figures, two of them female, and at the base smaller squatting figures are carved on just three faces. It may have come from a nearby hilltop sanctuary. Now in the Archaeological Museum of Krakow in Poland, it is dated to the ninth century AD and may depict several aspects of a Slavic deity or a whole pantheon. Some believe it to be a representation of the god Svantovit. A wooden idol of this four-headed god was destroyed in the twelfth century

30.4—The Zbruch idol.

in the Slavic sanctuary at Arkona on the Baltic island of Rügen, and other smaller four-faced images are known in the Baltic region.

There are no good parallels in insular Iron Age iconography for a pillar like that from Ballybritain, with four protruding human heads and distinctly carved hair. Though some Continental images of the human head of Iron Age date have hair depicted, this is not a common feature of Irish carvings. This sort of representation of hair is, however, an occasional feature of medieval sculpture in Ireland—as on the 1.27m-tall wooden image of St Molaise of Inishmurray of thirteenth- or early fourteenth-century date now in the National Museum of Ireland. It is quite possible that the Ballybritain idol dates from this general period too.

Whatever the date of the Ballybritain carving, the continuation of cremation and the historical references to pagan rites of one sort or another do imply that pagan practices and Christian beliefs occupied a shared ground in Ireland for many centuries.

We may get a fascinating hint of this in a later medieval addition to the *Amra Choluim Chille*, a eulogy for St Columba, or Colum Cille, who died in the late sixth century. A priest of the Cenél Conaill in Donegal, who had been carried away by the Devil, confessed that he had built a church with an altar of precious stones that also contained images of the sun and moon. We have no idea what form these *delb* or images took but various writers have considered this a reference to a pagan cult. The priest was absolved of his sins and became a follower of the saint, but it is an intriguing possibility that symbols of the old and new religions were once worshipped in a Donegal church in an attempt to reconcile the two traditions.

The perpetual fire maintained by nuns at St Brigid's monastery in County Kildare is probably another instance of this sort of accommodation, assuming that it was constantly maintained into the medieval period by the successors of the devotees of the goddess. The conspicuous absence of any mention of the fire ritual in the seventh-century life of St Brigid by Cogitosus may be a deliberate omission and an indication of its pagan nature.

Such activities may not be the same as idol worship but to what extent should some former folk customs be considered pagan practice? Following the French historian of religions Jean Delumeau, it is likely that only a minority had acquired the rudiments of religious understanding in medieval and early modern Europe. The greater part of the population inhabited an uncertain world in which magic and superstition were stronger than any Christian religious belief. As he said in 2010: 'While a veneer of Christianity was superimposed on medieval life, a closer look revealed evidence that remnants of paganism persisted among the people. The saints of the Church now assumed many of the functions that had been formerly reserved to pagan gods.' This was probably true of Ireland too.

While the quarterly feasts of the old Irish year, Lughnasa, Samhain, Imbolc and Bealtaine, were undoubtedly important ritual occasions in ancient times, the popular traditions associated with Lughnasa in historic times had many of the characteristics of a harvest festival. For the most part they seem to have lacked a religious dimension and any action clearly directed at a non-Christian entity. The same may be true in the case of the custom of devotion at 'holy wells'. They are a Europe-wide phenomenon and around 3,000 examples survive in Ireland today. It is fair to say that the traditions at many or most of these may be only a few centuries old and appear to represent a thoroughly Christianised phenomenon. Some, however, have probable origins in pre-Christian times and may go back at least to the time of St Patrick, if not before. He is more than once said to have encountered druids at such sacred places.

Struell Wells, near Downpatrick, Co. Down, was, according to an eighth-century hymn, visited by the saint, who immersed himself in its waters. By the eleventh or twelfth century it is said to have healing powers. There are two wells on the site, one for drinking and one for eye cures. One was also traditionally associated with St Patrick, who, in a seventeenth-century account, is claimed to have spent the greater part of the night there as 'an untiring athlete … stark naked, singing psalms and spiritual songs'.

30.5—Struell Wells today. The eye well is on the left, the men's and women's bathhouses are on the right.

Both wells were enclosed in stone cells in later medieval times, and two other stone structures were built at later dates for male and female bathing rites. It was an important place of pilgrimage at midsummer too, but all activities here were suppressed in the nineteenth century. Finbar McCormick has argued that the unusual and popular practice of communal naked bathing there at midsummer had its origins in a pre-Christian pagan cult. The story of St Patrick's odd naked activities possibly reflects its conversion to Christian practice. It is interesting to note that wells do seem to have been a particular focus of Patrician attention and (in Tírechán's seventh-century *Collectanea*) the saint encountered or baptised new converts at no fewer than eight named wells.

Among these is a remarkable account of pagan devotion at one holy well that evidently included the practice of votive offerings to pagan gods. Tírechán, who enumerated the churches that St Patrick was reputed to have founded, wrote an account of the saint's visit:

'Patrick went to a well in Findmag called Slán ['whole, healthy'], since it had been told to him that druids pay homage to this well and offer gifts to it as if it were a god. The well was square-shaped, with a square stone on its opening, and water would flow over the stone, that is through the joints like a royal trace (?). The incredulous said that a certain deceased prophet made a casket for himself underwater under the stone so that he might purify his bones forever, because he feared being burned with fire. Hence they worshipped the well like a god. Now the background to this cult was explained to Patrick, and he, fired by the zeal of the living God, said, "It is untrue what you say, namely, that this well is the King of Waters" (for they had named it "King of Waters"). The local druids and pagans congregated at the well, along with an enormous crowd, and Patrick said to them, "Lift the stone. Let us see what is underneath, whether there are bones or not. For I say to you there are no bones of any man down here, but only, methinks, a little of the gold and silver from your false offerings that has seeped through the joints of the stone structure". They could not, however, lift the stone. And so Patrick and his servants blessed the stone, and he said to the multitude, "Stand aside for a little while, so that you may see the strength of my God who lives in heaven". With his hands raised he lifted the stone from off the mouth of the well and positioned it just beyond the opening, and it has remained there ever since. And they found nothing in the well except water, and they believed in God the Most High. A certain man sat apart near to the stone which Patrick had fixed in the ground, and Patrick blessed him, baptized him, and said to this person, whose name was Caeta or Cata, "Your seed will be blessed for ever".

In blessing the stone and miraculously moving it to one side of the well and fixing it erect in the ground, Patrick permanently alters a pagan site and triumphantly reveals that there is nothing in the well—no dead sage, no bones. He also shows that there is no substance to the belief in a 'royal trace' or some sort of mark of a 'King of Waters'. The allusion to fire in the water is interesting, for this notion of a burning or brilliant element hidden in water is an ancient Indo-European motif. In J.F. Nagy's words, a monument to pagan power is transformed into a memorial to a saintly miracle.

This place is named as 'Slanpatrick' in the thirteenth century and has been identified with a church and well in the townland of Ballynew, near Castlebar, Co. Mayo. According to John O'Donovan, writing in 1838, a pattern was once held at the well on Garland or Reek Sunday, the last Sunday in July. The well is a rectangular stone structure and local folklore records that one stone with two indentations bears the marks of St Patrick, who knelt to pray on it. The well is now dry but a 1938 account in the National Folklore Collection states that 'at the right-hand side of it, there is a split in the rock in the bottom, and out of this the water springs up, and at the other end there is an outlet. At one side of it there is a large flag, and it is said that when St Patrick was in Ireland, he was passing by he knelt down to get a drink, and the mark of his knees are still in it.'

A holy well in the townland of Coolatoor, Co. Westmeath, is located on the western slope of Knockastia, where the summit of the hill is crowned by a major Bronze Age cemetery mound. The well may have been the focus of ritual in pre-Christian times. The well of Nechtan, near Carbury Hill, Co. Kildare, which figures prominently in the mythology of the River Boyne, may also have had a prehistoric importance. It too was associated with an illuminating and brilliant feature, that of wisdom. Some wells at major pagan cult centres are also likely to be of pre-Christian date and include several on the hill of Tara and a number at Rathcroghan.

A very few holy wells have produced some Roman and Romano-British votive material. These include a brooch and a sherd of Samian ware found at St Anne's well at Randalstown, Co. Meath, and an oculist's stamp from a well near Golden, Co. Tipperary. The latter is a small, inscribed stone used to impress the name and nature of various concoctions onto small sticks of eye ointment. Finds like these are thought to indicate the development of a Romano-British well cult with curative possibilities.

The first edition of the Ordnance Survey map records the position of a 'thorn'

30.6—Prayer at a holy bullaun stone and a rag tree on Church Island, near Bellaghy, Co. Derry, in 1836, as depicted by Charles W. Ligar in the Ordnance Survey Memoirs.

at Struell Wells in 1834. Though nothing more is known, this was undoubtedly a holy rag tree, for these are common enough at wells of this sort. In 1836 Charles W. Ligar, a youthful civil assistant in the Ordnance Survey, visited Church Island on Lough Beg, near Bellaghy, Co. Derry. This is an ancient church site associated with a St Taoide, about whom very little is known. The water that collects in the hollow of a bullaun stone there is said to have curative properties, especially for warts and eye problems. Ligar painted a sombre picture of a crippled man seated in prayer at the site. Behind him stands a rag tree bedecked with pieces of cloth. These are poignant offerings left there in the hope of a cure and, it has been claimed, as the material on the tree slowly rots, so the affliction ceases.

Almost a century and a half later, Seamus Heaney, writing of this part of his home ground in County Derry, saw a landscape that sustained a diminished structure of lore and superstition, and half-pagan, half-Christian thought and practice. He remembered as a schoolboy:

'On Church Island Sunday in September there was a pilgrimage out to the place because St Patrick was supposed to have prayed there, and prayed with such intensity that he branded the shape of his knee into a stone in the old church yard. The rainwater that collected in that stone, of course, had healing powers, and the thorn bush beside it was pennanted with the rags used by those who rubbed their warts and sores in that water.'

Wells and trees with a distinctly Christian veneer aside, other folkloric practices may also have ancient roots but retained a more obvious non-Christian focus. John Carey has drawn attention to some of the cult practices connected with that god of the dead, Donn, who is associated with Tech Duinn and is the subject of widespread folklore. He is also linked to Knockfierna, a prominent hill near Ballingarry, Co. Limerick. It was once a Lughnasa assembly site and there are the remains of a large cairn on its summit—now defaced by a modern concrete cross with a telecommunications mast nearby. Here he was known as Donn Fírinne, 'Donn of truth', because he was invoked as a guarantor of oaths and promises. This recalls an invocation in an early text: 'let the dead be summoned, let them be made to live by oaths sworn in the places where they dwelt'. Small animals were also sacrificed to Donn. One nineteenth-century writer mentions some of the gifts left on this hill: 'they bury eggs in hay, in crops of corn, and also parts of dead animals'. Other folkloric accounts record the sacrifice of a cock: 'they took a cock which was no good to be plucked to let his blood run out and throw him either into the wood or under a hill, and it was said they threw it out for Donn Fírinneach'.

These practices are reminiscent of those offerings at Rathcroghan recorded by William Wilde in the early nineteenth century already mentioned. In 1852 he also wrote:

'it was not unusual, some fifteen or twenty years ago, to bleed a whole herd of cattle upon a May morning, and then to dry and burn the blood. We have more than once, when a boy, seen the entire of the great Fort of Rathcroghan, then the centre of one of the most extensive and fertile grazing districts of Connaught, literally reddened with the blood thus drawn upon a May morning. Bleeding the cattle at this period of the year was evidently done with a sanitary intention, as some of the older medical works recommended in the human subject; but choosing that particular day, and subsequently burning the blood, were evidently vestiges of some Heathen rite.'

In some districts blood was mixed with meal and consumed as a hot drink, even though the Church had long condemned the drinking of animal blood. According to a medieval Penitential, anyone who ate the flesh of a horse or drank the blood or urine of an animal had to do penance for three years and a half, and anyone who drank the blood of a cat had to undertake three fasts. The latter prohibition is surprisingly specific and would seem to imply a peculiar form of unchristian cat abuse about which we know nothing. It is, however, an interesting possibility that this is a guarded allusion to witchcraft and that cats were associated with witches at this early date.

We have no difficulty in describing the Iron Age deposits of shellfish in the megalithic tomb at Altar in west Cork as pagan gifts to the Otherworld 4,000 years ago. Presumably the offerings at places like Knockfierna and Rathcroghan in more recent times were not much different, and pagan and Christian beliefs lived comfortably together as they had for over 1,000 years. The story of Christianity and its accommodation of paganism seems to have been a long and uneven process that continued into the early nineteenth century. The middle of that century witnessed great social change that included the consequences of apocalyptic famine, language loss and a devotional revolution in Catholic religious practice. Up until then it is fair to say that the pagan past was never dead. It was not even past.

References

Introduction: a pagan tapestry

T. Insoll, *Archaeology, ritual, religion* (London, 2004), xiii.

J.P. Mackey, 'Christian past and primal present', *Etudes Celtiques* **29** (1992), 285–97.

A. Norenzayan, *Big gods: how religion transformed cooperation and conflict* (Princeton, 2013).

A. Norenzayan, A.F. Shariff, W.M. Gervais *et al.*, 'The cultural evolution of prosocial religions', *Behavioral and Brain Sciences* (2016) (doi: 10.1017/ S0140525X14001356,e0).

H.C. Peoples, P. Duda and F.W. Marlowe, 'Hunter-gatherers and the origins of religion', *Human Nature* **27** (2016), 261–82 (doi: 10.1007/s12110-016-9260-0).

K. Werthmann, 'Local religion or cult-shopping? A sacrificial site in Burkina Faso', *Anthropos* **109** (2014), 399–409.

1. Manipulating bones and bodies

F. Beglane and C. Jones, 'Hares, juvenile domesticates, structured deposition, and ritual in the Neolithic court tomb at Parknabinnia, Ireland', *Journal of Archaeological Science: Reports* **35** (2021), 102672.

S. Bergh, F. Gallagher, R. Hensey and P. Meehan, *A baseline survey of the passage tombs of County Sligo 2021* (Sligo, 2021).

J.A. Boyle, 'The hare in myth and reality: a review article', *Folklore* **84** (1973), 313–26.

J. Geber, R. Hensey, P. Meehan, S. Moore and T. Kador, 'Facilitating transitions: postmortem processing of the dead at the Carrowkeel passage tomb complex, Ireland (3500–3000 cal BC)', *Bioarchaeology International* **1** (1–2) (2017), 35–51.

T. Kador, L.M. Cassidy, J. Geber, R. Hensey and S. Moore, 'Rites of passage: mortuary practice, population dynamics, and chronology at the Carrowkeel passage tomb complex, Co. Sligo, Ireland', *Proceedings of the Prehistoric Society* **84** (2018), 225–55.

B. Lincoln, *Myth, cosmos, and society. Indo-European themes of creation and destruction* (Harvard, 1986).

R.I. Lohmann, 'The afterlife of Asabano corpses: relationships with the deceased in Papua New Guinea', *Ethnology* 44 (2005), 189–206.

C. Manning, 'A Neolithic burial mound at Ashleypark, Co. Tipperary', *Proceedings of the Royal Irish Academy* 85C (1985), 61–100.

J.C. Muller, 'Mort, autopsie et funérailles chez les Dìi de l'Adamaoua (Nord-Cameroun)', *Anthropologie et Sociétés* 37 (2013), 161–75.

M. Nic an Airchinnigh, 'Ól na fola i dtraidisiún na hÉireann', *Eighteenth-Century Ireland* 29 (2014), 130–41.

2. Veneration of the sun

U. Boser, 'Solar circle', *Archaeology* 59 (4) (2006), 30–5.

S. Burrow, 'Bryn Celli Ddu passage tomb, Anglesey: alignment, construction, date, and ritual', *Proceedings of the Prehistoric Society* 76 (2010), 249–70.

M. Cahill, 'Here comes the sun ...', *Archaeology Ireland* 29 (1) (2015), 26–33.

L.M. Cassidy, R. Ó Maoldúin, T. Kador *et al.*, 'A dynastic elite in monumental Neolithic society', *Nature* 582 (2020), 384–8 (https://doi.org/10.1038/s41586-020-2378-6).

R. Hensey, *First light: the origins of Newgrange* (Oxford, 2015).

C. Jeunesse, 'Les premiers sanctuaires construits. Les enclos circulaires en bois et en terre de la Préhistoire récente européenne', *L'Archéologue* 154 (2020), 34–7.

K. Kristiansen, 'Rock art and religion. The sun journey in Indo-European mythology and Bronze Age rock art', in Å.C. Fredell, K. Kristiansen and F. Criado-Boado (eds), *Representations and communications: creating an archaeological matrix of late prehistoric rock art* (Oxford, 2010), 93–115.

J.D. Moore, 'Rituals of the past: final comments', in S.A. Rosenfeld and S.L. Bautista (eds), *Rituals of the past. Prehispanic and colonial case studies in Andean archaeology* (Boulder, Colorado, 2017), 295–311.

W. O'Brien, *Iverni: a prehistory of Cork* (Cork, 2012), 163.

F. Prendergast, *Solar alignment and the Irish passage tomb tradition*, Archaeology Ireland Heritage Guide 82 (Dublin, 2018).

F. Prendergast, M. O'Sullivan, K. Williams and G. Cooney, 'Facing the sun', *Archaeology Ireland* 31 (4) (2017), 10–17.

P.L. Van Den Berghe and G.M. Mesher, 'Royal incest and inclusive fitness', *American Ethnologist* 7 (1980), 300–17.

J. Waddell, *Archaeology and Celtic myth* (Dublin, 2014), 36.

K. Williams, 'Rekindling the solstice light', *Archaeology Ireland* 33 (4) (2019), 19–24.

3. The cosmic circle

M. Bayle, 'Réflexions pour une architecture significative: univers symbolique et matériel de la maison chez les Inuit du Nunavik (Note de recherche)', *Études Inuit Studies* **44** (1–2) (2020), 161–82.

T.O. Beidelman, 'The Kaguru house', *Anthropos* **67** (1972), 690–707.

G. Bordin, 'Le corpus lexical de l'habitat Inuit de l'Arctique oriental canadien', *Journal de la Société des Américanistes* **89** (1) (2003), 95–123.

J. Brück, 'Houses, lifecycles and deposition on Middle Bronze Age settlements in southern England', *Proceedings of the Prehistoric Society* **65** (1999), 145–66.

M. Carver, 'Early Scottish monasteries and prehistory: a preliminary dialogue', *Scottish Historical Review* **88** (226) (2009), 347.

M. Eliade, *The myth of the eternal return, or, cosmos and history* (Princeton, 1991), 76.

L. Nees, 'The colophon drawing in the Book of Mulling: a supposed Irish monastery plan and the tradition of terminal illustration in early medieval manuscripts', *Cambridge Medieval Celtic Studies* **5** (1983), 67–91.

E. O'Brien, *Mapping death: burial in late Iron Age and early medieval Ireland* (Dublin, 2020), 77.

T. Ó Carragáin, *Churches in early medieval Ireland* (Yale, 2010), 38.

S. Ó Nualláin, 'A survey of stone circles in Cork and Kerry', *Proceedings of the Royal Irish Academy* **84C** (1984), 45.

R. Sherlock, 'Killydonoghoe AR7—settlement', in K. Hanley and M.F. Hurley (eds), *Generations: the archaeology of five national road schemes in County Cork*, Vol. 1 (Dublin, 2013), 142.

C. Thomas, *The early Christian archaeology of north Britain* (Oxford, 1971), 38.

J. Waddell, *Archaeology and Celtic myth* (Dublin, 2014), 19.

G.F. Willmot, 'Three burial sites at Carbury, Co. Kildare', *Journal of the Royal Society of Antiquaries of Ireland* **68** (1938), 130–42.

4. Small offerings in hallowed places

E. Bhreathnach, *Ireland in the medieval world AD 400–1000* (Dublin, 2014), 139.

A. Cooper, D. Garrow, C. Gibson, M. Giles and N. Wilkin, *Grave goods: objects and death in later prehistoric Britain* (Oxford, 2022), 206.

R. Lash, 'Pebbles and *peregrinatio*: the taskscape of medieval devotion on Inishark Island, Ireland', *Medieval Archaeology* **62** (2018), 83–104.

R. Lash, I. Kuijt, E. Alonzi, M.S. Chesson and T. Burke, '"Differing in status, but one in spirit": sacred space and social diversity at island monasteries in Connemara, Ireland', *Antiquity* **92** (362) (2018), 437–55.

E. O'Brien, *Mapping death: burial in late Iron Age and early medieval Ireland* (Dublin, 2020), 119.

W. O'Brien, *Sacred ground: megalithic tombs in coastal south-west Ireland* (Galway, 1999), 91, 141.

W. O'Brien, 'Megaliths in a mythologised landscape', in C. Scarre (ed.), *Monuments and landscape in Atlantic Europe* (London, 2002), 152–77.

W. O'Brien, *Local worlds: early settlement landscapes and upland farming in south-west Ireland* (Cork, 2009), 187.

R.J. Schulting, M. McClatchie, A. Sheridan, R. McLaughlin, P. Barratt and N.J. Whitehouse, 'Radiocarbon dating of a multi-phase passage tomb on Baltinglass Hill, Co. Wicklow, Ireland', *Proceedings of the Prehistoric Society* **83** (2017), 305–23.

T. Thompson, 'Clocha geala/clocha uaisle: white quartz in Irish tradition', *Béaloideas* **73** (2005), 111–33.

W. Wilde, *Irish popular superstitions* (Dublin, 1852).

5. Crouched burial

M. Cahill and M. Sikora (eds), *Breaking ground, finding graves—reports on the excavations of burials by the National Museum of Ireland, 1927–2006*, Vol. 1 (Dublin, 2011), 540.

L.M. Cassidy, R. Martiniano, E.M. Murphy, M.D. Teasdale, J. Mallory, B. Hartwell and D.G. Bradley, 'Neolithic and Bronze Age migration to Ireland and establishment of the insular Atlantic genome', *Proceedings of the National Academy of Sciences of the United States of America* **113** (2016), 368–73.

E.E. Evans-Pritchard, 'Burial and mortuary rites of the Nuer', *African Affairs* **48** (1949), 56–63.

A.P. Fitzpatrick, 'The arrival of the Bell Beaker Set in Britain and Ireland', in J.T. Koch and B. Cunliffe (eds), *Celtic from the West 2: Rethinking the Bronze Age and the arrival of Indo-European in Atlantic Europe* (Oxford, 2013), 41–70.

M. Furholt, 'Re-integrating archaeology: a contribution to aDNA studies and the migration discourse on the 3rd millennium BC in Europe', *Proceedings of the Prehistoric Society* **85** (2019), 115–29.

L. Hackett and J. Twomey, 'Final report on archaeological investigations at Site E2972, in the townland of Mullamast, Co. Kildare' (2010). TII Excavation Report (https://repository.dri.ie/catalog/4q77v686d).

C. McSparron, *Burials and society in Late Chalcolithic and Early Bronze Age Ireland* (Oxford, 2021).

C. Mount, 'Adolf Mahr's excavations of an early Bronze Age cemetery at Keenoge,

County Meath', *Proceedings of the Royal Irish Academy* **97**C (1997), 1–68.

E. O'Brien, *Mapping death: burial in late Iron Age and early medieval Ireland* (Dublin, 2020), 34, 54, 155.

P. Ucko, 'Ethnography and the archaeological interpretation of funerary remains', *World Archaeology* **1** (1969), 262–80.

6. The funeral pyre

M. Gowen, *Three Irish gas pipelines: new archaeological evidence from Munster* (Dublin, 1988), 106, 193.

E. Grogan, L. O'Donnell and P. Johnston, *The Bronze Age landscapes of the Pipeline to the West* (Dublin, 2007), 45, 116, 337.

P. Johnston and J. Kiely, *Hidden voices: the archaeology of the M8 Fermoy–Mitchelstown motorway* (Dublin, 2019), 61.

M. McQuade, B. Molloy and C. Moriarty, *In the shadow of the Galtees* (Dublin, 2009), 130, 213, 230.

J.P. Mallory, *In search of the Irish dreamtime: archaeology and early Irish literature* (London, 2016), 257.

C. Mount, 'Early Bronze Age burial in south-east Ireland in the light of recent research', *Proceedings of the Royal Irish Academy* **97**C (1997), 101–93.

M. Ó Briain, 'Snáithín san uige: "loisc agus léig a luaith le sruth"', in M. Ó Briain and P. Ó Héalaí (eds), *Téada dúchais. Aistí in ómós don Ollamh Breandán Ó Madagáin* (Indreabhán, 2002), 256.

L. O'Donnell, 'The power of the pyre', *Journal of Archaeological Science* **65** (2016), 161–71.

F. Reilly, 'Bronze Age cremation burials and funeral practices at Carmanhall, Co. Dublin', *Journal of the Royal Society of Antiquaries of Ireland* **139** (2009), 9–34.

R. Rosenblum, 'David's "Funeral of Patroclus"', *The Burlington Magazine* **115** (846) (1973), 567–77.

B. Wilkins, 'Pyre, post-pits and burnt mound at Newford', in J. McKeon and J. O'Sullivan (eds), *The quiet landscape: archaeological investigations on the M6 Galway to Ballinasloe national road scheme* (Dublin, 2014), 54–6.

H. Williams, 'Death warmed up: the agency of bodies and bones in Anglo-Saxon cremation rites', *Journal of Material Culture* **9** (2004), 263–91.

7. Inversion and reversal

M. Dowd, *The archaeology of caves in Ireland* (Oxford, 2015), 149.

P. Johnston and J. Kiely, *Hidden voices: the archaeology of the M8 Fermoy–Mitchelstown motorway* (Dublin, 2019), 47.

J. Lehane and D. Lee, 'Archaeological excavation report. Prehistoric site with enclosure, structures, two ring ditches and associated cist burials at Ballynacarriga 3, Co Cork' (2010). TII Excavation Report (https://repository.dri.ie/catalog/bk12nr78m).

B. Lincoln, 'On the imagery of paradise', *Indogermanische Forschungen* **85** (1980), 151–64.

C. Lynn, 'House-urns in Ireland?', *Ulster Journal of Archaeology* **56** (1993), 70–7.

L. Olivier, 'Processus mortuaires et rites funéraires dans les sépultures sous tumulus du domaine hallstattien occidental: une approche des représentations collectives de la mort à l'âge du Fer', *Antiquités Nationales* **35** (2003), 95–110.

E.M. Prendergast, 'Bronze Age burials in Co. Westmeath', *Journal of the Royal Society of Antiquaries of Ireland* **75** (1945), 107–11.

I.M. Stead, *Iron Age cemeteries in east Yorkshire* (London, 1991), 224.

J. Waddell, *Archaeology and Celtic myth* (Dublin, 2014), 61.

8. A chosen few

D. Bayley and S. Delaney, 'Chalcolithic and Bronze Age settlement and burials', in S. Delaney, D. Bayley and J. McKeon, *Around the Bay of Dundalk: archaeological investigations along the route of the M1 Dundalk Western Bypass* (Dublin, 2020), 54.

A.L. Brindley and J. Lanting, 'Radiocarbon dates from the cemetery at Poulawack, Co. Clare', *Journal of Irish Archaeology* **6** (1992), 13–17.

H.-M. Faure, 'Rites mortuaires chez les M'Bérés', *Journal de la Société des Africanistes* **1** (1931), 111–15.

E. Grogan, 'Bronze Age cemetery at Carrig, Co. Wicklow', *Archaeology Ireland* **4** (4) (1990), 12–14.

H.O'N. Hencken, 'A cairn at Poulawack, County Clare', *Journal of the Royal Society of Antiquaries of Ireland* **65** (1935), 191–222.

C. Jones, *Temples of stone* (Cork, 2007), 120.

C. Mount and P.J. Hartnett, 'Early Bronze Age cemetery at Edmondstown, County Dublin', *Proceedings of the Royal Irish Academy* **93C** (1993), 21–79.

9. Gifts to an Otherworld

L. Bourke, *Crossing the Rubicon: Bronze Age metalwork from Irish rivers* (Galway, 2001).

P. Busse, 'River names', in J.C. Koch (ed.), *Celtic culture: a historical encyclopedia* (Santa Barbara, 2005), 1511–12.

G. Eogan, *The hoards of the Irish later Bronze Age* (Dublin, 1983), 117, 151.

J. Feehan, *The bogs of Ireland: an introduction to the natural, cultural and industrial heritage of Irish peatlands* (revised edn) (Dublin, 2008), 169, 415.

R. Johnston, *Bronze Age worlds: a social prehistory of Britain and Ireland* (Abingdon, 2021), 4, 241.

K. Leonard, *Ritual in Late Bronze Age Ireland: material culture, practices, landscape setting and social context* (Oxford, 2015), 74.

P. Macdonald and J. Ó Néill, 'Investigation of the find-spot of the Tamlaght hoard, Co. Armagh', in G. Cooney, K. Becker, J. Coles, M. Ryan and S. Sievers (eds), *Relics of old decency: archaeological studies in later prehistory* (Dublin, 2009), 167–79.

R. O'Flaherty, 'The crane-bag of the Fianna', *Archaeology Ireland* **10** (1) (1996), 27–9.

A. Rosse, 'The Dowris Hoard', *Irish Arts Review* **2** (1) (1985), 25–8.

P. Stastney, 'A question of scale? A review of interpretations of Irish peatland archaeology in relation to Holocene environmental and climate change', *Proceedings of the Royal Irish Academy* **120**C (2020), 51–81.

P. Stastney, D.S. Young and N.P. Branch, 'The identification of Late-Holocene bog bursts at Littleton bog, Ireland: ecohydrological changes display complex climatic and non-climatic drivers', *The Holocene* **28** (4) (2018), 570–82.

R. Warner, 'The Broighter hoard—a question of ownership', in G. O'Brien (ed.), *Derry & Londonderry: history and society* (Dublin, 1999), 69–90.

R. Warner, 'The Tamlaght hoard and the Creeveroe axe', *Emania* **20** (2006), 20–8.

10. The puzzle of fragments

J. Brück, *Personifying prehistory: relational ontologies in Bronze Age Britain and Ireland* (Oxford, 2019), 94.

M. Cahill, 'Reclaiming Mrs Tyrrell's field: reprovenancing and reconsidering a hoard of gold lunulae from Ballinderry, Co. Kildare', *Proceedings of the Royal Irish Academy* **122**C (2022), 1–47.

M. Cahill and M. Sikora (eds), *Breaking ground, finding graves—reports on the excavations of burials by the National Museum of Ireland, 1927–2006*, Vol. 1 (Dublin, 2011), 71, 269.

K. Cleary, 'Broken bones and broken stones: exploring fragmentation in middle and late Bronze Age settlement contexts in Ireland', *European Journal of Archaeology* **21** (2018), 336–60.

E. Cotter, 'Ballybrowney Lower 1—nucleated settlement', in K. Hanley and M.F. Hurley (eds), *Generations: the archaeology of national road schemes in County Cork*, Vol. 1 (2013), 93–104.

G. Eogan, *The hoards of the Irish later Bronze Age* (Dublin, 1983), 147.

B. Ó Ríordáin, 'Early Bronze Age hoard from Co. Leitrim', *Journal of the Royal Society of Antiquaries of Ireland* **88** (1958), 143–5.

R. Warner and M. Cahill, 'The Downpatrick hoards: an analytical reconsideration', in J.R. Trigg (ed.), *Of things gone but not forgotten: essays in archaeology for Joan Taylor* (Oxford, 2012), 95–108.

11. What's in a name?

E. FitzPatrick, E. Murphy, R. McHugh, C. Donnelly and C. Foley, 'Evoking the white mare: the cult landscape of *Sgiath Gabhra* and its medieval perception in Gaelic *Fir Mhanach*', in R. Schot, C. Newman and E. Bhreathnach (eds), *Landscapes of cult and kingship* (Dublin, 2011), 163–91.

D. Lavelle, *An archaeological survey of Ballinrobe and district, including Lough Mask and Lough Carra* (Castlebar, 1994), 3.

M. Lohan, 'Ceremonial monuments in Moytura, Co. Mayo', *Journal of the Galway Archaeological and Historical Society* **51** (1999), 77–108.

C. Newman, 'The sacral landscape of Tara: a preliminary exploration', in R. Schot, C. Newman and E. Bhreathnach (eds), *Landscapes of cult and kingship* (Dublin, 2011), 22–43.

T. Robinson, *Stones of Aran: pilgrimage* (Dublin, 1986), 23.

T. Robinson, 'Twilight on old stones', *Field Day Review* **3** (2007), 42–51.

J. Waddell, *Foundation myths: the beginnings of Irish archaeology* (Dublin, 2005), 103, 134.

12. Mountains of the mind

O. Alcock (ed.), *Archaeological inventory of County Galway, Vol. II: North Galway* (Dublin, 1999), 6.

S. Bergh, 'Transforming Knocknarea—the archaeology of a mountain', *Archaeology Ireland* **52** (2000), 14–18.

S. Bergh, *Neolithic Cúil Irra, Co. Sligo—Knocknarea/Carrowmore/Carns*, Archaeology Ireland Heritage Guide 78 (Dublin, 2017).

S. Bergh, 'Making space—creating place', *Building Material* **24** (2022), 171–86.

F. Coyne, *Islands in the clouds: an upland archaeological study on Mount Brandon and The Paps, County Kerry* (Tralee, 2006), 20.

M. MacNeill, *The festival of Lughnasa: a study of the survival of the Celtic festival of the beginning of harvest* (Oxford, 1962), 71.

S. Moore, *The archaeology of Slieve Donard: a cultural biography of Ulster's highest mountain* (Downpatrick, 2012), 25.

L. Morahan, *Croagh Patrick, Co. Mayo: archaeology, landscape and people* (Westport, 2001), 18.

D. Ó hÓgain, *Myth, legend, and romance: an encyclopaedia of Irish folk tradition* (London, 1990), 212.

13. On the edge of the world

C. Cotter, *The Western Stone Forts Project: excavations at Dún Aonghasa and Dún Eoghanachta* (2 vols) (Dublin, 2012).

J. de Courcy Ireland, 'The maritime history of the Aran Islands', in J. Waddell, J.W. O'Connell and A. Korff (eds), *The Book of Aran* (Kinvara, 1994), 163.

M.V. García Quintela, 'Celtic elements in north-western Spain in pre-Roman times', *e-Keltoi: Journal of Interdisciplinary Celtic Studies* **6** (10) (2005), 531 (https://dc.uwm.edu/ekeltoi/vol6/iss1/10).

M.V. García Quintela and C. González-García, 'The rock sanctuary of Baroña hill-fort as an exchanger, interface and cross-roads among the world layers of Celtic cosmology', *Mediterranean Archaeology and Archaeometry* **18** (4) (2018), 387–94 (doi: 10.5281/zenodo.1477034).

A.T. Lucas, 'Washing and bathing in ancient Ireland', *Journal of the Royal Society of Antiquaries of Ireland* **95** (1965), 99.

B. Malinowski, *Argonauts of the western Pacific* (London, 1922), 81.

K. Meyer, 'Conall Corc and the Corco Luigde', *Anecdota from Irish manuscripts*, Vol. 3 (Dublin, 1910), 60.

R. Ó Maoldúin, 'In search of amber: long distance directional movement between Bronze Age Ireland and Denmark', in P. Suchowska-Ducke and H. Vandkilde (eds), *Mobility of culture in Bronze Age Europe*, Vol. 2 (Oxford, 2014), 115–22.

B.G. Scott and J. Ó Néill, 'Bronze Age Rathlin', in W. Forsythe and R. McConkey (eds), *Rathlin Island: an archaeological survey of a maritime landscape* (Belfast, 2012), 91.

J.P. Singh Uberoi, *Politics of the kula ring: an analysis of the findings of Bronislaw Malinowski* (Manchester, 1971), 139.

R.A. Smith, *British Museum: a guide to the antiquities of the Bronze Age in the Department of British and Medieval Antiquities* (London, 1920), 110.

R. Van de Noort, 'Argonauts of the North Sea—a social maritime archaeology for the 2nd millennium BC', *Proceedings of the Prehistoric Society* **72** (2006), 267–87.

R. Van de Noort, 'Exploring the ritual of travel in prehistoric Europe: the Bronze Age sewn-plank boats in context', in P. Clarke (ed.), *Bronze Age connections: cultural contact in prehistoric Europe* (Oxford, 2009), 159–75.

J. Waddell, *Archaeology and Celtic myth* (Dublin, 2014), 52.

D.M. Williams, 'Marine erosion and archaeological landscapes: a case study of stone forts at cliff-top locations in the Aran Islands, Ireland', *Geoarchaeology* **19** (2) (2004), 167–75.

14. Aristocratic feasts

K. Becker, 'Irish Iron Age settlement and society: reframing royal sites', *Proceedings of the Prehistoric Society* **85** (2019), 273–306.

S. Gerloff, *Atlantic cauldrons and buckets of the late Bronze and early Iron Ages in Western Europe* (Stuttgart, 2010), 143.

B. Hayden and S. Villeneuve, 'A century of feasting studies', *Annual Review of Anthropology* **40** (2021), 433–49.

M. Kitts, 'Sacrificial violence in the Iliad', *Journal of Ritual Studies* **16** (2002), 19–39.

K. Leonard, 'Birds of the Otherworld: sacral symbolism and the Dunaverney fleshhook', *Journal of Irish Archaeology* **23** (2014), 123–42.

K. Leonard, 'Commensality and casting: a discussion of Irish late Bronze Age cauldrons', in D. Brandherm (ed.), *Aspects of the Bronze Age in the Atlantic archipelago and beyond* (Hagen, 2019), 239.

R. Madgwick, V. Grimes, A.L. Lamb, A.J. Nederbragt, J.A. Evans and F. McCormick, 'Feasting and mobility in Iron Age Ireland', *Nature Research Scientific Reports* **9** (2019), 19792 (https://doi.org/10.1038/s41598-019-55671-0).

R. Ó Maoldúin, 'Seachtain i nDaingean an Umha Aois (A week in Bronze Age Dingle): a personal perspective', *Archaeology Ireland* **28** (2) (2014), 40–3.

S. Sherratt, 'Feasting in Homeric epic', *Hesperia* **73** (2004), 301–37.

R.A. Smith, *British Museum: a guide to the antiquities of the Bronze Age in the Department of British and Medieval Antiquities* (London, 1920), 104, 110.

15. The power of skulls

I. Armit, *Head hunting and the body in Iron Age Europe* (Cambridge, 2012).

G. Burenhult, *The archaeology of Carrowmore* (Stockholm, 1984), 67.

N. Carty, '"The halved heads": osteological evidence for decapitation in medieval Ireland', *Papers from the Institute of Archaeology* **25** (1) (2015), 1–20 (doi: http://dx.doi.org/10.5334/pia.477).

N. Carty and P. Gleeson, 'Kingship, violence and *Loch Da Gabhor*: royal landscapes and the production of authority in early medieval Brega', *Ríocht na Midhe* **24** (2013), 1–44.

K. Cleary, 'Skeletons in the closet: the dead among the living on Irish Bronze Age settlements', *Journal of Irish Archaeology* **14** (2005), 23–42.

R.M. Cleary, 'Later Bronze Age settlement and prehistoric burials, Lough Gur, Co.

Limerick', *Proceedings of the Royal Irish Academy* **95**C (1995), 1–92.

R.M. Cleary, *The archaeology of Lough Gur* (Dublin, 2018), 101.

I. Doyle, 'A prehistoric ring-barrow in Kilmahuddrick, Co. Dublin', *Archaeology Ireland* **15** (4) (2001), 16–19.

E. Grogan, L. O'Donnell and P. Johnston, *The Bronze Age landscapes of the Pipeline to the West* (Dublin, 2007), 94.

H.O'N. Hencken, *Cahercommaun: a stone fort in County Clare* (Dublin, 1938), 22.

N. Kissane, *Saint Brigid of Kildare: life, legend and cult* (Dublin, 2017), 115.

C.J. Lynn, 'Trial excavations at the King's Stables, Tray Townland, County Armagh', *Ulster Journal of Archaeology* **40** (1977), 42–62.

C. Lynn, *Navan Fort: archaeology and myth* (Bray, 2003), 55.

C. Newman, 'Ballinderry Crannog No. 2, Co. Offaly: the Later Bronze Age', *Journal of Irish Archaeology* **8** (1997), 91–100.

C. Newman, M. O'Connell, M. Dillon and K. Molloy, 'Interpretation of charcoal and pollen data relating to an Iron Age ritual site in eastern Ireland: a holistic approach', *Vegetation History and Archaeobotany* **16** (2007), 349–65.

E. O'Brien, *Mapping death: burial in late Iron Age and early medieval Ireland* (Dublin, 2020), 141.

B. Raftery, 'The Loughnashade horns', *Emania* **2** (1987), 21–4.

16. The language of the stones

G.G. Bracken and P.A. Wyman, 'A Neolithic or Bronze Age alignment for Croagh Patrick', *Cathair na Mart: Journal of the Westport Historical Society* **12** (1992), 1–11.

C. Corlett, 'Prehistoric pilgrimage to Croagh Patrick', *Archaeology Ireland* **11** (2) (1997), 8–11.

G. Eogan and K. Cleary, *Excavations at Knowth 6. The passage tomb archaeology of the great mound at Knowth* (Dublin, 2017).

R. Hensey, 'Assuming the jigsaw had only one piece: abstraction, figuration and the interpretation of Irish passage tomb art', in A. Cochrane and A.M. Jones (eds), *Visualising the Neolithic: abstraction, figuration, performance, representation* (Oxford, 2012), 161–78.

R. Hensey, *First light: the origins of Newgrange* (Oxford, 2015), 89, 120.

H. Morphy, 'What circles look like', *Canberra Anthropology* **3** (1) (1980), 17–36.

M.J. O'Kelly, *Newgrange: archaeology, art and legend* (London, 1982).

G. Robin, 'Spatial structures and symbolic systems in Irish and British passage tombs', *Cambridge Archaeological Journal* **20** (2010), 373–418.

G. Robin, 'The figurative part of an abstract Neolithic iconography', in A. Cochrane and A.M. Jones (eds), *Visualising the Neolithic: abstraction, figuration, perform-ance, representation* (Oxford, 2012), 140–60.

J. Valdez-Tullett, *Design and connectivity: the case of Atlantic rock art* (Oxford, 2019).

M.A.M. van Hoek, 'The prehistoric rock art of the Boheh Stone, Co. Mayo', *Cathair na Mart: Journal of the Westport Historical Society* 13 (1993), 1–15.

17. A tripartite ideology

W. Fitzgerald, 'Mullaghmast: its history and traditions', *Journal of the Kildare Archaeological Society* 1 (1891–5), 379–90.

P. Harbison, *The high crosses of Ireland*, Vol. 1 (Bonn, 1992), 351.

R. Hicks, 'The rout of Ailill and Medb: myth on the landscape', *Emania* 24 (2018), 25.

J. Irwin, 'The Axis Mundi and the phallus: some unrecognised east–west parallels', in V.J. Newall (ed.), *Folklore studies in the twentieth century: proceedings of the centenary conference of the Folklore Society* (Woodbridge, 1980), 250–9.

C.J. Lynn, *Navan Fort: archaeology and myth* (Bray, 2003).

C.J. Lynn, 'Suggested archaeological and architectural examples of tripartite struc-tures', *Journal of Indo-European Studies* 34 (2006), 111–41.

J. Nicholls, 'Geophysical survey: Mullamast, Ballitore, Co. Kildare' (2004). Unpub-lished report funded by the Heritage Council, Margaret Gowen & Co. Ltd.

R. Poulton, 'Farley Heath Roman temple', *Surrey Archaeological Collections* 92 (2007), 1–147.

B. Raftery, *A catalogue of Irish Iron Age antiquities* (Marburg, 1983), 272.

C. Thomas, *The early Christian archaeology of north Britain* (Oxford, 1971), 123.

J. Waddell, *Archaeology and Celtic myth* (Dublin, 2014), 106.

R.J. Williams, P.J. Hart and A.T.L. Williams, *Wavendon Gate: a late Iron Age and Roman settlement in Milton Keynes* (Aylesbury, 1996), 64, 155.

18. Kingship and sacrifice

C. Doherty, 'Kingship in early Ireland', in E. Bhreathnach (ed.), *The kingship and landscape of Tara* (Dublin, 2005), 3–31.

D. Fickett-Wilbar, 'Ritual details of the Irish horse sacrifice in *Betha Mholaise Dai-minse*', *Journal of Indo-European Studies* 40 (2012), 315–43.

C. Newman, 'Procession and symbolism at Tara: analysis of Tech Midhchúarta (the "Banqueting Hall") in the context of the sacral campus', *Oxford Journal of Archaeology* 26 (2007), 415–38.

T.G. Ó Canann, 'Carraig an Dúnáin: probable Ua Canannáin inauguration site',

Journal of the Royal Society of Antiquaries of Ireland **133** (2003), 36–67.

J.J. O'Meara, *The first version of the Topography of Ireland by Giraldus Cambrensis* (Dundalk, 1951), 94.

J. Waddell, *Archaeology and Celtic myth* (Dublin, 2014), 127.

J. Waddell, *Myth and materiality* (Oxford, 2018), 37.

M. Warmind, 'Once more the Celtic horse-goddess', *Proceedings of the Harvard Celtic Colloquium* **36** (2016), 231–40.

19. In search of the ritualists

M. Aldhouse-Green, *Rethinking the ancient druids: an archaeological perspective* (Cardiff, 2021).

J. Borsje, 'Druids, deer and "words of power": coming to terms with evil in medieval Ireland', in K. Ritari and A. Bergholm (eds), *Approaches to religion and mythology in Celtic studies* (Newcastle, 2008), 122–49.

J. Borsje, *The Celtic evil eye and related mythological motifs in early Ireland* (Leuven, 2012), 101.

J. Carey, 'Saint Patrick, the druids, and the end of the world', *History of Religions* **36** (1) (1996), 42–53.

J. Carey, 'An Old Irish poem about Mug Ruith', *Journal of the Cork Historical and Archaeological Society* **110** (2005), 113–34.

G. Coffey, 'On the excavation of a tumulus near Loughrea, Co. Galway', *Proceedings of the Royal Irish Academy* **25** (1905), 14–20.

H. Duday, *The archaeology of the dead: lectures in archaeothanatology* (Oxford, 2009), 15, 19–20, 79–81.

G. Eogan, *Hoards of the Irish later Bronze Age* (Dublin, 1983), 151.

A.P. Fitzpatrick, 'Druids: towards an archaeology', in P. de Jersey, C. Gosden, H. Hamerow and G. Lock (eds), *Communities and connections: essays in honour of Barry Cunliffe* (Oxford, 2007), 287–315.

J.D. Hill, 'Wetwang chariot burial', *Current Archaeology* **178** (2002), 410–12 (https://www.britishmuseum.org/collection/object/H_2001-0401-20).

U. Holmberg, 'The shaman costume and its significance', *Annales Universitatis Fennicae Aboensis*, ser. B, **1** (2) (1922), 3–36.

C.J. Knüsel, 'The unwritten history of medical treatment: evidence for ritual-healers and their activities in the pre-literate past', *International Journal of Paleopathology* **34** (2021), 206–16.

K. Mannermaa and T. Kirkinen, 'Tracing the materiality of feathers in Stone Age north-eastern Europe', *Current Swedish Archaeology* **28** (2020), 23–46.

E. O'Brien, *Mapping death: burial in late Iron Age and early medieval Ireland* (Dublin, 2020), 114, 187.

G. Ó Crualaoich, 'Reading the *Bean Feasa*', *Folklore* **116** (1) (2005), 37–50.

S. Ó Duinn, *Forbhais Droma Dámhgháire. The Siege of Knocklong* (Cork, 1992), 103.

R. Ó Floinn, 'A bog burial from Derrymaquirke and other related finds from County Roscommon', *County Roscommon Historical and Archaeological Journal* **4** (1992), 71–2.

A. O'Leary, 'Constructing the magical biography of the Irish druid Mog Ruith', in A. Classen (ed.), *Magic and magicians in the Middle Ages and early modern time: the occult in pre-modern sciences, medicine, literature, religion and astrology* (Berlin, 2017), 219–29.

L.K. Pharo, 'A methodology for a deconstruction and reconstruction of the concepts "shaman" and "shamanism"', *Numen* **58** (2011), 6–70.

M. Porr and K.W. Alt, 'The burial of Bad Dürrenberg, central Germany: osteopathology and osteoarchaeology of a Late Mesolithic shaman's grave', *International Journal of Osteoarchaeology* **16** (2006), 395–406.

B. Raftery, *A catalogue of Irish Iron Age antiquities* (Marburg, 1983), 262.

A. Reymann, 'Part-time females and full-time specialists? Identifying gender roles in ritual behaviour and archaeological remains', in J.K. Koch and S. Needs-Howarth (eds), *Gender transformations in prehistoric and archaic societies* (Leiden, 2019), 368.

N.L.C. Stevens, 'A new reconstruction of the Etruscan heaven', *American Journal of Archaeology* **113** (2) (2009), 153–64.

J. Waddell, *Archaeology and Celtic myth* (Dublin, 2014), 118.

J. Waddell, *Myth and materiality* (Oxford, 2018), 74.

20. Wooden idols

E. Campbell and R. Ó Maoldúin, 'Idols, ards and severed heads', *Archaeology Ireland* **36** (1) (2022), 9, 14–19.

J. Carey, 'Irish parallels to the myth of Odin's eye', *Folklore* **94** (1983), 214–18.

B. Coles, 'Anthropomorphic wooden figures from Britain and Ireland', *Proceedings of the Prehistoric Society* **56** (1990), 315–33.

E. Corcoran, 'Bog enigmas', *Archaeology Ireland* **17** (3) (2003), 12–13.

Å.C. Fredell and M.V. García Quintela, 'Bodily attributes and semantic expressions: knees in rock art and Indo-European symbolism', in Å.C. Fredell, K. Kristiansen and F. Criado Boado (eds), *Representations and communications: creating an archaeological matrix of late prehistoric rock art* (Oxford, 2010), 75–92.

H. Hayen, 'Hölzerne Kultfiguren am Bohlenweg XLII (Ip) im Wittemoor (Gemeinde Berne, Landkreis Wesermarsch)', *Die Kunde* (N.F.) **22** (1971), 88–123.

C. McDermott, C. Moore, C. Murray and M. Stanley, 'Bog standard?', *Archaeology Ireland* **17** (4) (2003), 20–3.

M. Stanley, 'Anthropomorphic wooden figures: recent Irish discoveries', in J. Barber, C. Clark, M. Cressy *et al.* (eds), *Archaeology from the wetlands: recent perspectives* (Edinburgh, 2007), 183–90.

Z.S. Strother, 'A terrifying mimesis: problems of portraiture and representation in African sculpture (Congo-Kinshasa)', *RES: Anthropology and Aesthetics* **65–6** (2014–15), 128–47.

21. The sacred tree

M. Brennand and M. Taylor, 'The survey and excavation of a Bronze Age timber circle at Holme-next-the-Sea, Norfolk, 1998–9', *Proceedings of the Prehistoric Society* **69** (2003), 1–84.

C. Cusack, *The sacred tree: ancient and medieval manifestations* (Newcastle upon Tyne, 2011), 75.

E. Lenihan and C.E. Green, *Meeting the other crowd: the fairy stories of hidden Ireland* (Dublin, 2003), 12.

C. Manning, 'A note on sacred trees', *Emania* **5** (1988), 34–5.

K. Simms, 'The poetic Brehon lawyers of sixteenth-century Ireland', *Ériu* **57** (2007), 121–32.

J. Waddell, *Myth and materiality* (Oxford, 2018), 106.

R. Wyss, 'The sword of Korisios', *Antiquity* **30** (1956), 27–8.

22. Agrarian rites and sacrifices

N. Alonso, F.J. Cantero, R. Jornet, D. López, E. Montes, G. Prats and S. Valenzuela, 'Milling wheat and barley with rotary querns: the *Ouarten* women (Dahmani, Kef, Tunisia)', *AmS-Skrifter* **24** (2014), 11–30.

C.R. Batten and M. Williams, '*Erce* in the Old English *Æcerbot* charm: an Irish solution', *Notes and Queries* **67** (2020), 168–72.

S. Bergh, F. Gallagher, R. Hensey and P. Meehan, *A baseline survey of the passage tombs of County Sligo 2021* (Sligo, 2021).

G. Burenhult, *The archaeological excavation at Carrowmore, Co. Sligo, Ireland* (Stockholm, 1980), 37, 67.

C. Green and C. Gosden, 'Field systems, orientation, and cosmology', in C. Gosden, C. Green, A. Cooper *et al.*, *English landscapes and identities: investigating landscape change from 1500 BC to AD 1086* (Oxford, 2021), 248.

F. Kelly, *Early Irish farming* (Dublin, 1997), 439.

A.H.M. Kirk-Greene, 'A Lala initiation ceremony', *Man* 57 (1957), 9–11.

B. Mag Fhloinn, *Blood rite: the feast of St Martin in Ireland* (Helsinki, 2016).

J.F. Nagy, 'A pig for Samhain?', in D. Minkova and T. Tinkle, *Chaucer and the challenges of medievalism: studies in honor of H.A. Kelly* (Frankfurt, 2003), 311–25.

S. Ó Súilleabháin, *Irish folk custom and belief* (Dublin, 1967), 17, 45.

B. Raftery, *La Tène in Ireland: problems of origin and chronology* (Marburg, 1984), 244.

B.A. Rosenberg, 'The meaning of Æcerbot', *Journal of American Folklore* 79 (313) (1966), 428–36.

L. ten Harkel, T. Franconi and C. Gosden, 'Fields, ritual and religion: holistic approaches to the rural landscape in long-term perspective (*c.* 1500 BC–AD 1086)', *Oxford Journal of Archaeology* 36 (2017), 419.

C. Tolley, 'The mill in Norse and Finnish mythology', *Saga-Book* 24 (1995), 63–82.

V. Turner, 'Sacrifice as quintessential process prophylaxis or abandonment?', *History of Religions* 16 (3) (1977), 209.

S. Watts, 'The symbolism of querns and millstones', *AmS-Skrifter* 24 (2014), 51–64.

W. Wilde, *Irish popular superstitions* (Dublin, 1852), 55.

T. Zachrisson, 'Rotary querns and bread—a social history of Iron Age Sweden', *AmS-Skrifter* 24 (2014), 181–91.

23. Offerings in a midden

G. Burenhult, *The archaeology of Carrowmore* (Stockholm, 1984), 68, 331.

R. Gilchrist, 'Magic for the dead? The archaeology of magic in later medieval burials', *Medieval Archaeology* 52 (2008), 119–59.

L. Harney, 'Fasting and feasting on Irish church sites: the archaeological and historical evidence', *Ulster Journal of Archaeology* 73 (2016), 182–97.

B.C. Leon, 'Mesolithic and Neolithic activity on Dalkey Island—a reassessment', *Journal of Irish Archaeology* 14 (2005), 1–21.

F. McCormick, M. Gibbons, F.G. McCormac and J. Moore, 'Bronze Age to medieval coastal shell middens near Ballyconneely, Co. Galway', *Journal of Irish Archaeology* 7 (1996), 77–84.

I.J. McNiven, 'Ritualized middening practices', *Journal of Archaeological Method and Theory* 20 (2013), 552–87.

N. Milner and P. Woodman, 'Deconstructing the myths of Irish shell middens', in N. Milner, O.E. Craig and G.N. Bailey (eds), *Shell middens in Atlantic Europe* (Oxford, 2007), 101–10.

E.V. Murray, 'Molluscs and middens: the archaeology of "Ireland's early savage race"?', in E.M. Murphy and J.J. Whitehouse (eds), *Environmental archaeology in*

Ireland (Oxford, 2007), 119–35.

E. O'Brien, *Mapping death: burial in late Iron Age and early medieval Ireland* (Dublin, 2020), 42.

24. The magic of ironworking

J. Carey, *Magic, metallurgy and imagination in medieval Ireland* (Aberystwyth, 2019), 31.

N. Carlin, 'Ironworking and production', in N. Carlin, L. Clarke and F. Walsh (eds), *The archaeology of life and death in the Boyne floodplain* (Dublin, 2008), 87–112.

S. Chirikure, *Metals in past societies: a global perspective on indigenous African metallurgy* (New York, 2015), 89.

B. Dolan, 'Making iron in the Irish midlands: the social and symbolic role of Iron Age ironworkers', *Journal of Irish Archaeology* 25 (2016), 31–48.

R.G. Goodchild, 'A priest's sceptre from the Romano-Celtic temple at Farley Heath, Surrey', *Antiquaries Journal* 18 (4) (1938), 391–6.

R.G. Goodchild, 'The Farley Heath sceptre', *Antiquaries Journal* 27 (1–2) (1947), 3–5.

P.M. McNutt, 'The African ironsmith as marginal mediator: a symbolic analysis', *Journal of Ritual Studies* 5 (2) (1991), 75–98.

R. Poulton, 'Farley Heath Roman temple', *Surrey Archaeological Collections* 92 (2007), 1–147.

R. Schot, 'Forging life amid the dead: crafting and kingship at Iron Age Tara', *Discovery Programme Reports* 9 (2018), 107–28.

J. Zeidler, 'Gobannos and his namesakes in the framework of Indo-European textual and cultural reconstruction', in W. Spickermann (ed.), *Celtic theonyms as an individual option?* (Rahden, 2013), 77–122.

25. The bodies in the bog

M. Aldhouse-Green, *Bog bodies uncovered: solving Europe's ancient mystery* (London, 2015).

J. Carey, 'The encounter at the ford: warriors, water and women', *Éigse* 34 (2004), 23.

C. Fredengren, 'Becoming bog bodies: sacrifice and politics of exclusion, as evidenced in the deposition of skeletal remains in wetlands', *Journal of Wetland Archaeology* 18 (2018), 1–19.

M. Giles, *Bog bodies: face to face with the past* (Manchester, 2020).

R. Hutton, 'What did happen to Lindow Man?', *The Times Literary Supplement*, 30 January 2004, 12–13.

E.P. Kelly, 'Secrets of the bog bodies: the enigma of the Iron Age explained', *Archaeology Ireland* **20** (1) (2006), 26–30.

E.P. Kelly, *Kingship and sacrifice. Iron Age bog bodies and boundaries.* Archaeology Ireland Heritage Guide 35 (Dublin, 2006).

E.P. Kelly, 'An archaeological interpretation of Irish Iron Age bog bodies', in S. Ralph (ed.), *The archaeology of violence: interdisciplinary approaches* (New York, 2013), 232–40.

T. Ó Cathasaigh, 'The threefold death in early Irish sources', *Studia Celtica Japonica* **6** (1994), 53–75; reprinted in M. Boyd (ed.), *Coire Sois: the Cauldron of Knowledge* (Notre Dame, 2014), 101–20.

R. Ó Floinn, 'Recent research into Irish bog bodies', in R. Turner and R.G. Scaife, *Bog bodies: new discoveries and new perspectives* (London, 1995), 137–45.

G. Plunkett, N.J. Whitehouse, V.A. Hall, D.J. Charman, M. Blaauw, E. Kelly and I. Mulhall, 'A multi-proxy palaeoenvironmental investigation of the findspot of an Iron Age bog body from Oldcroghan, Co. Offaly, Ireland', *Journal of Archaeological Science* **36** (2009), 265–77.

I.M. Stead, J.D. Bourke and D. Brothwell, *Lindow Man: the body in the bog* (London, 1986).

W. Wilde, *A descriptive catalogue of the antiquities of animal materials and bronze in the museum of the Royal Irish Academy* (Dublin, 1861), 276.

26. Lost mythologies

J. Bagnall Smith, 'Votive objects and objects of votive significance from Great Walsingham', *Britannia* **30** (1999), 21–56.

J. Carey, 'Irish parallels to the myth of Odin's eye', *Folklore* **94** (1983), 214–18.

P.-M. Duval, *Monnaies gauloises et mythes celtiques* (Paris, 1987), 22.

P.-M. Duval, 'Le groupe de bas-reliefs des "Nautae Parisiaci"', in P.-M. Duval, *Travaux sur la Gaule (1946–1986)* (Rome, 1989), 433–62.

É. Espérandieu, *Recueil général des bas-reliefs, statues et bustes de la Gaule romaine,* IV (Paris, 1911), no. 3429.

M. Green, *Symbol and image in Celtic religious art* (London, 1989), 180.

M.J. Green, 'Crossing the boundaries: triple horns and emblematic transference', *European Journal of Archaeology* **1** (2) (1998), 219–40.

V. Kruta, 'Les bronzes de Castiglione delle Stiviere: carnyx ou effigie d'un échassier?', *Études celtiques* **39** (2013), 41–60.

W. O'Brien, *Iverni: a prehistory of Cork* (Cork, 2012), 233.

M.J. O'Kelly, 'The Cork Horns, the Petrie Crown and the Bann Disc: the technique of their ornamentation', *Journal of the Cork Historical and Archaeological Society*

66 (1961), 1–12.

L. O'Toole, 'The Eurasian crane (*Grus grus*) in Ireland—another extinct bird or a key species for an ancient belief system?', *Irish Naturalists' Journal* **33** (2014), 53–65.

G.S. Olmsted, *The gods of the Celts and the Indo-Europeans* (Budapest, 1994), 403.

S. Read, M. Henig and L. Cram, 'Three-horned bull', *Britannia* **17** (1986), 346–7.

J. Rood, 'The cult of Óðinn in the early Scandinavian warrior aristocracy', in E. Lyle (ed.), *Myth and history in Celtic and Scandinavian traditions* (Amsterdam, 2021), 197–218.

A. Ross, *Pagan Celtic Britain: studies in iconography and tradition* (London, 1967), 302.

R.M. Scowcroft, 'Abstract narrative in Ireland', *Ériu* **46** (1995), 140.

G. Unterberger, 'Taureau tricornu. Der keltische Dreihorn-Stier und der Ursprung des Dreihorn-Motivs', in W. Spickermann (ed.), *Celtic theonyms as an individual option?* (Rahden, 2013), 273–99.

J. Waddell, *Myth and materiality* (Oxford, 2018), 33, 134.

J. Wade, 'The castrated gods and their castration cults: revenge, punishment, and spiritual supremacy', *International Journal of Transpersonal Studies* **38** (2019), 31–58.

27. Graven images

T.J. Barron, 'Some beehive quernstones from Counties Cavan and Monaghan [and the Corleck gods]', *Clogher Record* **9** (1) (1976), 98.

R. Baumgarten, 'Creative medieval etymology and Irish hagiography (Lasair, Columba, Senán)', *Ériu* **54** (2004), 74.

A. Bergholm, 'The idols of the pagan Irish in the medieval literary imagination', in E. Lyle (ed.), *Myth and history in Celtic and Scandinavian traditions* (Amsterdam, 2021), 117–34.

M. Duignan, 'The Turoe stone: its place in insular La Tène art', in P.-M. Duval and C. Hawkes (eds), *Celtic art in ancient Europe: five protohistoric centuries* (London, 1976), 201–17.

H. Hickey, *Images of stone* (Belfast, 1976), 26.

M. MacNeill, *The festival of Lughnasa* (Oxford, 1962), 172.

E. Markey and J. Clarke, *Knockbride: a history* (Monaghan, 1995), 12.

E. O'Brien, *Mapping death: burial in late Iron Age and early medieval Ireland* (Dublin, 2020), 86.

P. Ó Riain, *A dictionary of Irish saints* (Dublin, 2011), 401, 582.

A. O'Sullivan, 'Saint Brecán of Clare', *Celtica* **15** (1983), 128–39.

B. Raftery, 'A decorated Iron Age horse-bit fragment from Ireland', *Proceedings of the Royal Irish Academy* **74C** (1974), 1–10.

A. Ross, 'Chain symbolism in pagan Celtic religion', *Speculum* **34** (1959), 39–59.

A. Ross, 'A Celtic three-faced head from Wiltshire', *Antiquity* **41** (1967), 53–6.

R. Stalley, 'Iona, the Vikings and the making of the Book of Kells', *History Ireland* **21** (3) (2013), 17.

J. Waddell, 'On Turoe and Castlestrange', *Ulster Journal of Archaeology* **74** (2018), 20–5.

P.F. Wallace and R. Ó Floinn (eds), *Treasures of the National Museum of Ireland: Irish antiquities* (Dublin, 2002), 142.

28. Warriors, wolves and swords

D.W. Anthony, 'Migration, ancient DNA, and Bronze Age pastoralists from the Eurasian steppes', in M.J. Daniels (ed.), *Homo migrans: modeling mobility and migration in human history* (New York, 2022), 55–77.

D.W. Anthony and D.R. Brown, 'The dogs of war: a Bronze Age initiation ritual in the Russian steppes', *Journal of Anthropological Archaeology* **48** (2017), 134–48.

A. Dooley and H. Roe, *Tales of the Elders of Ireland. A new translation of Acallam na Senórach* (Oxford, 1999), 6.

D.S. Farrer and J.D. Sellmann, 'Chants of re-enchantment: Chamorro spiritual resistance to colonial domination', *Social Analysis: the International Journal of Anthropology* **58** (1) (2014), 127–48.

R.J. Harrison, *Symbols and warriors: images of the European Bronze Age* (Bristol, 2004).

R. Haussler, 'Apollo Cunomaglos, Lord of the Wolves', *Bandue: Journal of the Spanish Association for the Sciences of Religions* **9** (2018–19), 65–82.

A.T. Lucas, 'The social role of relics and reliquaries in ancient Ireland', *Journal of the Royal Society of Antiquaries of Ireland* **116** (1986), 17.

K. McCone, 'Werewolves, cyclopes, *díberga* and *fíanna*: juvenile delinquency in early Ireland', *Cambridge Medieval Celtic Studies* **12** (1986), 1–22.

K. McCone, 'The Celtic and Indo-European origins of the *fían*', in S.J. Arbuthnot and G. Parsons (eds), *The Gaelic Finn tradition* (Dublin, 2012), 14–30.

B. Malinowski, 'War and weapons among the natives of the Trobriand Islands', *Man* **20** (1920), 10–12.

J.P. Mallory, *In search of the Irish dreamtime: archaeology and early Irish literature* (London, 2016), 177.

R. Megaw and V. Megaw, 'The Italian job: some implications of recent finds of Celtic scabbards decorated with dragon-pairs', *Mediterranean Archaeology* **2**

(1989), 85–100.

C. Newman, 'The sword in the stone: previously unrecognised archaeological evidence of ceremonies of the later Iron Age and early medieval period', in G. Cooney, K. Becker, J. Coles, M. Ryan and S. Sievers (eds), *Relics of old decency: archaeological studies in later prehistory* (Dublin, 2009), 425–36.

J. Rodríguez-Corral, 'The empowerment of imagery: stone warriors in the borders', *Cambridge Archaeological Journal* 23 (2) (2013), 283–306.

C. Scott Littleton, 'From swords in the earth to the sword in the stone: a possible reflection of an Alano-Sarmatian rite of passage in the Arthurian tradition', in E.C. Polomé (ed.), *Homage to Georges Dumézil. Journal of Indo-European Studies Monograph 3* (1982), 53–67.

B. Slavin, 'Coming to terms with druids in early Christian Ireland', *Australian Celtic Journal* 10 (2009), 1–27.

M.A. Valante, 'Family relics and Viking kingship in Ireland', *Eolas: Journal of the American Society of Irish Medieval Studies* 6 (2013), 88–106.

J. Waddell, 'The elusive image', in G. Cooney, K. Becker, J. Coles, M. Ryan and S. Sievers (eds), *Relics of old decency: archaeological studies in later prehistory* (Dublin, 2009), 341–9.

J. Waddell, *Archaeology and Celtic myth* (Dublin, 2014), 66.

J. Wade, 'Going berserk: battle trance and ecstatic holy warriors in the European war magic tradition', *International Journal of Transpersonal Studies* 35 (2016), 21–38.

29. The old gods

J. Carey, *A single ray of the sun: religious speculation in early Ireland* (Aberystwyth, 2011), 1–38.

J. Carey, 'Ogmios and the eternal word', *Cosmos* 30 (2014), 1–36.

A.J. Daubney, *Portable antiquities, palimpsests, and persistent places: a multi-period approach to Portable Antiquities Scheme data in Lincolnshire* (Leiden, 2016), 156.

M. Egeler, 'Some thoughts on "Goddess Medb" and her typological context', *Zeitschrift für celtische Philologie* 59 (2012), 67–96.

P. Gleeson, 'Making provincial kingship in early Ireland: Cashel and the creation of Munster', *Proceedings of the British Academy* 224 (2019), 346–68.

M. Herbert, 'Transmutations of an Irish goddess', in S. Billington and M. Green (eds), *The concept of the goddess* (London, 1996), 141–51.

F. Hunter, M. Henig, E. Sauer and J. Gooder, 'Mithras in Scotland: a Mithraeum at Inveresk (East Lothian)', *Britannia* 47 (2016), 119–68.

N. Kissane, *Saint Brigid of Kildare: life, legend and cult* (Dublin, 2017), 83.

H. Lanigan Wood, 'Dogs and Celtic deities: pre-Christian stone carvings in Armagh', *Irish Arts Review* **16** (2000), 26–33.

B. Lincoln, 'The lord of the dead', *History of Religions* **20** (1981), 224–41.

P. Mac Cana, *Celtic mythology* (London, 1970), 34.

P. Mac Cana, *The cult of the sacred centre* (Dublin, 2011), 221.

J.P. Mallory, *In search of the Irish dreamtime: archaeology and early Irish literature* (London, 2016), 74.

M. Ní Dhonnchadha, 'Síd Crúachan and its names', *Celtica* **20** (2022), 113–26.

W. O'Brien, *Iverni: a prehistory of Cork* (Cork, 2012), 259.

J.J. O'Meara, *The first version of the Topography of Ireland by Giraldus Cambrensis* (Dundalk, 1951), 64, 71.

A. Ross, *Pagan Celtic Britain: studies in iconography and tradition* (London, 1967), 81, 146.

N. Tolstoy, *The mysteries of Stonehenge* (Stroud, 2016), 465, 478.

R.B. Warner, 'The Armagh "pagan" statues: a check-list, a summary of their known history and possible evidence of their original location', *Ulster Journal of Archaeology* **72** (2013–14 [2016]), 55–69.

R.E.M. Wheeler and T.V. Wheeler, *Report on the excavation of the prehistoric, Roman, and post-Roman site in Lydney Park, Gloucestershire* (Oxford, 1932), 87.

30. The pagan continuum

N.B. Aitchison, 'Votive deposition in Iron Age Ireland: an early medieval account', *Emania* **15** (1996), 67–75.

J. Carey, 'The old gods of Ireland in the later Middle Ages', in K. Ritari and A. Bergholm (eds), *Understanding Celtic religion: revisiting the pagan past* (Cardiff, 2015), 51–68.

S. Daffy, 'A site for sore eyes: a Hiberno-Roman curative cult at Golden, Co. Tipperary', *Archaeology Ireland* **16** (2) (2002), 8–9.

A. Day, *Glimpses of Ireland's past* (Dublin, 2014), 190.

J. Delumeau, *Le péché et la peur: la culpabilisation en Occident, XIIIe–XVIIe siècles* (Paris, 1983).

J. Delumeau, 'The journey of a historian', *Catholic Historical Review* **96** (3) (2010), 435–48.

R. Dunne, 'Ballynew cemetery', in National Folklore Collection, UCD, Schools' Collection, Vol. 0089, 453.

P. Gleeson and R. McLaughlin, 'Ways of death: cremation and belief in first-millennium AD Ireland', *Antiquity* **95** (2021), 382–99.

E.J. Gwynn, 'An Irish penitential', *Ériu* **7** (1914), 147, 151.

S. Heaney, 'The poet as a Christian', reprinted in *The Furrow* **64** (10) (2013), 541–5.

E.P. Kelly, 'Antiquities from Irish holy wells and their wider context', *Archaeology Ireland* **16** (2) (2002), 24–8.

E. Larkin, 'The devotional revolution in Ireland, 1850–75', *American Historical Review* **77** (3) (1972), 625–52.

L. Lawrence, 'Pagan imagery in the early lives of Brigit: a transformation from goddess to saint?', *Proceedings of the Harvard Celtic Colloquium* **16–17** (1996–7), 39–54.

F. McCormick, 'Struell Wells: pagan past and Christian present', *Journal of the Royal Society of Antiquaries of Ireland* **139** (2009), 45–62.

F. McCormick, 'Struell: bathing at midsummer and the origins of holy wells', in C. Bis-Worch and C. Theune (eds), *Religion, cults and rituals in the medieval rural environment*: *Ruralia* **11** (2017), 69–77.

K. Müller-Lisowski, 'Contributions to a study in Irish folklore: traditions about Donn', *Béaloideas* **18** (1948), 156.

J.F. Nagy, *Conversing with angels and ancients: literary myths of medieval Ireland* (Dublin, 1997), 15, 129.

K.W. Nicholls, 'Tobar Finnmhuighe—Slán Pádraig', *Dinnseanchas* **2** (1966–7), 97–8.

C. O'Brien, 'Survey of the holy wells in Moycashel barony', in S. O'Brien (ed.), *Westmeath: history and society* (Dublin, 2022), 176.

T. Ó Carragáin, *Churches in the Irish landscape AD 400–1100* (Cork, 2021), 216.

C. Ray, *The origins of Ireland's holy wells* (Oxford, 2014).

K. Simms, *From kings to warlords: the changing political structure of Gaelic Ireland in the later Middle Ages* (Woodbridge, 1987), 27.

P. Stevens, 'Site 42-44, Ask Townland, Co. Wexford' (2011), TII Excavation Report (https://repository.dri.ie/catalog/h1291v592).

W. Stokes (ed.), 'The Bodleian Amra Choluimb Chille', *Revue Celtique* **20** (1899), 429.

D.Y. Telegin and J.P. Mallory, *The anthropomorphic stelae of the Ukraine: the early iconography of the Indo-Europeans* (Washington, 1994), 77–86.

J. Waddell, 'Equine cults and Celtic goddesses', *Emania* **24** (2018), 5–18.

W. Wilde, *Irish popular superstitions* (Dublin, 1852), 56, 121.

Index

References to illustrations are *italicised*.